Negotiating Privilege and Identity in Educational Contexts

I0042202

Recent efforts emphasize the roles that privilege and elite education play in shaping affluent youths' identities. Despite various backgrounds, the common qualities shared among these adolescents define their self-understandings and serve as means for them to negotiate their privilege. This improved self-knowledge helps them to feel more at ease with being privileged, foster a positive sense of self, and reduce the negative feelings associated with their advantages, thus managing expectations for future success.

Offering an intimate and comprehensive view of affluent adolescents' inner lives and understandings, *Negotiating Privilege and Identity in Educational Contexts* explores these qualities and provides an important alternative perspective on privilege and how privilege works. The case studies in this volume explore different settings and lived experiences of eight privileged adolescents who, influenced by various sources, actively construct and cultivate their own privilege. Their stories address a wide range of issues relevant to the study of adolescence and the various social class factors that mediate adolescents' educational experiences and identities.

Adam Howard is associate professor of education at Colby College, Waterville, Maine. Prior to teaching at the college level, he was an English teacher at an independent high school. He is co-editor of Educating Elites: Class Privilege and Educational Advantage and author of Learning Privilege: Lessons of Power and Identity in Affluent Schooling.

Aimee Polimeno is an undergraduate at Colby College, majoring in psychology with a minor in education. She is a research assistant for Professor Adam Howard in Colby's Education Program.

Brianne Wheeler is an undergraduate student at Colby College, majoring in psychology with minors in administrative science and human development. She is a research assistant for Professor Adam Howard in Colby's Education Program.

Routledge Research in Education

For a full list of titles in this series, please visit www.routledge.com.

89 **Family, Community, and Higher Education**
Edited by Toby S. Jenkins

90 **Rethinking School Bullying**
Dominance, Identity and School Culture
Ronald B. Jacobson

91 **Language, Literacy, and Pedagogy in Postindustrial Societies**
The Case of Black Academic Underachievement
Paul C. Mocombe and Carol Tomlin

92 **Education for Civic and Political Participation**
A Critical Approach
Edited by Reinhold Hedtke and Tatjana Zimenkova

93 **Language Teaching Through the Ages**
Garon Wheeler

94 **Refugees, Immigrants, and Education in the Global South**
Lives in Motion
Edited by Lesley Bartlett and Ameena Ghaffar-Kucher

95 **The Resegregation of Schools**
Education and Race in the Twenty-First Century
Edited by Jamel K. Donnor and Adrienne D. Dixson

96 **Autobiographical Writing and Identity in EFL Education**
Shizhou Yang

97 **Online Learning and Community Cohesion**
Linking Schools
Roger Austin and Bill Hunter

98 **Language Teachers and Teaching**
Global Perspectives, Local Initiatives
Edited by Selim Ben Said and Lawrence Jun Zhang

99 **Towards Methodologically Inclusive Research Syntheses**
Expanding Possibilities
Harsh Suri

100 **Raising Literacy Achievement in High-Poverty Schools**
An Evidence-Based Approach
Eithne Kennedy

101 **Learning and Collective Creativity**
Activity-Theoretical and Sociocultural Studies
Annalisa Sannino and Viv Ellis

102 **Educational Inequalities**
Difference and Diversity in Schools and Higher Education
Edited by Kalwant Bhopal and Uvanney Maylor

103 **Education, Social Background and Cognitive Ability**
The Decline of the Social
Gary N. Marks

104 **Education in Computer Generated Environments**
Sara de Freitas

105 **The Social Construction of Meaning**
Reading Literature in Urban
English Classrooms
John Yandell

106 **Global Perspectives on Spirituality in Education**
Edited by Jacqueline Watson,
Marian de Souza and
Ann Trousdale

107 **Neo-liberal Educational Reforms**
A Critical Analysis
Edited by David A. Turner and
Hüseyin Yolcu

108 **The Politics of Pleasure in Sexuality Education**
Pleasure Bound
Edited by Louisa Allen,
Mary Lou Rasmussen, and
Kathleen Quinlivan

109 **Popular Culture, Pedagogy and Teacher Education**
International Perspectives
Edited by Phil Benson and
Alice Chik

110 **Teacher Training and the Education of Black Children**
Bringing Color into Difference
Uvanney Maylor

111 **Secrecy and Tradecraft in Educational Administration**
The Covert Side of
Educational Life
Eugenie A. Samier

112 **Affirming Language Diversity in Schools and Society**
Beyond Linguistic Apartheid
Edited by Pierre Wilbert Orelus

113 **Teacher Leadership**
New Conceptions for
Autonomous Student Learning
in the Age of the Internet
Kokila Roy Katyal and
Colin Evers

114 **Test Fraud**
Statistical Detection and
Methodology
Edited by Neal M. Kingston and
Amy K. Clark

115 **Literacy, Play and Globalization**
Converging Imaginaries in
Children's Critical and
Cultural Performances
Carmen Liliana Medina and
Karen E. Wohlwend

116 **Biotechnology, Education and Life Politics**
Debating Genetic Futures from
School to Society
Pádraig Murphy

117 **Vernaculars in the Classroom**
Paradoxes, Pedagogy, Possibilities
Shondel Nero and Dohra Ahmad

118 **A Psycho-social Perspective on Professional Uncertainty**
Knowledge, Theory and
Relationship in the Classroom
Joseph Mintz

119 **Negotiating Privilege and Identity in Educational Contexts**
Adam Howard, Aimee Polimeno,
and Brianne Wheeler

Negotiating Privilege and Identity in Educational Contexts

Adam Howard, Aimee Polimeno, and Brianne Wheeler

Routledge
Taylor & Francis Group

NEW YORK AND LONDON

First published 2014
by Routledge
711 Third Avenue, New York, NY 10017, USA

and by Routledge
2 Park Square, Milton Park, Abingdon, Oxfordshire OX14 4RN

First issued in paperback 2016

*Routledge is an imprint of the Taylor & Francis Group,
an informa business*

© 2014 Taylor & Francis

The right of Adam Howard, Aimee Polimeno, and Brianne Wheeler to be
identified as authors of this work has been asserted by them in accordance
with sections 77 and 78 of the Copyright, Designs and Patents Act 1988.

All rights reserved. No part of this book may be reprinted or reproduced or
utilised in any form or by any electronic, mechanical, or other means, now
known or hereafter invented, including photocopying and recording, or in
any information storage or retrieval system, without permission in writing
from the publishers.

Trademark Notice: Product or corporate names may be trademarks or
registered trademarks, and are used only for identification and explanation
without intent to infringe.

Library of Congress Cataloging-in-Publication Data
Howard, Adam.
    Negotiating privilege and identity in educational contexts / by Adam
Howard, Aimee Polimeno, and Brianne Wheeler.
        pages cm. — (Routledge research in education)
    Includes bibliographical references and index.
    1. Upper class—Education—United States.   2. Elite (Social sciences—
Education—United States.   3. Educational sociology—United States.
4. Social classes—United States.   5. Social status—United States.
I. Polimeno, Aimee.   II. Wheeler, Brianne.   III. Title.
    LC4941.H694 2014
    371.826'210973—dc23
    2014003033

Typeset in Sabon
by IBT Global.

ISBN 13: 978-1-138-28693-1 (pbk)
ISBN 13: 978-1-138-02468-7 (hbk)

To Ellen Brantlinger

Contents

Foreword   xi

1   Making Privilege Visible   1

2   Meredith: Confidently Traveling   20
    WITH ANNA CARON, JENIFER GOLDMAN, KATIE GRIFFIN,
    CONNIE JANGRO, CELESTE LATTANZI, AND ADELE PRIESTLEY

3   Herman: A Scripted Life   41
    WITH CYNTHIA GARVIN, ERIKA JOHNSON, ETHAN MEIGS,
    AND MORGAN RUBLEE

4   Kayla: Dribbling toward the Goal   61
    WITH ADRIENNE BOWLES, JENIFER GOLDMAN, CELESTE LATTANZI,
    KATE O'CALLAGHAN, AND MORGAN RUBLEE

5   Marcus: On His Own   80
    WITH COURTNEY ERSKINE, CYNTHIA GARVIN, MOLLY HODSON,
    PEGGY MEYER, AND HANNAH O'BRIEN

6   Sarah: Alone in the Crowd   99
    WITH IAN BORTHWICK, ANNIE CHEN, KELSEY CROMIE,
    ANDREW RHOADS, AND HILLARY ROWSE

7   Leo: Uncertain Future, Certain Success   119
    WITH ANNIE CHEN

8   Olive: Creating Her Own Space   138
    WITH ANNIE CHEN

9   **Jacob: Dancing through Life**   157
    WITH KELSEY CROMIE

10 **Negotiating Privilege**   177

11 **Transforming Self-Understandings**   198
    WITH KELSEY CROMIE

    References   211
    Index   219

Foreword

Reading Adam Howard and his students' book, I find myself remembering being interviewed as a child by social workers, standing next to my mother and her hot shame. I was six and she was trying to get me in to see an ophthalmologist, something she was not sure she could afford on a waitress's salary—especially not to see the specialist who might actually be able to help my vision. My memories are hazy, but what I know is that she managed through simple determination and gritted teeth to get past the social worker and on to the doctor, but not without paying a high price—the onus of being interviewed by a student trainee who was oblivious to her self-consciousness and painful sense of embarrassment.

It's the examined life I find myself thinking about, those of us who are traditionally subject to such examinations. I am so grateful that Adam and his students have turned that examination on the classes who are so rarely subject to that kind of intensity. All the things I know or believe about this leave me shaking and exhausted, most of all because there has never been this kind of balance about examined lives. Poor people, people of color, Native Americans, the marginal, the queer, and the divergent—we are those who are always being subject to social analysis. The middle and upper classes are assumed to be the examiners, those with distance and a keen intellectual inquiry, no real emotional vulnerability in the enterprise. Those of us being examined have only our resentment and outrage and no justification for these emotions. After all, what do we have to question or resist? By what right may we refuse to be the subject of such study?

Oddly enough I find myself grateful that these chapters about the young of the middle and upper classes are not framed with any vestige of resentment or disdain. These young people's statements are vulnerable and forthright. It is almost as if they have permission to be fearless, to categorize their families and position in the world in terms as naked and revealing as fine poetry. To understand these issues requires compassion and high honesty, which are continually reflected in the pieces in which these young people make themselves so vulnerable. I read them with my mouth open—not only for the difference between their lives and my own, but for the revelations of a worldview that takes for granted what I have never felt could be trusted—a sense of purpose and meaning that renders all choices reasonable. Whatever comes next for these young people they will have these beautifully rendered versions of their own examined lives. Their sense of entitlement becomes the defining characteristic of a class that rarely realizes how different those assumptions are from those of us who have no such inherent sense of place and social membership.

Privilege does not always know itself as such. A sense of place, social membership, and entitlement obscure what it means for those who have no such defenses. Even the most sympathetic and insightful perspective that social science can create is obscured by what the social scientist or student cannot see, their own place in the hierarchy. The following chapters try valiantly to look past that obscurity, to look at what is so hard to examine, their own place in the larger world.

Dorothy Allison
Award-Winning Writer, Scholar, and Activist
Guerneville, California

1   Making Privilege Visible

Situated on top of Mayflower Hill overlooking a river valley and the small town of Waterville, Maine, Colby College enjoys a geographical prominence equal to its magnificent campus. Neo-Georgian–style buildings are positioned around expansive, terraced quadrangles. The most scenic route of arrival takes people along a six-acre pond with brick dormitories and Miller Library in the distance. At the highest elevation, Miller stands with a sailing-ship weathervane perched on a white tower, conveying a part of the college's history and representing the many directions students can take in life. In the evenings, the tower is illuminated in blue, making it visible to most of the surrounding areas. Although town residents have this constant visible reminder of Colby's presence, the college community mostly remains at a distance. The town's once thriving mill and factories are no longer sources of employment; nearly 23 percent of residents live below the poverty line and many others are barely making ends meet. The wealthy community on top of the hill has little contact with the drastically different life circumstances of so many living within this small town.

The incredible beauty and abundance of Colby allows most of us within this elite community to forget that these forms of human suffering, such as poverty, homelessness, and hunger, exist just beyond this isolated campus. We also rarely give thoughtful attention to the fabric of privilege that clothes our own community. As with most elite educational communities, we keep privilege invisible by ignoring and, at times, avoiding it. Collectively, we have not had the kinds of educational experiences that would enable us to work toward a critical understanding of our privilege. The twenty-four of us involved in the writing of this book gathered for the first time in February 2012 to begin our efforts of developing this awareness in a course focused on the influences of social class within educational contexts.

Before the first class session, Adam Howard, who taught the course, asked the twenty-three students enrolled that semester to bring in an artifact representing their social class and to avoid letting their classmates see what they brought. As students entered the classroom, they received additional instructions to place their artifacts on a table in the middle of the room. They dutifully did as they were told, glancing around to make sure no one noticed what they brought as they put their items in their proper place. Curious about what their classmates had added to the collection, the students began to study the objects before them; among the keys to a BMW, gold rings, and a lacrosse ball sat a used jelly jar and a page with pictures of houses that became progressively smaller. Howard gave them a few moments to form some initial thoughts about the differences reflected in this collection and then asked them each to select one of the artifacts that was not their own. As they made their selections, he further instructed, "Study the artifact that you've selected and decide two things: what this object reveals about someone's social class and who it belongs to."

After a few moments, Brianne began, "I have a receipt for some books. I assume the person brought it to represent how much they value education. But it could also mean something about how expensive books are and how they can afford to buy them."

"Who do you think the artifact belongs to?" Howard inquired.

"I don't know. It could be any of us because we all have to buy books," she replied.

Howard challenged, "I'm not letting you off that easy. Pick someone who you think brought this to represent something about their social class."

Brianne finally pointed to the student sitting directly across from her. "I pick Andrew," she said with some frustration.

The rest of the class took turns sharing their thoughts about the objects they had selected. As with Brianne, most of them identified who they believed owned the artifact with a fair amount of hesitation. Toward the end, Ian voiced concerns that many others shared: "We're just making a guess and randomly picking somebody. What's the purpose of that? It's pretty uncomfortable pointing someone out when you're just guessing."

Howard questioned, "What part of it makes you uncomfortable?"

"That we're saying something about someone we don't really know yet," Ian replied.

Howard responded with a question, "What is that something that you're referring to?"

Ian clarified, "It's supposed to be their social class and there's no way of knowing that. That something seems too personal to be guessing at." Howard ended the exchange by saying, "You're on to something," and then asked to revisit this point at the end.

Soon after, the students began the second phase of the activity, where they retrieved and explained the significance of their artifacts. Molly volunteered to go first. "You got the hat part right but it isn't for gardening," she told Aimee, as she picked up her item, "This is an old hat from a regatta that my dad sailed in. My family is really into sailing." Next, Adele stood up and headed toward Erika, who was sitting across the room. "I brought in my ski goggles, because although it is a passion and something I worked very hard for, skiing is an expensive leisure sport and is definitely a huge privilege that I've grown up with," she explained. Adele went on to say that she attended a ski academy during high school and continued her skiing career at Colby.

As they revealed what their artifacts represented about their social class, the students, to varying degrees, disclosed information about their activities, interests, tastes, families, friends, and life and schooling experiences. Courtney, one of the three students we eventually learned who did not identify as privileged, ended the activity by reclaiming the book receipt from Brianne. "I've been trying to figure out how much I'm going to share," she began. After an extended pause, she continued, "I brought a printout of the receipt for all the books I've purchased for this semester online. I couldn't afford to buy them from the campus bookstore. It's just too expensive."

While debriefing the activity, we returned to the point that Ian raised earlier. A few students questioned whether we should even try to identify someone's social class just by looking at them. "It seems like you're stepping into shaky ground when you're doing that," Katie reasoned. Others argued that we do this unconsciously on a regular basis, but as Erika confessed, "we don't like to admit it to ourselves." Hearing this, Anna, another student from a working-class background, quickly jumped in, "It's more about ignoring it. People don't talk about social class at Colby. I mean, people politely bring it up, but they aren't really talking about it; they're talking around it. And they especially don't talk about anything too personal or talk about someone else's social class, at least to their face."

Howard asked, "Why is that?"

"Because most people here have a lot of privilege and wealthy people don't talk about anything real when it comes to their privilege," she said with an assertive tone in her voice. Her comments halted our discussion. Several students squirmed in their seats, nervously looking away from Anna. A few students made eye contact with one another, and then quickly broke it to avoid the awkwardness of the moment. Anna had done something we rarely do in our community; she had made privilege visible.

This activity initiated our efforts to excavate privilege in order to understand how it works. Soon after, we embarked on a participatory action research (PAR) project developed to explore the individual and cultural processes involved in constructing and cultivating privilege. In so doing, we joined a growing number of researchers using collaborative approaches to study privilege.[1] Although no two projects are alike, a common understanding is that PAR is a collaborative approach, "founded on versions of justice, grounded in evidence, and working toward reform; it is a political use of research by community members to better understand and improve their communities."[2] Researchers are engaging in a variety of PAR projects, using a wide range of methods guided by an equally wide range of theoretical perspectives, to explore how privilege is reinforced by and through the daily practices of privileged individuals and the structures, policies, and practices of the institutions in which they occupy, study, and work. These recent endeavors are significantly advancing our understandings of how privilege works.

Encouraged by the potential of this collaborative approach, we conducted a research study to explore eight affluent adolescents' self-understandings and the role of these understandings in generating and reinforcing their privilege. Our project added a friendly amendment to how PAR is commonly understood by defining "our community" as privileged young people instead of just those within the Colby community. Our collective deliberately focused on privileged youth outside Colby so that we maintained enough distance from the participants to take nothing for granted. Over the course of the project, we read theory and previous research on adolescent identity development and privilege. We collaborated to formulate research questions, design the study, develop research instruments, collect and interpret data, and construct case studies. In the end and throughout the research, each of us involved in the project brought different forms of knowledge and expertise to our exploration. This book is the result of our collaborative efforts.

At the heart of this project are our empirical efforts to understand more fully how the workings of privilege are revealed through these eight affluent adolescents' understandings of self, others, and the world around them. But we did not cast our gaze only toward others in our critical inquiry of privilege. As members of an elite community, we are, to varying degrees, ourselves part of a privileged group. Our efforts to further develop a critical awareness of our own understandings are also central to this book. During this project, we submitted our own privilege to the same rigorous analysis as we did to understand the eight adolescents who participated in this research. Although this analysis of our understandings and privilege is mostly a subtext,[3] it gave shape to what we present in the pages that follow.

In the remaining sections of this chapter, we offer a brief discussion of the theoretical concepts that inform our analysis of the adolescents' self-understandings. We explore how privilege has been understood and studied before articulating a conception of privilege that highlights the relationship between advantages and identity formation. We then discuss some of the recent empirical efforts to understand the role that privilege plays in shaping affluent adolescents' experiences and identities. At the end, some background for the research reported in this book is described.

HOW PRIVILEGE WORKS

The ways in which inequalities are created and persist in the United States has been the subject of a considerable amount of debate in popular culture and in the social sciences. Various key concepts—such as exclusion, social/political/economic divisions, discrimination, disadvantage, powerlessness, marginalization, and oppression—have emerged from these debates to explain the dynamics that facilitate and maintain these inequalities. Although these concepts are important in explaining and exploring the various costs of inequalities for disadvantaged individuals and groups, they have done little in addressing the role played by those individuals and groups who benefit most from existing inequalities. Nor do they provide an adequate framework for examining how inequalities are reinforced by and through the actions of advantaged individuals and groups. Therefore, as Bob Pease argues, "We need to develop a new vocabulary to understand the ways in which various dimensions of privilege are interconnected and reproduced."[4] We begin to develop this new vocabulary just by "the very naming of privilege as opposed to discrimination, social exclusion, oppression and so forth [to give] another perspective from which to understand social inequality."[5]

Over the past twenty-five years, a few scholars have offered this new vocabulary and other perspectives by defining privilege and exploring how it works. This body of work has examined the ways in which race, gender, and sexuality, in particular, operate in all our lives and are inextricably involved with issues of power and power differences. Privilege has been conceived as consisting of the advantages that certain individuals have over others, which have been granted to them not because of what they have done but because of the social category (or categories) to which they belong.[6] Most often, these advantages are not recognized as such by those who have them. Individuals from dominant groups tend to have little awareness "of their own dominant identity, of the privileges it affords them, of the oppression suffered by the corresponding disadvantaged group, and of how they perpetuate it."[7] In fact, one of the functions of privilege is to structure the world in ways that conceal how privilege works, so that advantages remain invisible to those who benefit from them.[8] These scholars have argued that individuals' lack of awareness of their advantages, what some call "the luxury of obliviousness,"[9] is an important part of understanding how privilege works.[10]

One of the first writers to relate the concept of privilege to advantages that individuals receive because they belong to particular social and cultural groups was Peggy McIntosh. In her essay on what she calls the "invisible knapsack" of privilege, she identifies specific advantages that are available to her as a white person but not available to people of color. As she explains, "My skin color was an asset for any move that I was educated to make, I could think of myself as 'belonging' in major ways, and of making social systems work for me."[11] Before becoming aware of her white privilege, she took these advantages for granted as neutral, normal, and universally available to everyone. She encourages others who have privilege to follow her example by opening their "invisible knapsack" of privilege, which contains all their benefits from social, cultural, and economic positions. She urges them to take a critical look at all the various and often unconscious ways in which they enjoy advantages that others do not have.

McIntosh identifies two types of privilege, which other scholars have explored in more detail over the years. The first is "unearned entitlements," which are rights that all people should have, such as feeling safe, being respected, and having access to all the opportunities that life offers. Unearned entitlements become a form of privilege—what McIntosh calls "unearned advantages"—when they are restricted to certain groups of people. These unearned advantages give members of dominant groups a competitive edge that they are reluctant to acknowledge or give up; they are often thought of as outcomes brought about by hard work, good choices, and great effort. The other form of privilege is "conferred dominance," which occurs when one group has power over another. Cultural assumptions related to people's social positions help to determine assumptions about which group is meant to dominate another group. Conferred dominance is entrenched in cultural assumptions that establish patterns of control and maintain societal hierarchies.

According to McIntosh and most others who study privilege, we begin to confront privilege by becoming aware of unearned advantages and conferred dominance. This awareness allows privileged individuals to acknowledge that their advantages come at an expense to others. The more aware people are of their privilege, the better they can contribute to changing themselves and the systems that facilitate inequalities. Because privilege is rooted primarily in social systems, change does not happen only at the individual level; the systems that support privilege must be transformed as well. Privileged people, of course, need to contribute to the work necessary for changing these systems, but it is not enough for them simply to change.[12] Social change, however, can begin only when they do.

RETHINKING PRIVILEGE

The scholarship on privilege paved the way for us to examine the complex ways in which privilege works through memberships,[13] representations,[14] actions,[15] and language[16] to re-create itself, thereby perpetuating structures, systems, and practices that create and maintain inequalities.[17] This work established a critical foundation for making systems of privilege visible and revealing the ways in which advantaged individuals and groups work to reinforce privilege. While this work has generated useful understandings, limitations exist in the ways privilege is conceptualized and studied. By and large, scholars have constructed *commodified* notions of privilege. Privilege, in other words, has been understood extrinsically, as something individuals *have* or *possess,* rather than as something more intrinsic, something that reveals who they *are* or who they have *become* in a fundamental sense. Although some have acknowledged intrinsic aspects of privilege—in particular the influence of privilege on people's identities—the prominent views on privilege have ultimately fallen short in providing a framework for exploring those aspects.[18]

Allan Johnson, for instance, argues that privilege is formed from standards of comparison, or what he identifies as "reference groups."[19] Johnson explains that people use these reference groups to construct a sense of where they are located in the scheme of things in order to determine whether they are doing better or worse than others. People figuring out where they are located in comparison to others appears to be a very intrinsic process. However, Johnson goes on to argue that privilege is not derived primarily from how people feel they fit in or what they have done but is more about the social category to which they belong.[20] Privilege, therefore, is framed mainly as something individuals have (in this case, a particular social category) instead of their process of figuring out what they have and where they belong. Like others, he does not draw on a theoretical perspective that would allow him to explore the intrinsic aspects of privilege.

Moreover, several scholars emphasize the importance of social class in the study of privilege, but they rarely focus on it. Michael Kimmel argues that one reason for this lack of focus is that "class can be concealed and class feels like something we have earned all by ourselves. Therefore, class privilege may be the one set of privileges we are least interested in examining because they feel like they are ours by right, not by birth."[21] This is, as Kimmel further explains, "all the more reason to take a look at class."[22] Despite similar calls by others, class is situated in ways that make it seem less important than other forms of privilege.[23] Most often, class is unacknowledged and therefore remains invisible. This lack of attention to class is more than just a gap in the literature; it is a conceptual link missing in the understanding of privilege.

Departing from the ways in which privilege has been studied and understood up to this point, this book puts class front and center while recognizing privilege along the intersecting axes of race, gender, sexuality, and other social and cultural categories. With this focus on class privilege, we move beyond commodified notions of privilege to articulate a conception of *privilege as identity*.[24] As an identity or an aspect of identity, privilege is a lens through which individuals with advantages understand themselves, others, and the world around them. Their values, perspectives, assumptions, and actions are shaped, created, re-created, and maintained through this lens of privilege. This view of privilege is more concerned with people's self-understandings than their advantages. To think about privilege in this way is not to deny or diminish the importance of advantages that certain individuals and groups have over others, but it is, in fact, to underline the relationship between advantages and identity formation and thus to understand the ways individuals actively construct and cultivate privilege.[25]

Identity is rarely addressed explicitly in the study of privilege; instead, scholars use related concepts such as identification, membership, and social category. However, an implied view of identity emerges from this body of work that challenges traditional ways of thinking about identity as a distinctive and stable set of characteristics belonging to an individual or group. Instead, the common thinking is that identities develop within social and cultural groups and out of the socially and culturally marked differences and commonalities that permeate interactions within and between groups. According to this perspective, identities are marked by many categories: gender, race, ethnicity, sexuality, nationality, class, religion, and ability, to name the ones most commonly discussed. These different categories have meaning in the material and symbolic structures that organize social and cultural groups in societies. Groups are positioned in particular ways to put some groups at an advantage (and therefore others at a disadvantage) in the "accumulation of power, resources, legitimacy, dignity and recognition."[26] But larger structures in societies are constantly in flux; therefore identities are not fixed. What may be meaningful about identity at a particular moment or in a certain context may not be so meaningful at another moment or in another context. Because of this continuous placement and displacement of who people are, identities are viewed as multiple, contextual, and contingent.

In this book, we extend this view of identities as being constantly influenced by various contexts, structures, and interactions to establish a more useful framing for exploring intrinsic aspects of privilege. We primarily view identities as forms of *self-understanding*[27]: "People tell others who they are, but even more important, they tell themselves and then try to act as though they are who they say they are."[28] These self-understandings are not, however, simply individual, internal, psychological qualities or subjective understandings that emerge solely from self-reflection.[29] Identities, instead, link the personal and the social—they are constituted relationally[30]; they entail action and interaction in a sociocultural context[31]; they are social products that live in and through activity and practice[32]; and they are always performed and enacted.[33]

Our main focus is on what individuals *say* and *do* through the stories they tell that reflect their self-understandings. The analytic premise of this book is that when people describe their experiences, perspectives, beliefs, and ideas, they communicate and enact particular versions of their self-understandings. We agree with the many scholars who argue that it is through these stories that people create themselves.[34] As Ruthellen Josselson points out, "The self and identity become the entity which is enacting the particular story under construction."[35] People construct stories to share how they see themselves, others, and the world around them.[36] Stories are the linguistic form in which self-understandings can be expressed.[37] Like any story that reflects the realities of life, these stories are often nonlinear and filled with contradictions, unresolved issues, and tensions. However, constructed by a particular plot and around specific themes, each story reveals information about who a person is.

The portraits of the eight affluent adolescents presented in this book capture some of the stories they tell to themselves and others that reveal significant aspects of their self-understandings. Given that self-understandings are provisional, the stories that gave shape to these portraits will undoubtedly change and be told differently at future moments in their lives. This book provides a glimpse of the stories the adolescents tell now and what these stories reflect about their current self-understandings at this critical moment in the formation of their identities.[38]

RESEARCHING AFFLUENT ADOLESCENTS

Some relatively recent work in the study of adolescence suggests that understanding adolescence involves a consideration of how social categories such as race, class, gender, and sexuality affect individual development. This body of scholarship has challenged stage and phase theories of development, which tend to ignore the impact of these social categories on an individual's experience and identity. Scholars have increasingly argued that these theories are insufficient for explaining the complex influence these factors have on an individual's behaviors, beliefs, and sense of self. This research has also challenged the "storm and stress" model of adolescent development, which understands adolescence as a transitional period to adulthood filled with contradictory emotions and behaviors.[39] This perspective of adolescence—as a period of struggle before adulthood—had a profound influence on the study of adolescence during the twentieth century. However, versions of what is and is not normal during adolescence have been modified and challenged over the years.[40] In more recent work, scholars are increasingly accepting "many variations within their definitions of normality in adolescence."[41] This has made the study of adolescence "more inclusive in terms of who is studied, what questions are asked, and how experience is analyzed."[42]

Even with this more comprehensive and inclusive approach, the topic of class privilege in the study of adolescence, as in other fields, is underscrutinized. Even when researchers address various social class factors that mediate adolescents' experiences and identities, they have largely failed to interrogate the conditions and circumstances of class privilege. Committed instead to examining the adverse consequences of oppression, the gaze of researchers has fallen primarily upon adolescents from disadvantaged backgrounds. Although this work is important and still very much needed, researchers "have thereby left in the shadows the dynamics that facilitate and protect privilege . . . how resources, opportunities, dignity, and social rewards flow 'upward' and remain there, so as to appear both natural and deserved."[43] As Brett Stoudt further points out, "Infrequent are empirical efforts to understand privileged statuses on their own terms as lived identities . . . systemically connected to the many inequalities experienced by others."[44] The absence of this critical gaze on class privilege helps to normalize the mechanisms that reinforce privilege even further.

There are ways in which class privilege has remained invisible that are specific to the study of adolescence. Similar to the overgeneralizations that researchers made in the past by using particular groups of adolescents (mostly white middle-class males) to represent everyone,[45] some who study privileged adolescents or adolescents within privileged contexts position them as representative and their experiences the "norm." They do this in part by leaving class privilege unexamined and unexplored—and in some cases, completely ignored. For example, Denise Pope's study of five adolescents' perspectives on their educational experiences attending a school located in a wealthy California suburb altogether avoids an examination of privilege.[46] Although her study provides useful insight into the ways in which adolescents at an affluent high school "do school" in their pursuits of academic success, she makes only a fleeting reference to the elite nature of the school and the affluence of its student body. In so doing, she disregards the powerful ways in which privilege influences these adolescents' perspectives. Although it is possible that not all of her participants are from class-privileged backgrounds,[47] they all attend an elite school and their ways of knowing and doing are undoubtedly influenced by this context.

Affluent adolescents' experiences and perceptions have also been positioned as the norm in popular forms of inquiry and representation. For example, in the critically acclaimed film *Race to Nowhere*, most of the youths showcased are from class-privileged backgrounds, but this is not acknowledged. Instead, their experiences are used to make some broad claims about what adolescents in general are experiencing in "the high-stakes, high-pressure culture" of schools and the consequences of this culture: depression, burnout, stress, and disengagement. The film does a great job of convincing its viewers that this is what all youths are experiencing today. There is not one reference to the role that privilege plays in shaping these young people's experiences. Ironically, one of the experts repeatedly interviewed in the film, Madeline Levine, is an influential scholar-practitioner of the study of privileged adolescents.[48] However, Levine does not surface the topic of class privilege even when she clearly refers to experiences particular to affluent youth. Like others in the film, she frames their experiences as representative of all.

Some researchers do a better job at acknowledging privilege in their research of affluent adolescents but have largely failed at offering a critical analysis of privilege. This is certainly the case in the body of work that explores what Levine calls "the price of privilege"—that is, the various "disadvantages" that affluent adolescents encounter because of the circumstances and experiences associated with being privileged. Specifically, numerous studies show that affluent adolescents experience rates of depression, anxiety disorders, and substance abuse to a greater extent than adolescents of other social class groups.[49] These researchers argue that various factors associated with privilege—in particular, materialism, pressure to achieve, and disconnection—combine to create a crisis for affluent adolescents. Although these studies offer a valuable exploration of the various psychological costs associated with privilege, they research these costs in ways that ignore or at the very least minimize advantages. They study privilege as if it were separate from that which creates and maintains the advantaged circumstances of affluent adolescents. Privilege, therefore, is largely unacknowledged and unexamined even though these researchers are critical of it.

In recent years there has been a small yet important body of research on affluent adolescents that offers a more comprehensive exploration of privilege. This work has revealed the contours and consequences of privilege that shape affluent adolescents' experiences and identities. For example, Shamus Khan, in his study of adolescents at the elite St. Paul's School, finds that privilege remains a constant, powerful influence on students' learning despite the demographic shifts in the institution.[50] Similarly, Rubén Gaztambide-Fernández demonstrates that the unchanging nature of an elite school influences the ways in which privileged and nonprivileged adolescents become a part of that school's culture.[51] In another recent study, Adam Howard finds that affluent adolescents within the schooling context learn incredibly important lessons about their place in the world, their relationships with others, and who they are; these embrace particular norms, perspectives, dispositions, and ideologies that reinforce and regenerate privilege.[52] Likewise, Sarah Chase's analysis of gender performances at an elite boarding school highlights how affluent adolescents learn to preserve their privilege.[53] She joins others who have explored the ways in which gender and class intersect and interact to shape affluent adolescents' overall experiences within elite schools.[54]

These are just a few of the recent empirical efforts to understand not only the role that privilege plays in shaping affluent adolescents' experiences and identities but also the ways in which their life and schooling advantages are sustained and further generated. While these recent advances in scholarship represent a dramatic shift in the study of affluent adolescents, there is much ground yet to cover and important questions that remain to be addressed. This body of work has focused primarily on institutional arrangements, policies, and practices of elite schools that maintain and advance affluent adolescents' advantaged circumstances. The focus, then, has been mainly on institutions and not on affluent adolescents themselves. Specifically, we know little about their self-understandings and the role of these understandings in developing and cultivating their privilege.[55]

This book therefore breaks new ground in the study of affluent adolescents. Expanding on recent efforts to emphasize the role that privilege plays in shaping affluent youths' identities and experiences, we explore the complicated and, at times, conflicting qualities of eight affluent adolescents' self-understandings. Although this small sample is too limited to be representative, the portraits presented in this book offer a view of their diverse and similar understandings of self, others, the world around them, and the role of these understandings in constructing and cultivating privilege.

PORTRAITS OF SELF-UNDERSTANDINGS

As a group, the eight adolescents who are at the center of this book reflect the diversity of what Khan identifies as the "new elite."[56] They are not all born into wealthy families. Their families are not all the same—some of their parents are divorced and some of them have siblings. They are not all white; one is Asian American, one is Latino, and one is biracial (Arab American and Native American). They are not all Christian—one is an atheist, one is Jewish, and one is Muslim. They do not all attend private schools—five attend (or attended) public schools. They live in different regions of the United States—one in the Northeast, one in the Southeast, one in the Midwest, two on the West Coast, and two in the Northwest; and one lives abroad in Malaysia. There is an even split between females and males. There are also some differences in relation to their sexuality—six identify as straight, one as gay, and one as questioning. Although there are differences within the group, all of them are between the ages of 16 and 19; they are all U.S. citizens from affluent families and identify (and were identified by the research team) as privileged.[57]

In our research we rely on the categories that Jean Anyon outlined in her seminal work on class divisions in schooling to define what we mean in referring to the participants as "privileged." All of the participants come from families with characteristics of those whom Anyon identified as affluent professional and executive elite (what others commonly refer to as "upper middle class" and "upper class").[58] Unless they are independently wealthy,[59] the participants' parents are either executives or high-status professionals, and most are college-educated. The participants' families have an annual income that places them in the top 10 percent—although only two of the families fall below the top 5 percent and three are in the top 1 percent.

To keep the focus on the adolescents' self-understandings, we limited our data collection mainly to interviews with the adolescents. All eight adolescents participating in this study were interviewed five times by one member of the research team, with each interview lasting sixty to ninety minutes. Building on the data collected from these interviews, we kept in contact with the adolescents to ask follow-up questions as we constructed the portraits. We also gathered some additional information about the schooling and community contexts in which the participants were situated to provide a more complete background for these contexts. This additional information was not used to contradict or interpret what the adolescents told us during the interviews and follow-ups. Hence the experiences and perceptions captured here are rooted in the words of the young people themselves.

They played a critical role in giving shape to the portraits. As such, this book is primarily descriptive; the portraits evolved mainly through what the interviewees shared and revealed to us about their self-understandings.

As evident through these portraits, the eight adolescents are more different than they are similar. They live and attend school in different settings, ranging from a small, homogenous suburban community in Massachusetts to a diverse city of 7 million people in Malaysia and from a large public school in Kentucky to an elite boarding school in California. Their lives are marked by distinct experiences, from living a sheltered life to traveling throughout the world, from managing the stresses of a demanding academic program to spending days surfing and playing music, from relying on a supportive family to enduring an abusive home life. They are pursuing different life and career goals, from aspiring to become a professional dancer to preparing to enter the finance and business world, from wanting to make as much money as possible to intending to spend as much time as possible serving the poor. Even with the particularities of the adolescents' experiences, immediate worlds, and aspirations, six common qualities of their self-understandings—*confident, isolated, certain, independent, hardworking, and scripted*—emerge from their stories of self, others, and the world around them.

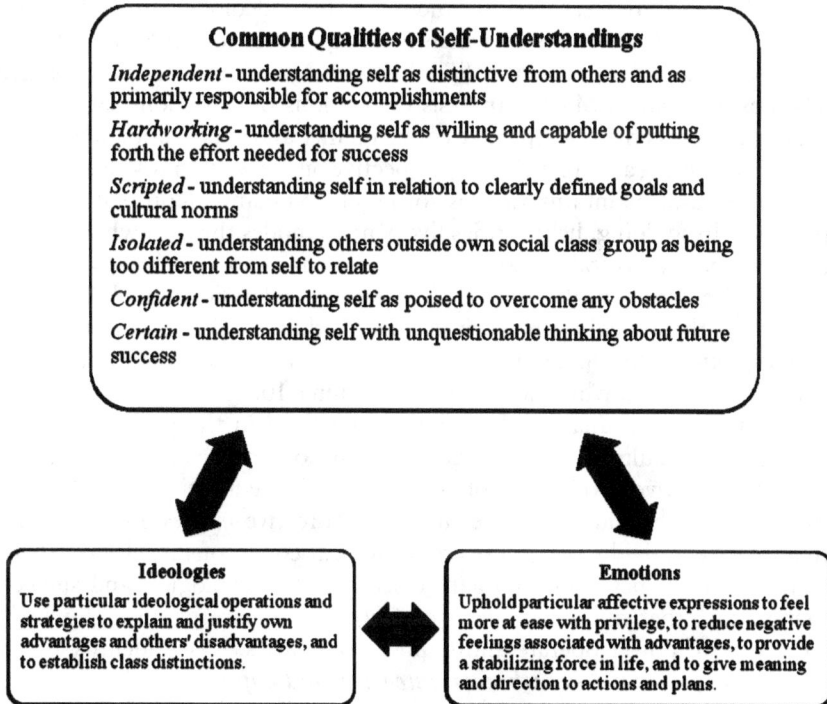

Common Qualities of Self-Understandings

Independent - understanding self as distinctive from others and as primarily responsible for accomplishments

Hardworking - understanding self as willing and capable of putting forth the effort needed for success

Scripted - understanding self in relation to clearly defined goals and cultural norms

Isolated - understanding others outside own social class group as being too different from self to relate

Confident - understanding self as poised to overcome any obstacles

Certain - understanding self with unquestionable thinking about future success

Ideologies
Use particular ideological operations and strategies to explain and justify own advantages and others' disadvantages, and to establish class distinctions.

Emotions
Uphold particular affective expressions to feel more at ease with privilege, to reduce negative feelings associated with advantages, to provide a stabilizing force in life, and to give meaning and direction to actions and plans.

Figure 1.1 Constructing and cultivating privilege.

It is important to note that these six qualities provide only a partial view of the adolescents' overall self-understandings. Given the differences among them, it is not surprising that there are other qualities—such as lonely, caring, energetic, and rebellious, for example—threaded through some adolescents' self-understandings but not shared by all. However, their common understandings of self, others, and the world around them help us to see the individual and cultural processes involved in the production and maintenance of their privilege. These common qualities reveal how privilege is a lens through which the adolescents form their self-understandings. Through this lens of privilege, they negotiate their identities in ways to preserve and possibly even advance their advantages in life. As represented in Figure 1.1, various ideologies and particular emotions play important roles in the processes involved in forming and sustaining this lens. Their self-understandings are constituted in relation to and coordination with specific ideologies and emotions to construct and cultivate privilege. Their privilege is more than what they have; it is a crucial part of themselves and their self-understandings, which they renew, recreate, defend, and modify ideologically and affectively.

To identify and analyze the adolescents' use of various ideological operations and strategies, we are guided heavily by British sociologist John B. Thompson's critical conceptualization of ways that ideologies intersect with relations of power. To study and understand ideology, argues Thompson, "is to study the ways in which meaning serves to establish and sustain relations of domination."[60] Starting with Marx's concept of ideology, Thompson expands Marx's analysis of relations of class domination and subordination as the principal axes of inequality and exploitation in human societies, offering a more inclusive perspective on the ways in which ideology establishes and maintains various forms of dominant-subordinate power relations. In so doing, he identifies five general modes through which ideology can operate to establish and sustain relations of domination: "legitimation, dissimulation, unification, fragmentation, and reification."[61] We make use of this theoretical framework to unearth those of the adolescents' ideologies that are "in the service of power,"[62] and to analyze the significance of these ideologies, which we discuss in Chapter 10.

To identify and analyze the emotions involved in the process of constructing and cultivating privilege, we draw on the emergent efforts to map the affective production of privilege in elite educational contexts.[63] Informed by this literature, we interpret "affective expressions as more than merely individual responses to structural conditions . . . [but rather] as the interface between dominant discourses [or ideologies] and subjectivities, such that embodied affects constitute an apparatus through which structures of power operate and impose boundaries."[64] We identify three affective expressions—*worthiness, integrity, and happiness*—that interact with their ideologies to uphold a necessary framing of self to feel more at ease with their privileged status, to reduce negative feelings associated with their advantages, to provide a stabilizing force in their lives, and to give meaning and direction to their actions and plans. Although the meanings that form and support their self-understandings involve an amalgam of emotions, the portraits emphasize these three emotions, which are most powerfully involved in the production of privilege.

The first portrait explores the understandings of Meredith, who welcomes any opportunity to leave her everyday privileged world to travel to contrary realities. Believing that people living in poverty are often born into circumstances that are beyond their control, she dreams of one day serving the poor as a doctor in Central America. She is confident that even if this ideal position does not pan out, she will adjust her goals as necessary in achieving inevitable success. This sense of security, derived mostly from her close family relationships, characterizes much of Meredith's existence, allowing her to explore the world on community service trips, become involved in challenging activities, take demanding courses in school, and embrace the unfamiliar without much hesitation.

An air of mystery surrounds Herman. An aspiring screenwriter, he has created a cautious script for his own life. He speaks with quiet confidence, carefully considering every word so he stays in character. Rare moments when he slips out of character reveal that he wants to express ideas that are in conflict with his scripted world. But he quickly falls back into his normal role, concealing his inner self from those around him. Elusive yet friendly, Herman prefers being alone—catching up on the latest films, reading books, or writing scripts—to spending time with family or friends. Either alone or surrounded by others, his thoughts often drift toward the future. With his love of writing and the knowledge and skills he has gained through his private school education, he confidently looks at the road ahead toward becoming the next great cinematic writer.

Wanting nothing more than to gain admissions to an elite college, academics are Kayla's highest priority. She daydreams of going abroad for a year between high school and college but knows deep down that this will never happen. Unable to veer off the direct path to success, she plans to continue her educational career without interruptions. Kayla puts much effort into demonstrating her intelligence to those around her, especially her family. Watching her older sisters wander aimlessly through their schooling, she is determined to do the opposite. She wants everyone around her to know that she is headed toward success. Her plans for what lies ahead often collide with what her father envisions for her future. Noticing her exceptional skills and abilities, he pressures her to take over the family business one day. Kayla, however, has no interest in following in his footsteps. She wants to find her own career and make it on her own through hard work and dedication.

As a self-proclaimed entrepreneur, Marcus has no trouble staying busy with his numerous endeavors. While attending a small elite private college in New England, he somehow finds the time to hold an internship at a computer software company as well as create his own website for hopeful college athletes who are looking for a way to get their names and talents into the recruiting circuit. As an athlete himself, he has created an idea that he believes will transform the college recruiting process. Marcus is keen on becoming a completely self-made businessman, independent from his family's wealth. He has no plans to rely on his life and schooling advantages to achieve what he wants out of life but instead wants to make it on his own.

Sarah juggles her multiple responsibilities as a student in the competitive Science and Math Magnet Program in Kentucky. Her academic responsibilities consume most of her time and social life, but she would never give it up to be a "general" student at Anderson High School, the public school in which the program is housed. Sarah confidently has her sights set on becoming a chemical engineer, something she has been working toward since the eighth grade. No obstacles will discourage her from achieving her goals, not even her learning difference. She often feels that peers outside her prestigious magnet program are not as motivated in school or achieving academically at the same level. In her peripheral vision she sees the "general" students at her school blurring into failure, but straight ahead she clearly sees her own isolated path to success clearly laid out.

Whether it is building a fish tank or learning to play the guitar, Leo accomplishes anything he sets his mind to do. School, however, was never something that grabbed his interest. After almost dropping out from his junior year of high school, Leo barely managed to graduate from an alternative high school program. His immediate future plans involve playing music, surfing, and avoiding any kind of restrictive nine-to-five work schedule. To those who surround him, Leo seems like a complete failure in comparison to the successful men in his family. But he is completely certain that his future is bright. When something sparks his interest and finally motivates him, he is well aware that nothing will stop him from achieving success and happiness on his own terms.

Fluent in Japanese, highly trained in ballet, involved in numerous activities, and academically high-achieving, Olive has the credentials to fill out a college application but has no specific direction at this point. Although college is assumed to lie in her future, she has been carefully sheltered from the world beyond her school, family, and secluded community. With a solid strain of rebellion running through her, Olive manages to carve out small areas of self-expression in a life where most of her choices are made by her parents. Although she often maintains a quiet presence, her rebellious spirit and confidence emerge most visibly and often through her love of hip-hop dancing. She constantly bargains with her parents to have the freedom to express her true self through this form of dance. Throughout her life she has found other ways to set herself apart from her family. Dreaming of attending college in a faraway large city, she is certain that she will eventually gain the freedom to explore the world in her own way.

On the stage, Jacob appears strong and graceful, but behind the scenes he is struggling to escape the painful realities of his home life. The hurts and disappointments of his family's rejection of him for being gay cast a massive shadow over his daily experiences. Although Jacob's family relationships improved after they moved to Malaysia two years ago, he avoids being around them whenever possible. He spends all of his time working on new choreography for dance shows, practicing for his upcoming performance, watching YouTube videos to learn new dance moves, and anything else that places him closer to realizing his dream of becoming a professional dancer. Above all, the world of dance is his escape. Wanting to move to New York City and sever ties with his parents, he is confident that he can make it on his own and forget his past forever.

These eight windows on affluent adolescents' self-understandings illuminate the relationship between advantages and self-understandings and reveal efforts to construct and cultivate privilege. As we listen to these stories, we see them through our own lenses—our own interpretations, influenced by our own assumptions, perspectives, beliefs, and self-understandings. As we talk and get to know these adolescents, we feel as though "we are in a hall of mirrors, seeing ourselves reflected in each other's eyes, hearing our conversations echoed in their stories."[65] Through our conversations and relationships with them, we explore our own privilege. We invite you to bring your own interpretations to these portraits. Listen to their stories to examine your own assumptions about privileged youth and to reflect upon your own self-understandings.

NOTES

1. For example, Stoudt, 2007, 2009; Stoudt, Fox, & Fine, 2012.
2. Stoudt, 2009, p. 8.
3. A discussion of this analysis is provided in Chapter 11.
4. Pease, 2010, p. 7.
5. Ibid.
6. For example, Jensen, 2005; Johnson, 2001; Kimmel & Ferber, 2010; Rothenberg, 2002.
7. Goodman, 2011, p. 22.
8. For further discussion on this point, see Bailey, 1998.
9. Johnson, 2001, p. 24.
10. Moreover, people from dominant groups are advantaged regardless of their individual attitudes. As Goodman (2011) points out, "They neither have to be aware of the advantages nor want to receive them" (p. 21).
11. McIntosh, 1988, p. 11.
12. See Bishop, 2002; Goodman, 2011; Hardiman & Jackson, 1997; Tappan, 2006.
13. For example, Jensen, 2002; Wise, 2002.
14. For example, Mantsios, 2003.
15. For example, Johnson, 2001.
16. For example, Kleinman & Ezzell, 2003.
17. For example, Jensen, 2005; Wise, 2005.

18. One of the very few exceptions is Khan's (2011) study of the elite St. Paul's School. He found that privilege became "inscribed upon the bodies of students and how students are able to display their privilege through their interactions. In being embodied, privilege is not seen as a product of differences in opportunities but instead as a skill, talent, capacity—'who you are'" (p. 16).
19. Johnson, 2001.
20. More specifically, Johnson (2001) argues, "When it comes to privilege . . . it doesn't really matter who we really are. What matters is who other people *think* we are, which is to say, the social categories they put us in" (p. 35).
21. Kimmel, 2010, p. 8.
22. Ibid.
23. For example, Johnson (2001) argues, "Class is fundamentally different from gender, race, and sexual orientation. The most important difference is that while we all have the potential to change our class position, the other forms of difference are almost impossible to change. Unlike class, differences of gender, race, and sexual orientation are associated with the body itself" (pp. vii–ix). This is a common perspective in the body of work on privilege.
24. Therefore this conception of class privilege, in particular, reflects the recent shift in thinking about class from simply an economic position to a central aspect of a person's identity. As Dowling (2009) explains, "Contemporary theorizations of class, unlike many of their predecessors, are less concerned with class as a form of socio-economic classification, a position in the labour market or as a relationship to the means of production, and more concerned with the ways class as an identity is forged and experienced" (p. 2).
25. In a previous work, Howard (2008) goes theoretically deeper into this concept of privilege as identity.
26. Stoudt, Fox, & Fine, 2012, p. 179.
27. Identity and self-understanding are used interchangeably throughout the book to emphasize this way of thinking.
28. Holland, Lachicotte, Skinner, & Cain, 1998, p. 3.
29. See Damon & Hart, 1988.
30. See Apple & Weis, 1983; Wexler, 1992.
31. Penuel & Wertsch 1995; Tappan, 2000, 2005.
32. Holland, Lachicotte, Skinner, & Cain, 1998.
33. Butler, 1990, 1991.
34. See, for example, Fischer-Rosenthal, 2000; MacIntyre, 1984; McAdams, 1999.
35. Josselson, 2004, p. 2.
36. Drawing on Bruner's (1990) narrative discourse, Gaztambide-Fernández (2009) uses this perspective in his notion of a discourse of distinction (pp. 13–15).
37. See, for example, Wortham, 2001.
38. Many scholars have argued that adolescence is a critical stage in identity formation. For a discussion on what makes this stage so critical in an individual's lifespan, see Part One in Garrod, Smulyan, Powers, & Kilkenny, 2012. Also see Erikson (1968), who helped shape our understandings—past and present—of identity formation in adolescence.
39. Hall, 1904.
40. See for example, Blos, 1962; Erikson, 1968; Freud, 1946; Mead, 1958.
41. Garrod, Smulyan, Powers, & Kilkenny, 2012, p. xv.
42. Ibid., xv.
43. Stoudt, Fox, & Fine, 2012, p. 179.
44. Stoudt, 2009, p. 8.

45. Feminist scholars, in particular, have pointed out this overrepresentation in the study of adolescence and other fields for decades. Michelle Fine has been one of the leading scholars—both in her theoretical work and research—to interrupt this tendency of situating white middle-class males as the norm and representative in social science research. See, for example, Fine & Gordon, 1992; Fine & Macpherson, 1992.
46. Pope, 2001.
47. Pope does not identify the adolescents' class backgrounds. She provides certain information about the adolescents suggesting that some of them are not from class privilege backgrounds. However, one can only assume this to be the case because she does not explicitly provide this information.
48. For example, Levine, 2006.
49. For example, Csikszentmihalyi & Schneider, 2000; Levine, 2006; Luthar & Becker, 2002; Luthar & D'Avanzo, 1999; Way, Stauber, Nakkula, & London, 1994.
50. Khan, 2011.
51. Gaztambide-Fernández, 2009.
52. Howard, 2008.
53. Chase, 2008.
54. For example, Proweller, 1999; Reichert, 2000; Stoudt, 2009.
55. Seider's (2010) research the impact of learning about homelessness on affluent adolescents' beliefs about homelessness, opportunity, and inequality is one of the few recent studies to explore affluent adolescents' self-understandings. See also Howard, 2010.
56. Khan, 2011.
57. During the process of selecting participants, we asked the adolescents if they identified as privileged and they all did. We realized that how they determined what it means to be privileged could possibly, or even likely, be different from our own understandings of what it means to be privileged. For the purposes of this study, however, we felt it was necessary that the adolescents themselves identified as privileged as a starting point for our discussions about their privilege.
58. Anyon, 1981.
59. "Independently wealthy" means that individuals have enough acquired wealth that their livelihood is not dependent on others. Some of the participants' parents did not have to work to maintain their wealth. They did certain kinds of work more out of interest than necessity. Their work would be considered neither high-status nor high-paying.
60. Thompson, 1990, p. 56.
61. Ibid., p. 60.
62. Thompson, 1984, p. 7.
63. For example, Maxwell & Aggleton, 2013.
64. Gaztambide-Fernández, Cairns, & Desai, 2013, p. 35.
65. Lawrence-Lightfoot, 2000, p. 13.

2 Meredith
Confidently Traveling

*with Anna Caron, Jenifer Goldman,
Katie Griffin, Connie Jangro,
Celeste Lattanzi, and Adele Priestley*

I've figured out so much about myself by traveling to so many different places.

As soon as seventeen-year-old Meredith steps off the plane in Costa Rica and walks through the jetway, she senses the unfamiliar smells and sights that she vaguely remembers from her last visit. Feeling both excited and nervous, she becomes lost in her thoughts about all the unknowns of the service trip she is about to begin. She snaps out of her distraction when she nearly bumps into a young boy running over to his mother. She manages to avoid a collision as he rushes by her. Redirecting her attention, she overhears an exchange between the boy and his mother.

"¿Me puedes dar dinera para comprar un dulce?" he asks while pointing to a nearby shop.

His mother replies, "No, acabas de comer. Quédate aquí; nos vamos pronto."

He pleads, "¡Por favor! ¡Quiero un chocolate!"

"Te dije que no. Siéntate y deja de pedirme. No voy a cambiar mi decision," she responds in a raised voice.

Meredith lingers nearby for a few moments, watching the boy pout and continue to beg for money to buy a candy bar. Then it occurs to her that she understood every word of their exchange. At that moment, she realizes why her father insisted that she become fluent in Spanish. "He always told me that I needed to learn another language so I can interact with more groups of people worldwide and connect with them more because I know their language," she reports. Even though she has heard her father say this on numerous occasions, she never fully understood what he meant but his words now make sense. She does not directly interact with the boy or his mother; she only observes them from a distance. By knowing their language, though, she feels a connection with them. As she explains, "It's not like I really knew them, but it felt that way." By forming this "pseudorelationship," Meredith begins to feel more at ease in this unfamiliar place.

She meets the other volunteers of the program at baggage claim. After gathering their luggage, Meredith and the rest of her group begin their journey to the mountain village where they will be working alongside residents of the community on a variety of service projects, such as clearing forest trails, teaching English to students at the local elementary school, and painting community-owned buildings. When they arrive at their temporary home, Meredith and the other volunteers have only a few minutes to settle in before orientation begins. They spend the rest of the day learning about the village and program, breaking into teams, engaging in community-building activities, and preparing for the week. For the remainder of the trip, the volunteers follow a similar schedule each day. After breakfast, they set out in small teams to work on a service project, break for lunch, take a short nap, and enjoy recreational activities. During more unstructured time, Meredith takes pictures, roams the area "without any real specific purpose," writes journal entries, and hangs out "with new friends from the program and village." This trip ends up being everything she had hoped. "I got to meet new people, helped others and did things that people needed done, and learned a lot," she reports.

Shortly after returning from her service trip, she begins making plans for her next adventure. "I want to see as much of the world as possible and experience new things and places and meet different people," she explains. Traveling is an important part of Meredith's life. Since she was a toddler, her family has gone on several trips each year, visiting her father's family in Spain at least once a year and taking "other trips in Europe and Central America." With her mother, whose family lives in Rhode Island, she has visited East Coast locations on a regular basis. They have also taken "smaller road trips in the Midwest" and traveled to places throughout the U.S. After entering high school, she began taking annual service trips on her own to different states and other countries and short trips with her friends to places near and far. Like her parents, she takes advantage of every opportunity to leave her Midwest suburban community to explore unfamiliar places, meet new people, and gain additional learning experiences.

Meredith claims that her traveling experiences have been the most important factors in fostering her awareness of self and others, setting her future goals, and becoming independent and confident. Through her travels, she has "figured out who I am and what I want to do with my life." To a lesser extent, her traveling also allows her to satisfy the part of her that has "difficulty sitting still for very long and always want[ing] to do something." When at home, her desire to stay busy leads her to maintain a jam-packed schedule. While handling the challenges of a rigorous curriculum at her public high school, she maintains a fashion blog, tutors at a local elementary school, and participates in school-sponsored community service activities. She is also an avid member of her school's Feminist Club and Model United Nations, and plays lacrosse and field hockey. She rarely has free time and is completely fine with that.

She believes that these activities as well as her traveling experiences are leading her down the path to a successful future. Next year, Meredith is certain that she will be attending an elite university and majoring in "pre-med with a focus in biology and public health." During her college years, she is also confident that she will maintain the same pace to which she is accustomed; in fact, she has already prepared a "must-do list" of her eventual extracurricular activities. Without any doubts, she knows that she will reach her goal of becoming a physician. Meredith has a very clear path laid out and sees everything she has already done, and continues to do, as fitting into her plans for the future.

INEVITABLE SUCCESS

Meredith attends a public high school located in Riverside, her hometown on the outskirts of a large city in Illinois, where she has lived for the past twelve years. Eighty-five percent of Riverside's eleven thousand residents are Caucasian, and the median annual household income is over twice the national median. Although it is a small suburban village, Riverside is home to two higher educational institutions, several public schools, three private schools with religious affiliations, and two other secondary private schools, which reflects the community's strong emphasis on education. Seventy-six percent of the residents over the age of 25 hold at least a bachelor's degree and 85 percent of the teachers at Meredith's high school have master's degrees in the subject they teach. Within this mostly affluent, white suburban community, "education is valued almost above anything else. Everybody is really highly educated or on their way to be; it's just a main value among people."

Meredith's own values and her beliefs about success, which she defines as "achieving goals that you set for yourself," have been deeply influenced by her community's emphasis on educational achievement and higher learning. She points out, however, "This doesn't mean that I don't have my own beliefs about what it means to be successful; success means something different for everybody." For Meredith, "I would only think that I've become successful later on if I had a fulfilling career, made enough money for a comfortable lifestyle, and had a family." She goes on to say that this path to success is inextricably linked to "getting into a really good college, then attending medical school, and then becoming a doctor." These are the steps that she has deemed necessary to achieve *her* success. Although her idea of success closely corresponds with the prominent mindset within her community, she insists, "I have my own version of what it'll take to be successful. It may seem like what other people think, but nobody will do the exact same thing as somebody else." She recognizes the impact of her community's culture of academic achievement on her thinking but firmly believes that she holds an individualized understanding of success.

Even though Meredith places importance on being different from others in her community, she acknowledges, "My family is pretty much like everybody else in [Riverside]." Both her parents came from wealthy families, attended elite undergraduate colleges, and went on to earn graduate degrees. In fact, they met during graduate school, where they both studied economics, and then married soon after. When Meredith was younger, her mother worked as an economist for "a nonprofit tax watchdog company," but eventually left the working world to focus on her family. After graduate school, her father worked in corporate finance and then became an economist for a law firm, where he continues to work today. Like the majority of Riverside residents, her family is firmly situated in the upper class.

The only difference that sets Meredith's family apart from most others is that "my dad wasn't born in the U.S.; he's from Spain." But she goes on to say, "We're not really that different when it comes to racial stuff." Identifying as white, Meredith sees herself as similar to the vast majority of those within her community and does not "feel like an outsider or something like that 'cause [my dad is] from another country." She reasons, "Everybody's family is originally from some other place."

Meredith describes her school of over 3,000 students, East Park High School, as having a "wide variety of people." She encounters more diversity there than within the other contexts that she occupies on a regular basis. Although East Park is located in a predominantly white, affluent community, its student body is fairly diverse, with students coming from neighboring communities that are much more diverse in terms of race and, to a lesser extent, social class for its reputation as one of the best high schools in the country.[1] Students of color make up nearly 45 percent of the student body and just over 20 percent of students are economically disadvantaged. Meredith claims that "race and class don't really play a big role at [East Park]"; instead, the main divisions within the student body are "between the typical honor student and people who are also athletes and then there's kind of a gap with like a lower section of students academically."

She also lists additional social groups that divide students, such as athletes, the dance team, a religious group, and "artsy" kids. She identifies her group of friends as "athletes but also really focused on school." Even though she and her friends are "always busy with school work and our sports," they still find time to "hang out maybe one weekday night and then Friday and Saturday." As she further explains, "We really make time to just hang out and take a break from everything. It's just something that's a priority and helps us maintain a balance—a balance between work and fun." Meredith sees her closest friends as "always incredibly supportive," which she considers essential for "managing" the academic demands of the honors program.

As is typical of schools throughout the country,[2] East Park's diversity virtually disappears in the honors program, where the vast majority of students are white and affluent. For most of the school day, Meredith is surrounded by students very similar to her and is mostly separated from students who are not enrolled in the honors program. Her closest friends, who are also honors students, "come from pretty much the same types of families, have the same interests and values, all try hard in school and stuff, and all just mesh together well." Meredith claims that she and her friends "don't really think about our financial situations at home that much and don't always think about how we're similar in that way." However, they and other East Park students are "pretty aware" of others' social class in that "you have to meet people's approval based on what you wear and how much money they think you have. I guess they want to make sure that you're the same as them or something." Not seeing this as contradicting her earlier statement that social class does not "play a big role" within the student body, she further explains, "Social class matters because you tend to hang out with people in your same economic group, but that doesn't really cause a lot of problems." Meredith partially acknowledges that social class is a dividing force at her school, but she does not consider these divisions to be detrimental because "it's only natural for you to hang out with people similar to you."

Meredith feels "really comfortable being myself" around her closest friends because they hold similar interests, values, and attitudes toward education and are also on a path to guaranteed success. Feeling entirely at ease to be her true self, she is unafraid to reveal "my vulnerable side 'cause I know they'll be there to support me." She further explains, "They empathize when I need them to, when I'm facing challenges or something like that and then they push me to be persistent and overcome those challenges." Without a doubt, she knows that they will be there to help her whenever she needs support, not only because "they know that I'll be there for them if they need it" but also because "they're facing similar challenges as I am or have in the past." She goes on to say,

> My friends help me because a lot of them are in a similar situation, so it's just like solidarity. And some of them who are a few years older than us are like in med school right now; they've achieved a lot so they know what we're going through because they've been there. Because my friends are in the same situation they know when I need help; I sometimes don't even need to ask for it.

Their support and encouragement have been "invaluable" in achieving the success she has experienced so far, and they have "provided a solid foundation and given me more confidence" for pursuing what she wants to achieve later in life.

Although Meredith feels she can always turn to her friends when she needs help, she finds no one more supportive than her parents. She claims that their "unquestionable support" has fostered a "solid and close" relationship. As she explains,

> I'm very close with both of my parents at the same level even though they're divorced. I talk to them a lot. I think I hang out with my family more than most teenagers . . . I even feel more comfortable around them than my friends, which I know sounds weird. But I can act the most like myself around them.

The closeness she experiences with her parents allows her to feel that "they'll always support me no matter what. I know them well enough and they know me enough that that's not even questionable." She quickly points out, though, "Just because they're supportive doesn't mean they're pushovers. Like, they set pretty high expectations for me but they're a good balance of encouraging but not punishing me if I ever don't achieve as highly as they wanted me to or as I wanted to." With her parents' high expectations and support, Meredith is confident that they are guiding her toward a successful future.

At the same time, however, she feels that her future is ultimately in her own hands. Her parents have allowed her "to make my own decisions about things; they don't make really important decisions for me but want me to figure things out on my own." She further explains,

> They expect me to do well, but they don't necessarily push me in a particular direction or punish me if I don't. They know that I want to do well for myself and they trust me to make the right decisions, so they're not necessarily always watching me and like, talking to me about it. They think I can do whatever I want as long as I work hard. They have confidence in me.

Their confidence in Meredith, in turn, has fostered her self-confidence. "Knowing that my parents trust me and believe in me kind of like spills over into me believing that too," she claims. With absolute certainty, she knows that she will accomplish what she wants in life. As she explains, "It's really up to me; I just need to work hard enough to accomplish my goals and I know that I will, no question about that." Even though she has ambitious goals for her future, her certainty coupled with confidence allows her "not [to be] really stressed about what's in front of me. I know it's going be difficult at times but I'll get over those obstacles. I guess that I just don't worry about everything."

Without worries, Meredith casually speaks about every step that is before her in achieving her certain success:

> My most immediate goal would be to get into a really good college and then graduate from college and then go to medical school and then

become a physician. My end goal would be either working at a hospital or working at a clinic in Central America, maybe like part time so I can do other things. Wherever I end up working as a doctor I know it'll be the place for me, like where I really want to be.

She does not "see myself as having any major disadvantages that I can't overcome" in accomplishing each step because "all of these goals are fairly realistic and I'm sure everything will just like fall into place as I'm going from one step to the next one." She adds, "I've proven to myself thus far I've achieved my goals, like I'm on the right track, so there's really no reason that I would think anything would change."

As a high school senior, Meredith's most immediate step in her plan for certain success is gaining admissions to a college "that will be good enough to get into a really good medical school." To accomplish this first step, "I just need to do as well as I can in my class so I graduate with honors and have a good GPA and continue doing all my stuff in addition to my classes so that it helps me get into a good school." Because she has nearly a perfect GPA, high SAT scores, and phenomenal array of extracurricular and service activities, "I don't really see any difficulties with going where I want to go." Although she has applied to multiple schools, Meredith has her eyes set on a prestigious university not too far from home. According to her, this choice makes "the most sense for me" and "will keep me on the right path."

She is just a few weeks away from finding out whether she has been admitted to her first-choice college. Waiting to hear the outcome, she feels "a bit stressed," but "not because I think everything will fall apart if I don't get in." She goes on to say, "It's just the waiting that's a bit stressful. I just want to know whatever it is and get it over with. I guess it's just the whole process that makes you feel stressed. I mean, this is something that you've been working toward your whole life and right now you're just in this waiting game." If by chance she does not get into her first-choice college, she has "back-up plans for my back-up plans." No matter what, she will stay on the "right track" toward achieving her goals.

VALUE OF TRAVELING

"In the hills of Central Appalachia, up winding, mountain roads, is a place where children and families face unthinkable conditions, living without what most Americans take for granted," Diane Sawyer reported in *A Hidden America: Children of the Mountains*.[3] Before watching this and other eye-opening reports about such extreme poverty in the Appalachian Region, Meredith believed that this level of poverty only existed in other countries. "I know there's dire poverty in the U.S. but had seen this kind of poverty only in third-world countries—I didn't think it was here in the U.S.," she explains. After learning such poverty existed relatively close to her,[4] she was called to action; "I wanted to find a way that I could help."

Soon after coming to this awareness, Meredith took a service trip with the Appalachia Service Program (ASP), a Christian initiative that aims to make the homes of low-income Appalachians warmer, safer, and drier by recruiting volunteers to help repair and rebuild them. Although she is not particularly religious, this organization offered volunteers the types of service experiences that she wanted. "ASP has you doing work that's really needed and I wanted to feel like I was helping people out and not just taking another trip to someplace that I haven't been to," she reports. For a week, Meredith joined a group of other ASP volunteers from the Midwest to help rebuild the houses of several families living in extreme poverty in Appalachia. During this experience, she had the opportunity to develop some meaningful relationships not only with fellow volunteers but also those whom she served.

Her relationships and interactions with several people from the area "made me more aware about what it's like living in poverty and their different lifestyles and mindsets." She recalls,

> We saw the type of places that they live and their whole town and stuff, so like for example, people either didn't have a job or they would do odd jobs around town. The biggest employer was Wal-Mart, and so that was like their only option. We met a bunch of teenagers that were still in school, but they didn't have any expectations of leaving their town to do anything different. So it was a completely different mindset and a different lifestyle.

These interactions also provided her opportunities to think more about her own advantaging circumstances.

The family with whom Meredith worked gave her a particularly transformative perspective on her own privilege. She helped drywall the bedroom of an 8-year-old girl who lived in a small trailer with her parents. Although she was partially aware of class differences within the U.S., Meredith felt that this experience taught her about her own social class even further. She claims,

> This little girl showed me how I had taken a lot of things for granted. She was living in such horrible conditions, but she was still very optimistic. She had all her career plans and wanted to make something out of her life. She wanted to be a teacher. We were in the middle of July, but she was doing all this extra homework and stuff. I guess she showed me how I shouldn't take it for granted. I thought to myself just how lucky I am and how unlucky so many other people are.

By the end of the week, her understandings of self and others changed. Although she went into the experience for the sole purpose of helping others in need, "the people there also helped me in some ways. They helped me learn things that I didn't know. I felt like I left there somewhat a different person than I was at the beginning and it was because of them."

According to Meredith, this service trip allowed her to gain understandings of self and others that she would not otherwise have. She believes, "You can only get those perspectives when you go someplace else and are around different people." Although the week spent in the Appalachian Mountains was a particularly meaningful learning experience, she claims that her other service activities and traveling adventures with family across the U.S. and throughout the world have similarly "opened my eyes and let me learn things that most kids around my age haven't learned." During her annual trips to Spain, for example, she explains,

> It's like adapting to a new culture each time I'm there, and since we live with our family there, they taught me to understand and accept these people who have different values, and I kind of had to blend in. These trips had an effect on me because it gave me a more global outlook and more chances to be independent and more confident.

She believes that her travels have allowed her to understand the world more fully, become more aware of people different from herself, and develop a strong sense of independence and a global outlook.

Meredith gives her parents partial credit for what she has learned through traveling, especially her global awareness and independence. Her parents emphasize that an important aspect of traveling is being exposed to the differences between oneself and others in order to develop an awareness of inequalities between groups of people. They also believe that traveling provides unique opportunities for developing independence and a holistic global outlook. For as long as she can remember, Meredith's parents have sought opportunities for her to travel as much as possible to foster her learning of self and others. She has learned from her parents that trying new things and immersing oneself in a different culture are vital to achieving a better understanding of the world, other people, and different cultures.

She quickly points out, however, "I don't have to always be far away to learn all this either." Even leaving her suburb community to visit different neighborhoods of her home city has helped her learn more about other people. She recalls,

> We would go to a predominantly Hispanic neighborhood, like close to downtown, and there we would walk around, nothing really planned other than paying attention to what is around us. There was a museum we'd often go to, restaurants and stuff, like go to little stores and then we just did a lot of different things like going biking together, going to explore neighborhoods, just trying out new things. We didn't have to

be in a totally different country to be exposed to different people and different places because that was all just downtown.

Although she has learned a great deal by exploring different local neighborhoods, she has been, at times, uncomfortable in situations and places where "being white or upper middle class is the minority." But as she explains, "I think this is part of a learning experience, stepping outside your comfort zone. It doesn't feel good all the time but you have to be willing to do that if you really want to learn about other people and different places."

She values not being completely immersed in "a blindly privileged community" all the time but, instead, having multiple opportunities to go "outside [that] bubble to see how and where other people live and being exposed to different social classes." By leaving her community, she believes, "I can see things about my neighborhood that I really couldn't notice if I didn't leave it, if that makes sense. I can see how my living conditions compare to other people's." She further explains,

> I really couldn't learn all this just in school and just reading books. I really needed the first-hand experiences, seeing it myself, being different places and meeting different people instead of reading about those places and people. Being educated is very important, but just going out into the world it gives you a wider scope of experiences.

Meredith believes that traveling provides her opportunities to explore "the diversity of the world" with which she does not regularly have the chance to interact.

She believes that the combination of these traveling experiences to far and near places and frequent conversations with her parents about social class differences has allowed her to form an awareness of her own privilege and the disadvantages of others. With this increased awareness, she feels obligated "to act upon what I know by giving back to the less fortunate [and] making the world a better place for everybody, especially the really disadvantaged." She again credits her parents for forming a commitment "to give back." As she explains,

> My mom emphasizes that we should give back as much as possible, really both [of my parents] emphasize this. My parents always tell me that you have to act upon what you know from like education and just like traveling and seeing the conditions that other people live in. They tell me that when you become aware that something is wrong with the world, and if we can do anything to fix it, we should.

Meredith has taken her parents' lessons to heart, hoping that "someday I can really make a difference in the world."

Although she regularly participates in service activities in local and distant communities, "I really think that it will be later on in my life before I can really make a difference, like I want to." She thinks that she can make this difference in the future by becoming a physician and working in a clinic in "some really poor community in Central America." This idea first emerged during a family trip to Costa Rica when she observed, "the people living there were without basic needs." She further explains, "I think healthcare, basic healthcare, is a human right. It was seeing how there are many places where people don't have clean water, which really affects health, and like all of these barriers for them. They need doctors working on this basic human right." During this trip, she decided that eventually "I could really make a difference in a place like that. I could help others and become a doctor and dedicate my life to making sure people have these basic needs." Seeing the differences between her life circumstances and the disadvantages of many others motivated Meredith to find some way, either as a physician or in some other capacity, to use her advantages to benefit others.[5] "This will be what I end up doing in my life," she states confidently.

COMING TO CLASS

Meredith's first-grade teacher began a lesson on measurements by asking students to use the ruler and sheet of paper that she placed on top of their desks before class to draw a 6-inch line. Meredith had no problem completing the task and eagerly waited for further instructions. "I figured we were starting out with a really easy task and then it would get harder," she recalls. After about ten minutes into the lesson, she realized, "this isn't going to get any harder," and felt that "what my teacher was having us do was way too easy."

Without raising her hand to ask permission to speak, Meredith blurted out, "This is too easy. Why aren't we doing something harder?"

After her teacher responded with a disapproving look, Meredith had no idea what she did wrong. "Was she upset because I didn't raise my hand before saying something out loud?" she asked herself.

The teacher then gave the students another task and told them that she was going to step out of the classroom very briefly. While the students completed the task, the teacher gently tapped Meredith on her shoulder and whispered, "Come with me for a moment."

When they got outside the classroom, her teacher asked, "Do you know why I gave you that look and asked you to come out here?"

"Because I didn't raise my hand," she replied nervously.

"No, no, although you should raise your hand. It's because you said something that could be really hurtful to others in class. What's easy to you may not be for others. Not everyone has already learned what we're doing today like you have. Does that make sense?" her teacher explained.

Unable to respond verbally because she felt embarrassed, Meredith nodded to indicate that she understood. For the rest of the school day, "I was thinking a lot about what she said because it was like the first time that I realized that not everybody had the same chances as I had at home to learn things." This experience changed her thinking about herself in relation to others in powerful ways and provided the beginnings of coming to understand that "some other people live a very different life than I do and I have to take that into consideration." From this experience, she also learned to be mindful "of other people's feelings and what they're thinking." She further explains, "You may not always know what other people are feeling and thinking, but you need to try to evaluate the situation."

This experience during first grade marked the beginning of her efforts to understand and be mindful of the differences that exist among people. She became more committed to seeing the world from the perspectives of others. It took a few more years, however, before she sufficiently grasped "what my teacher was trying to tell me that day." As she gained new life experiences from her extensive travels and new knowledge from the "open conversations" with her parents, she eventually understood more fully "what it means to see something through someone else's eyes . . . [and] keep noticing that not everybody and everything are like you."

Just before entering high school, she became especially intrigued with class differences and began questioning why those differences exist. In one of the first conversations she had with her parents about class differences, she recalls, "I started asking them about our neighbors' social class and my friends' social class. I wanted to know, were they like us? Like their parents' jobs and how that relates to how much money their family has compared to us." She reports that her parents initially did not know how to answer her questions. "They basically just said, 'People spend money differently and some spend it in a more showy way.' I didn't see how that was an answer to my question," she remembers. Yet their inadequate response still had an impact on Meredith's thinking and actions. As she explains, "I started to pay more attention to material things like the size and type of house we have, and vacations we take, clothes that we buy, or type of car that we have. Then compare all that to everybody else. I tried to figure out what these differences mean."

The more conversations she had with her parents about social class differences, though, "the better they got about answering my questions. They started to discuss other things like values and what you know, your education and stuff like that." From these conversations, "I would pay even more attention to differences in regard to social classes, especially looking at the differences between neighborhoods around us." In her own community, she observed "a lot of nice parks and facilities and community centers and stuff around here. There were big houses and people had cars with garages and driveways. Nice looking schools and plenty of room everywhere to walk and kids go out and play." In contrast, "there were these other neighborhoods that had run-down buildings, really small houses that were also run down, and schools that aren't in good shape and not as nice as our schools. It felt more crowded and looked dirtier." Through these observations, she came to realize more fully that "not everybody lives like people in my neighborhood do." This realization led to her identifying her own status as upper middle class. As she explains, "I could see that there were a lot of places that were not well off at all on the west side of [the city] so I could tell that my neighborhood was higher class. And I started to think about what all this really means not just about other people but for us also. This is really the first time that I really understood we were higher class."

Since these earlier conversations and observations, Meredith believes that she has become "very aware that I've been given a lot of advantages in my life" through her family circumstances, schooling, community, and close relationships with family and friends. "I know there are a lot of people who don't have all these advantages and face way more obstacles because they don't have them," she explains. The only disadvantage she identifies in her life "is the fact that my parents are divorced, which can sometimes make things more difficult." But she then goes on to explain, "This hasn't really been a really big disadvantage like other people have. I have a close relationship with both my parents." After further reflection, she concludes, "I guess [my parents' divorce] isn't really a disadvantage, it's something else, like something that I wish was different but doesn't really affect me negatively."

Both of her parents equally influence her thinking about social class in general and more specifically her own class privilege. They regularly discourage her from taking "what we have for granted, our advantages and stuff." She tries to stay mindful of this lesson but admits,

> It's really hard to think about this all the time. I sometimes take things for granted like having a nice house, clothes that I need, good healthy food all the time, that I go to a good school that is preparing me for college and what I want to do later on, that I live in a good neighborhood, a safe neighborhood. I just don't think about it because it's what I'm used to. They're too normal so I don't always think of these things like I need to pay attention to them; they're just there.

Even though the taken-for-granted realities of her advantaging circumstances are just "too normal" for her to be always conscious of them, Meredith insists that she is committed to an awareness of her advantages. At the moment, just having this commitment meets her parents' expectations sufficiently. "I know and they know that when I get older I will not take things for granted like I do now. I just have to show them that I'm trying not to take things for granted and they'll be happy with that," she explains.

One of the main ways in which Meredith attempts to value her advantages is by noticing the social class differences in her daily life. According to Meredith, "It's hard not to think about your advantages when you see people that don't have them and see how that manifests in their life." In these observations, she has attempted to wrap her head around what causes social class differences and what factors determine a person's social class. Through this reflection, she has developed an understanding of privilege as "a combination of somebody's occupation, salary, values, opportunities, and environment." She further explains,

> I would say that privilege is mostly defined by socioeconomic class, so what type of job you have, whether it is like the white-collar lawyers or businessmen, doctors, which determines your salary. And that is also related to like what type of neighborhood you live in because the more money you have the better neighborhood you live in. But it's also about opportunities. [Privileged people] have had a head start in life. Someone who has money, like lives in a nice neighborhood, with nice schools, a good background, good beliefs and values, that all helps them achieve their goals.

Although she partially acknowledges that privilege is more than economic factors, she believes, "How much money you have is probably the most important part of it."

Meredith goes on to claim that there are both "controllable and uncontrollable factors" in people's lives that determine their privilege. Particularly adamant about the uncontrollable factors, she explains, "There are just so many things out of people's control, like what family they're born into and what they're given the minute they're born." Finding it difficult to identify other uncontrollable factors of privilege, she instead discusses the ones related to disadvantages. She explains, "Disadvantages, like privileges, aren't something people necessarily deserve. They haven't done anything to have those disadvantages. It's like their family had something going on or their parents just have different types of jobs or something. It's not really something they did to cause their situation." She attributes their disadvantaging circumstances to the "vicious cycle" that makes it so difficult to escape poverty. Identifying what stands in the way of social and economic mobility within this "vicious cycle," she says, "There are so many things that make it difficult [to get out of poverty] but probably the main things are a lack of education, lack of money, unsafe environments, just things that limit your opportunities."

In her understandings about the other end of the social class spectrum, she believes that privileged people "definitely have an easier time because they don't have all these obstacles; they can achieve their goals easier than people who have a lot of things standing in their way to success." Meredith sees "favorable circumstances" as a necessary component of achieving success, but "it also takes hard work 'cause you can achieve what you want just because you have a better life." She further explains,

> I think at the beginning of your education, then maybe through middle school or something, a lot of it really depends on where you live and like your privilege, but then I don't think you can make it to the final step of achieving a career without hard work. Like, privilege could set you up so that you are in a good position to do it, then maybe with a little less work, but I feel like you always need hard work to actually achieve your success.

Conversely, she believes that those in poverty "would have to have a lot more luck" in order to succeed. Such sources of luck, according to Meredith, include the presence of mentors who would be willing to help someone of a disadvantaged background. She explains, "Even if they put in the hard work, they might not necessarily get there because the obstacles are too big. That's why luck plays a big part of it too."

Meredith partially believes that the meritocratic principle of hard work leads to success does not always hold true for disadvantaged people.[6] For instance, she considers the ways in which students are assigned to educational tracks at her school to be "unfair and really problematic." She believes that students' educational tracks are often not reflective of their true capacities and that luck and circumstance play "too much a big role" in their placement. In observing how students are placed, she notices, "The socioeconomic divide correlates with a racial divide and so I don't agree with stereotyping people of a different race or social class and like pigeonholing one certain type of person." At her school, she also sees teachers and other school officials "not really accommodating the needs of disadvantaged kids and minorities that have different learning styles and not good with tests and stuff like that." Overall, she observes her school "not offering the same opportunities to everybody." She concludes that privileged students, like her, "have a better chance to be successful in their academics."

Meredith also believes that privileged students at her school are successful because of their personal qualities. Drawing upon one of her own most prevalent qualities, Meredith cites confidence as a significant advantage for privileged students. She explains,

> When you're privileged you might think really highly of yourself because things have just worked out for you, and on the other end of the spectrum, if you're not privileged, you might think that it's something you've done when really you just didn't have the advantages that other people had. So I think it changes your outlook on your perseverance and your work ethic, just overall who you are.

She goes on to explain, "When you're confident then others have higher expectations for you and you get more support than if you're not confident." She recalls her experiences on her ASP service trip to clarify this point further. She believes,

The local people never left their poverty-stricken town 'cause they didn't have a lot of confidence that they could do that and be alright. And then because they didn't have confidence nobody expected them to leave. So I think that was a big thing, that they weren't going to strive for something that like nobody believed that they could do 'cause they didn't believe they could do it. It was this vicious cycle.

In contrast, she explains, "I've been successful not really because I've been doing my homework and stuff. It's different with me because my parents support me and believe in me. They want me to be highly educated and in my education they've given me really good opportunities. All this gives me the confidence to be successful."

For Meredith, opportunities and support "really determine a person's social class, I would say these parts are more important than other parts like how much money you have." Although she questions the meritocratic principle that the most talented and hardworking among us are the ones who are the most successful, she believes that "everybody can reach some level of success, no matter how disadvantaged they are. It will just be harder for some people and easier for other people." She points to her grandfather's life as evidence that success is achieved through hard work. As she explains, her grandfather—whom she considers to be "an inspiration because he's a doctor and he's achieved a lot"—grew up in a working-class family and "then he went to medical school and became a physician. So he made it like to the upper middle class because he worked really hard to get there and didn't let any obstacles prevent him from being successful." She goes on to say, "He made it his own and his determination, mostly, helped move him from working class into upper middle class." Her grandfather's example taught her that everyone could get what she or he wants out of life through hard work and determination. According to Meredith, these factors, above everything else, lead disadvantaged individuals down a path to success. Even though she believes that she will have an easier time in achieving her goals than those without the same advantages, "everybody has to work hard and focus on their dreams to achieve what they want."

TROUBLES WITH CLASS

Meredith believes that she has thought about social class issues and her own privilege more than most privileged individuals her age. Mainly because of her travels, conversations with her parents, and observations, she also believes that she has developed a fairly advanced understanding of the concepts of social class and privilege[7] and a strong commitment to ongoing learning. Even with her advanced understanding and strong commitment, she acknowledges, "There's just so much that doesn't make sense and with some things I still haven't figured them out." Struggling to make sense of what she observes and hears from various sources in her life, she often contradicts herself while explaining her thinking about various social class issues and her own social class position.

For the most part, she remains unaware of her contradictory statements. When she does realize that she is contradicting her previous opinions, however, she quickly sorts out that conflict by distancing herself from those earlier statements. Taking the safest route, she firmly reasserts her most current position, which often ends up corresponding with what she considers to be the most widely held belief on the topic. She avoids taking a potentially controversial stance, even if this appears to be what she actually believes. In these moments, her final position is not necessarily disingenuous but instead reflects that she is still figuring out what she truly believes. And until the conflict is resolved, she sides with the most acceptable position.

For instance, she struggles with her ideas about meritocracy, partly believing that unfair circumstances prevent disadvantaged individuals from achieving success while simultaneously believing that hard work leads everyone to success. She draws on her grandfather's path to success to reach her final decision that disadvantaged people can overcome obstacles to success through hard work and determination. While she is adamant about the difficulties within the "vicious cycle" of poverty that stand in the way of social and economic mobility, her overriding belief is that "anybody can overcome whatever stands in their way [to success], even if it's something really hard to get past."

To emphasize that this is indeed her primary position on the topic, she puts forth a hypothetical description of how she would overcome these challenging obstacles if "I was poor and didn't have all the advantages that I have right now." She confidently says, "I think that if I grew up in a lower social class I would find a way out of it somehow and would be successful and change my circumstances." She further claims,

> I would've either gone to a magnet school or like put in a lot of more work, or found some mentor or something to do the same things that I got to do in high school. Yeah, I think I might have ended up with the same goals, but I might not be as hopeful about them, because I didn't see other people in my situation like going out to be a doctor or a lawyer. But I wouldn't let this discouragement keep me from doing what I wanted.

While she claims that the people she observed and met on her ASP service trip were unable to escape their disadvantaging circumstances, she doubts that such difficulties would keep her from escaping poverty and achieving her goals. From her perspective, these disadvantages would be a source of discouragement that she could overcome. She therefore positions herself as superior to others who are unable to escape the cyclical nature of poverty even though she sees herself to be otherwise.[8] "I never put myself above other people," she believes.

Meredith thinks that she treats and interacts with others different from herself "not like somebody who's less than me." She claims to be strongly committed to breaking down the class hierarchies that separate and divide people from different social classes. In her daily life, however, she spends most of her time surrounded by people much like herself. In fact, the only time she comes in contact with disadvantaged individuals is during her community service activities. She justifies her isolation from people different from herself by explaining,

> Part of it is just the town that I went to elementary school and middle school in is primarily upper middle class and very white, and so when I was younger that was just the people who I had met. My high school is a little more diverse when it comes to both of those things, but I feel like there people already have ... I feel like different races have stereotypes of each other and so that's why at school, even though it's diverse, it tends to be somewhat segregated, like you are stuck with the same friends. And your friends tend to be the same as you, the same race and class.

Even though Meredith feels that she can overcome social class barriers through her community service and form meaningful relationships with those different from herself, she attributes her lack of diverse relationships in the other spheres of her life to "uncontrollable factors."

While she describes those in lower classes with largely positive characteristics, such as "they probably have more of a work ethic because they have had to earn things in their life," she seems to value the qualities of those who are similar to her the most. For instance, in describing another affluent group of peers at her school, she says,

> I guess there's another group at our school in our grade that are pretty similar to us, like to my group of friends. I admire all of them and I know a few of them individually. I don't know, like specifically why I admire them but I mean they're just fun, quirky individuals, a funny group together. They're all high achieving and athletes and really involved in things. I just see that my friends and me are like them in these ways.

Their confidence and high achievement are what she considers their most admirable traits. As she further explains,

> They're really confident as individuals, not trying to be something they're not. I guess it's confidence that makes them take really hard classes and not just trying to find the easy way in school. They know

they're going to be successful 'cause they're going to work hard enough to make sure of that.

Sharing these traits, she finds common ground with this other social group. In contrast, she describes another group as, "Not really involved in school and don't really care about their grades. They're always getting in trouble and doing risky stuff."[9] Meredith perceives that they are too different from her to find enough similarities to relate to them; she avoids them and remains far removed from those differences. She, instead, stays surrounded by her highly motivated, high-achieving, confident peers—those whom she has determined to be similar to herself.

In passing, she also acknowledges that these admirable peers and her close friends "also come from privileged families." She insists, however, "This isn't why I admire them or why we're close; it's, we share the same attitudes and values about school and want the same things." To stress this point further, she claims, "I don't see myself like a lot of privileged kids. A lot of them are really bratty and spoiled and don't appreciate that they've been given those advantages, not because of who they are, just because it happened to them and not somebody else." She makes a stark contrast between these "bratty and spoiled" privileged peers and herself and others "who don't take [our advantages] for granted." Restating a point that she frequently makes, "With our privileges in everything, we have a better chance to be successful . . . and some things make it where success does not totally happen because of what we do." While she denounces "ungrateful" privileged peers for believing that their own efforts have led to their success thus far in life, she admits, "I still think of myself as like having some control over achieving my goals. It's not just where I come from but I put in the time and energy."

After making this statement, she pauses, realizing that she has just contradicted herself. A few moments later, she continues,

> Me and my friends are just different than these kids. We know we have privileges and not everybody has our privileges but we're not taking them for granted and not just sitting there and letting success just happen [to us]. We're working hard for what we want in life. That's the big difference.

She questions whether she is being too harsh toward these other privileged peers and too generous toward herself and those similar to herself. "I think I'm making these other kids sound lazier than they are. I just don't think they're working very hard but they're still probably going to be as successful as we are and we're working hard. It's just frustrating," she admits. In thinking further about the role of advantages in her success, she acknowledges,

> It's just human nature to think positive about yourself and [people like you]. We want to accredit our successes to ourselves, but then we happen

to blame our failures on the environment or things that just happen to us. I guess that I do this somewhat. I want to think that it's mostly myself who's responsible for what I achieve and not something else. It would be difficult, for me at least, to think that I didn't deserve everything.

In the end, she sorts out this contradiction by toning down her criticisms of other privileged peers whom she considers to be different from herself and admitting a shortcoming.

Although Meredith has a strong commitment to make sense of "what's really going on around me" and to think further about her advantaging circumstances, she expresses an equally strong commitment to maintaining positive perceptions of self and others. She believes it is only "human nature" to avoid thinking negatively about oneself and partially extends this principle to others as well.[10] She tries to see herself and others only in a positive light, believing that people are influenced to some extent by their life circumstances and therefore not fully responsible for their actions.

At times she finds it difficult "to stay optimistic and be positive" in making sense of troubling class issues, especially ones related to the "vicious cycle" of poverty. This difficulty reminds her that she still has more to learn. Traveling, conversations with her parents, and observations of her daily life have been incredibly important in the development of Meredith's understandings of social class differences and her own privilege. While she plans to continue using these sources and finding additional ones for her continued education, she is reluctant to put her favorable understandings of self and others at risk. Similarly to the way in which she resolves her contradictory statements, she will continue transforming negative perceptions into positive ones whenever necessary.

NOTES

1. More specifically, East Park High School is ranked by *U.S. News and World Report*, *Newsweek*, and other sources as one of the top American high schools.
2. For more discussion on the lack of diversity in advanced programs even in heterogeneous schools, see, for example, Brantlinger, 2003; Oakes, 1985.
3. Tivnan & Goodman, 2009.
4. Although Meredith had knowledge of such poverty, she lacked understanding of it until she saw it on television. This example illustrates one of the significant differences between having knowledge and forming understanding when it comes to learning about the realities of those different from oneself.
5. Meredith's desire to use her advantages for the benefit of others through community service is consistent with what other studies have found regarding what motivates affluent adolescents to become committed to and involved in community service. For example, Howard (2011) found that privileged young people viewed being a resource as an important motivational factor for their involvement in community service and social justice efforts. Their view was useful in convincing themselves and others that they

were compassionate, kind, and giving; it also had considerable ideological value in diverting attention away from their privileged circumstances.

6. Meredith partially acknowledges the structural forces that contribute to maintaining and creating inequalities. As such, she holds an understanding of inequality that is different from that of most other affluent adolescents. More specifically, several scholars have found middle-class and affluent adolescents to be more likely than adolescents from poor and working-class backgrounds to characterize individuals as responsible for their economic status (Chafel & Neitzel, 2005; Cozzarelli, Wilkinson, & Tagler, 2001). Breaking this commonly held belief among affluent adolescents, Meredith argues that there are what she calls "uncontrollable factors" in determining economic status.

7. Privileged individuals, including adolescents, tend to have little understanding of their own privilege and the oppression suffered by disadvantaged groups (Wildman, 1996). In fact, privileged people tend to have little to no awareness of oppression and are likely to deny that it exists (Lazarre, 1996). Because Meredith has some understanding and awareness of oppression and privilege, she does indeed seem to have a more advanced understanding and awareness than most other privileged adolescents.

8. This is one of the clearest examples of Meredith rationalizing her own advantages by emphasizing her superior traits in comparison with those possessed by disadvantaged individuals. For more discussion on the ways in which affluent adolescents rationalize their advantages, see, for example, Brantlinger, 1993; Howard, 2008; and Proweller, 1999.

9. She indicates indirectly that this is a group of low-income students. Although she claims that "uncontrollable factors" play a greater role in their educational outcomes, she clearly believes that individualistic factors play a significant role as well. It is important to note that she often avoids discussing these individualistic factors in her efforts to maintain a positive image of others from disadvantaged backgrounds. This statement gives some indication, however, that she does not hold as positive an image of others as she repeatedly claims.

10. Meredith's desire to maintain a positive self-image is consistent with Baumeister's (1996) argument that the desire to think well of oneself is a fundamental and pervasive motivation of human psychological functioning. Part of what motivates Meredith to maintain a positive perception of disadvantaged individuals is that this is necessary for maintaining a positive self-image. For more discussion on how this motivation plays out in privileged individuals, see Brantlinger, 2003.

3 Herman
A Scripted Life

*with Cynthia Garvin, Erika Johnson,
Ethan Meigs, and Morgan Rublee*

I am in constant pursuit of an untrammeled mind and imagination.

Seventeen-year-old Herman is no stranger to the Southern California International Film Festival. Last year, Herman's screenplay was one of the few chosen for the student filmmaking competition. With a meager budget and less than two weeks to shoot, he was matched with a student director who attends a creative and performing arts high school nearby and a film industry mentor. In the end, Herman did not win first place; however, just being selected for the competition and seeing his screenplay come to life on the screen was rewarding enough for him.

This year Herman returns to the festival with a new screenplay, hoping for a different fate. He penned a story about a suicidal author reuniting with his lost love and best friends from high school, and, about two weeks ago, was matched with another student director to make a film. The local newspaper describes Herman as "one of the biggest threats in the high school competition." Although he did not win last year's competition, he won first place for a film he made and wrote at another film festival, making him a national award-winning screenwriter and filmmaker. Herman's success in the competition brought him unwanted attention, as his filmmaking was featured on National Public Radio, local television stations, and in newspapers and magazines. As is typical with these kinds of interviews, reporters posed as many questions about his personal life, experiences, and opinions as they did about his work. Speaking with an air of calm confidence, Herman answered reporters' questions concisely and reluctantly. Although he knows that these interviews are important for promoting his work, he does not enjoy having attention drawn to him. "My work should be center of attention, not me," Herman explains, but he also realizes that "this is part of the game and you have to play the game if you want to reach your goals."

For as long as he can remember, Herman has dreamed of becoming a screenwriter. Unwilling to wait until he gets older to realize this dream, he has worked feverishly on scripts and entered a number of local and national film competitions over the past few years. He explains,

From an early age, I have always known that I wanted a job that didn't feel like a job. Screenwriting is not an easy task—at times it's incredibly painful—however, I cannot imagine myself devoting my daytime hours to any other pursuit. At times, I must force myself to tackle a blank page, and consequently sit for hours staring at it. However, I find more joy in just attempting to write than *actually* doing anything else. I didn't find it necessary to wait until I finished college or at a later point in life to start my screenwriting career. I wanted to start living my dream.

Living the life of a screenwriter, Herman spends as much time as possible watching films, reading books and screenplays, and writing manuscripts. According to him, "When I don't have other responsibilities, like school, I'm working on my screenwriting career—studying other people's works and creating my own." Throughout the day, he finds himself constantly on the lookout for inspiration. "I listen to what people say and how they say it. I pay attention to what no one else is paying attention to. I listen and observe what's going on around me at any given point of the day," he explains.

Herman's passion for screenwriting is apparent to anyone who interacts with him. Because he is so focused on his career, most of his extracurricular activities are related to his screenwriting ambition. Even when he gets involved in a few unrelated activities, such as community service, he manages to find a connection with his interests. He explains, "I keep focused on what's really important to me and try to make the activity more interesting and relevant to my interests." But when he has a choice, he only participates in activities that directly relate to filmmaking and writing. His favorite activity is serving as a teacher's assistant for his school's film program, because "this is another opportunity to combine my primary interests with my academics." Herman explains that in this position, "I teach some lessons to my peers and convey some of my knowledge of screenwriting to them." Through this work, he has become even more convinced "that I've made the best choice for where I'm headed in the future."

Next year, Herman plans to take the next step in realizing his dream by attending a small elite liberal arts school in New England. Several small colleges in this region caught his attention while searching for a film program because "[these colleges] make me excited and also have an extremely rigorous curriculum and are academically competitive and challenging." As he further explains, "I know bigger universities have strong programs, and may have even better ones than smaller places, but they don't make me as excited as the smaller schools' programs. I'm just used to smaller schools and the more individualized attention and instruction." Although he wants to further his education at a college similar in size to his boarding high school, he explains, "I'm also looking forward to having new life experiences, which is why I want to go to the East Coast; I've spent my whole life on the West Coast, and I want to experience a different lifestyle." Whatever college he eventually chooses "will simply be a means to an end" for becoming a successful screenwriter. "These other aspects, like living in a totally different place, are exciting, but they are not what drive my decision on selecting my best option for this next step in reaching my goal," he insists.

Herman claims his entire world revolves around his dream of becoming a screenwriter. He finds a way for every film he watches, book he reads, and person with whom he interacts to bring him closer to his dream. As he explains,

> This is my aspiring vocation so it's a very important passion to me and it's something I try to better myself in. It's a very important part of my life and everything I do seems to relate to my passion because I'm always thinking about it. It's rare when I don't pose the question, 'How can this person, experience, opportunity, or whatever help me achieve my goal?' I get frustrated when things stand in the way of me spending time on my passion. After this year [when I graduate high school], I hope to devote more time to my writing when I have the freedom to and don't have as many obstacles to deal with.

Realizing that he will have to work hard to achieve success in this industry, Herman believes,

> Perseverance is the key to gaining success; it's the one attribute that successful screenwriters have and something that I'm good at. I know that I will persevere to achieve my goal and become a successful screenwriter. Besides perseverance, I possess the other skills that a screenwriter must have. I'm dedicated, can tell a good story, creative, well educated, and write well.

Not hesitant at pointing out his many strengths, Herman is confident that he has "what it takes to be one of the very few who actually make it in this competitive business."

Wanting to demonstrate his strengths, he returns to this year's International Film Festival competition more confident and determined. He is not necessarily focused on winning, although he will gladly accept the prize. Instead of winning, Herman explains, "I'm concentrating on the opportunity to show people, important people, that I have what it takes and I have considerable knowledge and skills." To a lesser extent, he also is looking for opportunities "to put my work out there in public and get feedback so that I can improve my skills and learn more about screenwriting and the industry." Above all else, Herman joins competitions to make contacts with "important people." Last year at the festival, for instance, he explains, "I met a woman who has since written me recommendations for my New York University summer program. She has worked in the screenwriting industry for years, and she's a valuable connection that I will benefit from for years." With her recommendation, he secured a spot in this highly selective dramatic writing program and will spend this upcoming summer "honing my craft" and learning more about the film industry. He also hopes that his involvement in this program leads to additional valuable contacts.

Herman takes advantage of opportunities to speak with anyone who he believes may help him realize his screenwriting dream, while avoiding individuals who may hold him back or serve as an obstacle along his path to success. "Especially in this industry," he explains, "it's all about making connections and contacts. Being in contact and aligning myself with the wrong people could inhibit the achievement of my goals." In an industry "where whom you know can make or break your chances of being hired," Herman is certain that he will be able to play the game with the best of them. "I have a lot to learn about the politics of the film business, I know that, but I'm aware that it's a very political, cutthroat industry. Just knowing that puts me ahead of most people who want to enter this business and naively think it isn't as political as it is."

Even though understanding the political nature of the business and making connections are essential, "what's most important, of course, is producing good work." After he finished his script for this year's competition, Herman immediately began working on his next screenplay. As he explains, "I started working on my next screenplay, which is set in the 1950s concerning a cosmologist going through a midlife crisis while the universe itself deteriorates. Both his personal world and the physical world are dissolving simultaneously. Its working title is *Simulacra*." Unlike the other screenwriters in the competition, "I wasn't on the set for the shooting and production process of the film. But the director had a clear vision for my script; he knew what I'm getting at with it." With his school responsibilities and unwavering commitment to his writing, Herman told the director and others that he was too busy to be on the set. Although he could have made room in his schedule, he decided that beginning his next writing project would be a better use of his time outside school.

Herman has yet to write a screenplay based on his life, but he uses aspects of his daily life as inspiration, and he already has a title in mind:

> If I adapted my life for the screen, I suppose the title would be *Cast Off Ye Shackles*. I'm not entirely sure why I chose 'ye' instead of 'the,' but it felt right after some rumination. My life as a young adult has been mostly comprised of removing mental barriers that I have unconsciously developed as I aged. I am in constant pursuit of an untrammeled mind and imagination.

He leaves it at that, with no further explanation of what burdens constrain him. As usual, he is reluctant to reveal too much about what he truly thinks or to go too deeply into his personal experiences. He remains guarded around others,[1] even those closest to him. Although friendly and eager to connect with others, Herman finds it difficult to establish intimate and meaningful relationships. He has created a script for his life and plays a distant and mysterious character.

ROUGH ACADEMIC WATERS

Paddling a canoe takes precision and balance. Putting too much effort on one side will lead a person in the wrong direction, and leaning just a little too far over the edge may send that person plunging into the water. It takes slow, steady paddle strokes to reach the destination. At school, Herman explains, "I feel like I am in a canoe, trying not to fall off a waterfall." With his school's rigorous academic expectations and the enormous pressure that he places on himself to earn top grades, "I feel like that I'm in a constant state where I'm about to fall right over the edge." However, he manages "to stay afloat in these rough waters" by keeping focused on his dream of becoming a successful screenwriter. "I know that the best way to reach my goals is by receiving a really good education, which I am, and then going to a [college] with a rigorous film program and thriving there," he believes.

Herman does more than just "stay afloat" at Chesthill Academy, his prestigious boarding school.[2] In his last two years of high school, he has maintained a nearly perfect GPA; ranked at the top of his class; received numerous academic awards from school and community organizations for his achievements in the classroom; won national, statewide, and local awards for his leadership; and represented his peers through student government. Featured throughout Chesthill's marketing and recruitment materials, he is identified as "a model student" and "academic powerhouse" by peers, teachers, and other community members. According to Herman, he has earned these achievements and recognitions while taking the "toughest course load at my school," because "I work hard at school, a lot harder than most, and learning genuinely excites me; I want to learn as much as I can." At some level, he realizes that he is as focused on earning top grades as he is on his learning. He explains, "I know grades don't necessarily reflect your learning, but maintaining a high GPA is important for achieving my most immediate task—getting into a good college—so I can achieve the ultimate goal." Although he enjoys school and his academic successes, there are downsides to the pressures placed on him by himself and others. Feeling like he is about to plunge over a waterfall, he handles this stress by isolating himself.

Keeping distance from others at his school is no easy feat to accomplish. Chesthill Academy is a small independent boarding middle and high school, with a total enrollment in the high school fewer than 170.[3] With a teacher-to-student ratio of one to five, class sizes are small enough to encourage close relationships between members of the community and to make sure that each student receives a tremendous amount of individualized attention. Although he avoids establishing close relationships with teachers and peers, "I like the smallness of the school, because it affords me opportunities that I wouldn't get at other schools."

Over the course of his schooling, Herman has attended five different schools, two of which were public schools. When his family lived in Nevada, he attended preschool at a private school, kindergarten at a public one, and then first through third grades at another private school. His family moved to California the summer before he entered fourth grade, where he attended a public school from fourth to sixth grade before attending Chesthill. Being in one school since seventh grade has provided stability and routine in his life. He says, "I think that I've been happier since being at [Chesthill]; I'm able to focus on learning and don't have distractions [caused by frequently moving]." He holds fond memories of each school that he has attended, believing both his public and private schools "fostered and produced academic success." Yet, he contends, "Academically, I feel like my needs were better met at the private schools, and I get a lot more out of my learning at the private schools versus the public ones."

Although he does not want to establish close relationships with his classmates, Herman discloses,

> I enjoy the majority of them. There are a few exceptions, of course. There are always the typical apathetic individuals [and] I tend to frown upon their way of life. I enjoy about 99 percent of the students that go here. Going to a private school that's obviously expensive there are always students that don't do anything. That kind of bothers me because I feel like an expensive opportunity like this there should be effort put into doing well. But there are a fairly good number of us who value what we have.

He puts a lot of pressure on himself to do well and to take advantage of the educational opportunities provided at Chesthill, and when he sees others wasting their opportunities, "it really frustrates me and I want to avoid being around those individuals." His frustration comes from his understanding that "we're fortunate enough to attend the school we're attending now and receive the education we're receiving, and a lot of people aren't given the opportunity to attend a school like ours, a private school." He goes on to say, "Frustrated may not be the proper word to describe how I respond to my peers not taking advantage of our education. It's just that I don't understand them and their actions. I can't fully grasp why they aren't taking advantage of the privileges afforded to them."

With the pressure that he feels to take advantage of his academic opportunities, Herman describes a monumental amount of stress in his academic life, believing "the stakes are high." In order to realize his screenwriting ambition, he believes, "I must attend a competitive college, so high grades are imperative. I know that I want to study film in college, but I have to first get into college, and grades will allow me to do that." The pressure he puts on himself in pursuit of his college-oriented desires makes him feel like he is inching toward a waterfall. "I'd say the waterfall is an accumulation of grades, SATs [Scholastic Achievement Tests], AP [advanced placement] classes, and college applications. It's just the whole [college admissions] process. I'm desperately paddling to keep from going over the waterfall in these rough waters," he explains.

Even before the time "when college was just around the corner," Herman claims, "There's always been this waterfall that I'm trying to avoid with the tremendous amount of work that my school demands of me." He sighs, "All the homework—I just stay mentally and physically exhausted." However, he remains certain that he will continue to achieve academic success, especially after having some time during his recent spring break to relax and gather his thoughts. "Before break, I was pretty disillusioned and burnt out with my academic experience, and I'd say I've garnered some motivation to continue and persevere and see the school year out instead of giving up on everything." In the end, he claims, "I always find a way to gather the strength that I need to keep on paddling and never go over the waterfall."

What helps Herman gather the strength to keep afloat is his ability "to keep focused on all the exciting and different experiences ahead of me when I'm in college." In addition to understanding college as the necessary step toward becoming a successful screenwriter, he also looks forward to furthering his education "for more personal reasons, not just ones that relate to my career goals." He explains,

> There are several personal reasons that lie behind my decision to attend college. College is kind of the status quo for the foundation of today's society and if you don't attend college then you work at McDonald's nowadays. So there's a benefit that comes from being college-educated in regards to your future employment. However, I want to go to college for a lot of reasons: to expand and to grow as a thinker, to have different kinds of life experiences. Yeah, achieving my career goals is the main reason for this being the next logical step, but it's not the only reason.

Though he partially acknowledges that his advantaging life circumstances would afford him more options than working at a minimum-wage job if he did not attend college, Herman argues, "You just can't be successful in life without being college-educated; you must receive a higher education to make something out of your life."

Herman cannot imagine any instances that would keep him from attending college, especially because "I work hard enough and have done everything that I need to do so I can continue my education after high school." He quickly points out, however, "I'm not looking to attend some local community college or state school. I'm looking for the specific film or creative writing oriented major, like-minded peers that intellectually stimulate me, and just a good atmosphere and vibe on campus. I'm definitely shooting for colleges that are harder to get into." After attending a small boarding high school, "I can only see myself attending an institution of equal or higher caliber for college. This would be the only type of college that I believe would continue to fit my specific needs."

Besides keeping his eyes on what lies immediately ahead of him, Herman's "somewhat competitive nature" is a source of motivation for enduring academic pressures and expectations. He claims to be "more of a friendly competitor with my classmates than anything else." As he further explains,

> Sometimes my peers in classes will do well on an essay, for example, an AP essay score better than myself, and that will motivate me to do more and work harder. But I don't feel like I want to do better than them for any malicious reason or that they want to do better than me most of the time. There isn't any animosity between us. I mean, it is just motivation to do better, not motivation to do better than someone else, I would say.

Although Herman feels motivated to do better when his peers outperform him, he insists, "Any competitive feelings that I have are rooted in bettering myself and improving my own performance and not wishing anything bad on others."

However, Herman acknowledges that within his small elite institution "the atmosphere is pretty competitive in one sense, a pretty alarming characteristic, but mainly it's not competitive at all." Recognizing his explanation sounds contradictory,[4] he clarifies,

> Students aren't competitive in terms of 'reaching full potential,' as [Chesthill's] motto states, but everyone wants to do well. They have a lot of other things going on in their lives other than academics and don't feel like that drives the competitiveness. It's more about reaching our potential and just doing your best. Is there competition among individuals? Yes. But it comes from a more productive internal source than just simply wanting bad things to happen to others so that you advance.

It is difficult for Herman to acknowledge the competitive nature of the Chesthill student body. He finds it even more difficult to admit his own competitive spirit. In the end, he concludes, "There may be this competitive atmosphere, but I don't involve myself in that," providing another opportunity to distance himself from others at Chesthill.

Despite his claims of "not being that competitive," Herman finds it difficult to accept moments when others outperform him academically despite putting his "best efforts into the task." In these moments, he quickly becomes frustrated and blames himself "for what I could've done differently." He believes that the main reason his peers occasionally outperform him in school "is because I need to learn how to prioritize my life better, especially lately." He further explains,

> This year I've learned that when I'm given a short amount of time and a certain amount of assignments, I will not be able to complete all of the assignments in that time. We are just assigned too much work to be completed like I was able to do in the past. I have to prioritize, which assignments are more valuable to my success in the class and which assignments I can sacrifice.

Over the past year or so, he has started to learn his limits. "It's been a process for me to discover that I can't do as well as I want in every subject. I have strengths in some, which means that I have weaknesses in others," he admits.

Although Herman usually exceeds in most subjects, he does struggle with the sciences. He admits that his difficulty with science has "humbled me and taught me even more about the power of hard work." For instance, "I'm taking biology this year, and biology is not my strong suit. My teacher is pretty intense, but I've managed to do well in class and power through, even though I don't enjoy it at all." He has been "relatively successful" in this class, but "it's still a hard pill to swallow that I'm not getting an A." When asked whether his grade reflects his performance accurately, he replies, "Third-party perspective would say that it's probably fairly accurate, but in my eyes not fair and doesn't reflect the amount of work I've put into it." He stops just short of blaming the teacher for his grade but is also reluctant to take full responsibility for not earning the grade he wants in this class.

Herman firmly believes that his Chesthill education is paving the way to certain success as a screenwriter, yet the academic pressures that he experiences make him feel as though he were constantly heading toward a waterfall in a one-person canoe. Despite the demanding expectations of his elite school, he does not blame these pressures on his teachers or his peers but instead on his intrinsic motivation to perform well in school. When these internal pressures consume and overwhelm him, he isolates himself from others and turns to screenwriting in order to stay afloat in the rough waters. He retreats into the world of writing, where he can determine how the story ends.

BACK-SEAT RELATIONSHIPS

I had decided to spend an afternoon in my room experimenting with ink and a roller, which is a common occurrence for me. After some time, I had created a splotch on the paper, which gave me an eerie sense of pleasure, so I hung it on the back of my door where I assumed

> *no one else would see it. I didn't really think much of it, but then my mother entered my room curious as to what I had been working on for such a long time. When she saw the inkblot that I had created on the page she smiled, and told me that I had an eye for modern abstract art, and then she left the room. I wasn't expecting any kind of praise, and I couldn't tell if she was serious, but it really made me very happy that she had paid me such a compliment.[5]*

Herman appreciates such "random expressions of affection and recognition," but insists, "I don't need people to do that to feel content with myself." He goes on to say, "I don't do things to get other people's attention like I see other people doing. Like attention is the only thing that motivates them and they can't just do something without being recognized for it. I'm not that way." Herman claims that intrinsic motivation plays a greater role in his actions and decisions. His lack of need for others' recognition and affection reflects his general attitude toward others; "I appreciate the people in my life, but they don't tend to be my priority." However, he quickly points out, "This does not necessarily mean that I don't have good relationships with my family members and friends and that I don't appreciate them. I just don't need them. I'm perfectly content being by myself, and I actually prefer that most often. It's really just that simple." Even though his family and friends "aren't an incredibly meaningful aspect" of his life, Herman feels comfortable and content with his relationships. According to Herman, "My family life is stable and enjoyable, and my social life is as well. I'm very content with the relationships that I have formed in my life."

Herman's parents are divorced, and even though his parents share joint custody, he lives mostly with his mother and "pseudo stepfather." As he explains, "My father travels a lot, and I switch off living with my parents when they're home. But I mostly live with my mother who, since the divorce, has been in a relationship with another man who I've been living with for six years now." Because his mother is a teacher at a local charter school, "she's home a lot more than my dad, so I live with her mostly because she's more available." Herman admits, though, that he probably would have the same living arrangements no matter what. "I guess I'm somewhat closer to my mom. Maybe it's because I've lived with her more, but she also gives me what I really want out of a relationship: cohabitation, compatibility, and an occasional intellectual conversation," he explains.

Though closer to his mother, Herman enjoys spending time with his father when he has the chance because "he's an inspiration for me since he works quite hard to put me through my schooling and to see me succeed. His selflessness is really inspiring to me." The only time he typically sees his father is on weekends, but once in a while his father finds more opportunities to spend time with him. He says, "My father tries to spend as much time with me as possible and that kind of epitomizes my relationship with him. He'll come over to my mother's house or just randomly pick me up from school. I like it that my father puts so much effort into seeing me because it lets me know that he loves and supports me." Although Herman appreciates his father's efforts, he goes on to say, "But there are times when I'm just too stressed and busy to enjoy spending time with him. It all depends on how much schoolwork I have or if I'm working on a [film] project or something like that."

Herman describes his parents as "different as night and day." As he puts it, "My father's more conservative, my mother's more liberal. My father has a Mac, and my mother has a PC. I don't think two people could be any more different from each other." Even though his parents are such opposites, they share a similar "hands-off" approach to parenting. "They give me the space that I need and let me make my own decisions with their guidance only when I need it," he explains. He goes on to say, "My parents don't really push me to get good grades or anything like that. They are just supportive and let me do my own thing. I feel like that is more conducive to my academic ability than them being more hands-on, so it works in my favor greatly." Herman appreciates that his parents "give me a lot of breathing room and don't hover over me, because it allows me to live and make decisions for myself."

Knowing how reserved Herman can be, "my parents put themselves in my shoes and respect that I'm an extremely independent and private person who doesn't like sharing a lot of information about myself. I know that they love me for who I am and not for who they want me to be." According to him, his parents' respect for his individuality is "another example of the singularly most important value that they try to live by and have tried to teach me, which is empathy and putting yourself in someone else's shoes." He further explains, "I guess if I was a different person that required them to be more attentive and affectionate then they would try to do that; that's just who they are. They try to see the world through my eyes and then respond accordingly." Although his family is not "necessarily affectionate," Herman and his parents have a comfortable and stable family structure that "is satisfying to all." Without question, he knows, "My parents will do anything in their power to help me succeed, and they'll be there to provide me whatever support I need when I need it." Knowing this, "I feel like I'm close with my parents. I've known them for a long time, so I feel I'm uninhibited around them more than anyone else. They provide for me and support me. I couldn't ask for anything else."

Like his relationship with his parents, Herman finds his relationships with friends "enjoyable and satisfying," but he still prefers not "to spend excessive amounts of time with them." Because he lives in a town "very divided in regards to where its inhabitants live," he essentially has two sets of friends who do not socialize with each other. Herman clarifies,

> It's kind of an odd town. There's a kind of ancient wine culture here, which brings a lot of yuppies to the vineyards and such, but it's kind

of a cowboy town too, so sprawling ranches to celebrities, and then we have trailer parks. So it's a pretty diverse place. I tend to have friends not in one particular group so they are as diverse as the town.

The diversity reflected in his friends partially results from Herman "not fitting perfectly into any of these social groups" and also from the fact that he enjoys "being a floater who can fit in anywhere." Beyond these reasons, though, his experience of attending both public and private schools within his community "has made my friends come from different parts of the town." He has had the chance to make friends with both the "vineyard kids" and "trailer-park kids." As he further explains, "My private school days are filled with people from the vineyards, whereas my public school was more of the trailer-park people. I enjoyed them both and made good friends. I always had good friends wherever I was."

Herman pays a little more attention to the social class differences between himself and his friends from his public school days who are less affluent than his private school friends, "many of whom are more well off than me." Although he claims that social class differences are not "an issue" in his friendships, he acknowledges, "They're more of an issue with my trailer-park friends than my other ones." However, he quickly points out, "They make it an issue, not me. I don't care where people come from, but some of them are embarrassed by their circumstances." For example, he recalls an awkward moment in middle school with a close friend:

> I had known one of my best friends months before he even let me see his home. I knew his family was poor or at least close to that level. But he kept making excuses to prevent me from coming over to his house. When I did finally get to see it, I found it humble but nothing to be ashamed of. However, my friend's actions seemed to demonstrate that he felt differently. He made it a much bigger deal than it needed to be.

Herman goes on to explain that when "the tables are turned and I have a friend over to my house and they have a nicer home than I do, I don't feel uncomfortable or embarrassed in that situation." He finds it difficult to understand why his middle-school friend "made it a bigger deal than it needed to be."

Social class is not a criterion that Herman uses to choose his friends. "I look for like-minded peers that intellectually stimulate me," he claims. He holds "intelligence at a very high standard," and those he chooses to call his friends "must be able to hold a conversation and share similar interests." Considering himself an extremely mature 17-year-old with little interest in the values and priorities of many of his peers, his friends "tend to be older than myself because we just have more in common." With his "friendships revolv[ing] around intellectual discussion and debate and exchange of ideas," he avoids sharing "personal information or engaging in personal subjects and topics." However, as with his parents, these kinds of impersonal friendships are the kinds of relationships that he seeks. "My peer friendships are satisfying and provide me everything I want," he insists.

Just as Herman expects his friends to be, he believes, "I'm really frank with my friends, uninhibited in expressing my opinion. At times it gets me in trouble, but I'm very blatant and honest with my friends and I think they respect that." He believes that honesty is one of the most important aspects of a relationship, especially in terms of sharing "your true opinions and beliefs and what you actually think about particular subjects." Communication is also very important in terms of maintaining relationships. He says, "I think there's a great amount of communication between my friends and myself about anything and any arguments we get into. We communicate, and that makes a sustainable friendship." Although he highly values honesty and communication in his relationships, "I'm not overly willing to share my private thoughts and feelings because that isn't necessary for maintaining a friendship."

Herman also does not believe that he needs to see his friends every day or even very often in order to uphold those relationships. What he needs more than almost anything is time spent alone, because "that is when I'm most at peace." He explains,

> I rely less on social stimuli and interactions and my friends. You know I'll spend the entire weekend without seeing any of my friends, because I've spent all day for five days seeing them and they don't understand why I don't want to socialize all the time. I definitely think I need interaction with others throughout my existence, but there are times that I have a great appreciation for time spent alone. For the most part, my friends accept this even though they don't understand this intense need I have for alone time.

Although he enjoys spending time with his friends, his alone time is "when I feel that I can get lost in a film or script and work on my craft, and I don't need to worry about putting up any fronts or anything like that." When he is alone, he feels most at ease with being himself. Even though he thinks of himself as "unpressured," meaning that he is not influenced by peer pressure, he still believes, "There is some need or pressure to be something different than oneself. No one, including myself, can be truly who they are around others." Despite being unable to escape peer pressure completely, he has never found much interest in trying drugs or alcohol even though "all my friends partake in those substances." He figures that he could instead be diving into a new movie, reading a novel, or writing a screenplay. He questions, "So why waste time at a becoming inebriated with my friends?"

Although Herman points out the numerous benefits of spending time alone, he acknowledges that there are "some downsides to my preferences for isolation." One of the negative consequences is that "I've been in a little bit of a romantic desert for most of high school." Unlike most of his peers, he has never had a romantic relationship. He insists, however, that this is not completely the result of his preference for solitude but "has to do more with me going to such a small school and there not being a lot of options for me." Attending a very selective small private school "does inhibit my choices for romantic options and has prevented me from finding the right person yet: someone I'm obviously attracted to, someone who is intellectually stimulating and on an intelligence level on par with myself. I need someone that I can respect, and someone interesting." Even though a part of him wants to be romantically involved with someone so "I know what that feels like," a greater part of him does not want "any distractions in my life that would break my focus from what's truly important."

Herman cares about those close to him, but with his screenwriting goals constantly looming over his head, he feels that he must prioritize "what is truly important." There is nothing more important to him than realizing his screenwriting ambition, and if some of his relationships suffer because of that, then they are not the type of relationships that he wants or needs. He acknowledges, "When it comes down to it, I'm grateful for all the support for my future from my family and friends, but my future is my own and not theirs. I wouldn't be too upset if where I'm going doesn't live up to other people's visions." In working toward achieving his goals, he pushes his relationships to the back seat, not only because he has other priorities in life but also because he is not entirely comfortable having deeply close and personal interactions with others. His relationships are characteristically shallow in nature, but he wants and expects nothing more.

PRIVILEGED ENOUGH

> *I was in a coffee shop with my father when I received notice I was accepted to my top-choice college. The allotted financial assistance package was immediately checked and found to be less than what my family was hoping for. We were expecting some assistance but just got a small scholarship. My father was undaunted. His words 'we'll make it work' both encouraged me and made me uneasy. A child is an economic burden on a family just by its existence, but college is another financial weight to bear. My father has always averred he would rather 'invest in my future than the stock market,' and his actions throughout my life have always supported that claim.*

When asked about his social class, Herman finds it difficult to communicate his beliefs in his usual eloquent and exact manner. It is one of the few moments when he seems at a loss for words. This is not to suggest that he experiences trouble defining the concept of social class or providing examples of class distinctions in his immediate and larger world, but he becomes confused and inarticulate with any question regarding his own social class. Not having previous opportunities to discuss social class with others, Herman does not have the well-planned and perfectly presented answers up his sleeve that he has for most other topics of discussion. The script that he has constructed for communicating his self-understandings is thrown out the window as he turns introspectively on his class privilege and attempts to discuss it with others. With great effort, he tries to gain a deeper understanding of his own social class but ends up even more confused than when he began. Eventually, he manages to sort out enough to admit reluctantly, "I'd say I'm privileged. I mean, privileged enough."

"My parents don't talk to me about social class," says Herman, "It's not a topic to bring up at the dinner table." He claims that his parents never saw a need for sitting him down to discuss their own advantaging circumstances in life or the social class differences existing in their immediate and larger world. Despite the lack of these discussions, he became aware of social class differences in his school and community around the age of 12, right around the time when his parents divorced. After their divorce, he briefly lived with his grandparents, who "are considerably more well off than my parents." When living with them, Herman noticed,

> Being more affluent changes your day-to-day life, including spending abilities and what people do with their time. I realized that after I moved back to my mom's house. Our lives weren't as leisurely as my grandparents' existence. My parents and I had more responsibilities that we couldn't just decide not to do. Living with my grandparents and then reflecting on that after I moved out, I became cognizant of money's effect on one's life and then noticing things around me that I didn't notice beforehand.

Although he became partially aware of how social class influences people's lives, he did not have opportunities to understand more fully what he was observing in the world around him. As with his parents, none of the adults in his life—including his grandparents, other family members, and teachers—created instructional settings to advance his understandings.

Despite his claims of being aware of his social class, Herman struggles to acknowledge his advantages. For instance, even though he realizes that not too many people are afforded the same educational opportunities he has received by attending a private school—where the annual tuition for day students is over $21,000 and over $47,000 for boarding students[6]—he makes certain claims to distance himself from those educational advantages. Initially, he proclaims, "My family could only afford to send me [to the school], because I receive financial aid and scholarships to cover about 85 percent of the tuition." Realizing that his statement seems too unbelievable, especially to others who know details of his family's financial circumstances,[7] he retracts his assertion by saying, "I'm not sure how much financial aid I get exactly, but it's a lot; more than what most people get." When asked specific questions about why he receives so much and how his school calculates financial aid, he avoids answering and redirects the conversation:

> A majority of the campus is pretty upper class and can fairly easily afford the tuition and other expenses. At the very least, everyone at the school is within the middle-class spectrum—whether lower, middle, or upper middle class—most of my friends are in that social class and not the upper class like most students.

More interested in talking about the social class of his classmates than his own, Herman continues describing the demographics of the student body. He successfully changes the subject but still manages to set himself apart from the affluent majority at his school by identifying his friends as middle class. Using his friends as a reference group,[8] he eventually discloses, "I'm also located somewhere within the middle-class spectrum; I would say that I'm within the lower upper middle class."[9]

Herman uses his friends as a reference group not only to distinguish himself from Chesthill's affluent majority but also to construct a sense of where he is socially and economically located within his community. Though amorphous and ambiguous, he identifies as being in the middle as a means of not associating with the class extremes. Locating himself in the neutral middle, he is neither a *have* nor a *have not*. He says,

> I drive past the vineyards on the way to school and know that I'm not a part of that group. But I'm not in the trailer park either. I'm in town. I don't really fit into those two sides of the economic spectrum. I guess that's why I position myself and my family somewhere in the middle and not part of either of these social classes. I don't live in their communities; I live between them, somewhere in the middle.

Although identifying in the middle, he partially acknowledges his advantages by locating himself in the upper part of the middle class, but he also eschews that identification and thus minimizes his advantages by pointing out that he is within the lower end. He also insists that others perceive him to be middle class. As he explains, "If someone was trying to guess my social class by just looking at me, they would think that I'm middle class. To quote the great Forrest Gump, 'You can tell a lot about a person by their shoes.' So I guess my wearing leather shoes puts me in the middle class."

Even though Herman downplays his advantages by identifying as middle class and setting himself apart from the majority at Chesthill, he recognizes "how extraordinarily fortunate I am for receiving the kind of education that I'm afforded at [Chesthill]." He further explains, "I'm attending a school that gives me opportunities that so many others don't have or will never have. I know this. I know how lucky that makes me, and I never take that for granted." He also partially acknowledges that he enjoys other educational advantages through his numerous academic and extracurricular activities. As he explains,

> I feel very fortunate to have the support that I need to pursue my filmmaking. Equipment for making films, like cameras and other materials, tend to be relatively expensive, but my parents always have managed to give me the financial support that I needed over the years to buy this equipment and pursue my budding filmmaking career as far as I can take it. My parents tell me, 'It's not your job to worry about the financial matters—that's our job.' I'm very fortunate they hold this attitude.[10]

Having the resources needed to develop his skills and knowledge in filmmaking has allowed Herman to enter numerous film competitions and attend selective filmmaking and screenwriting programs. To a certain extent he acknowledges that these opportunities have provided the kinds of experiences to put him at an advantage in vying for admission to an elite college. He explains, "I know that I'm going into the college application process in good shape, not only because I attend [Chesthill], but also because all these other relevant experiences make me a competitive applicant." He recognizes that these activities have allowed him to establish valuable connections to advance his goals. "I've tapped into a network of important people in the industry through these programs and competitions. I have people who can really help me and direct me to new opportunities," he reports.

Although Herman points out some of the advantages that come with these opportunities, he once again minimizes his advantaged circumstances. For instance, he was recently accepted to a prestigious summer program at a film school in New York City. He initially discloses, "I'm really excited about going there, but it's really expensive so I need to find financial aid to attend it. I've been sending inquiries and request letters trying to network around for aid, but so far I've [found] nothing." When questioned what will happen if he does not receive financial aid, he avoids the question by restating, "I need to find the financial support to attend the program; it's very expensive and will put a strain on my parents." Upon further questioning, he finally admits, "My parents have high hopes for me attending this program and will do whatever possible for me to attend." When asked whether he thinks he will qualify for financial aid, he responds, "The program doesn't offer financial aid. I mean, they do but you have to be really disadvantaged to get any. I'm trying to find financial help from local businesses and my networks." With some frustration by being asked about the financial aspects of the program, he concludes the discussion by saying, "I'm going to the program with or without financial aid; my parents will make sure of that, but I don't want to put that burden on them. I want to get the money from other sources so that they don't have to pay for it." It takes

Herman a while to divulge that his parents have the financial means to afford this opportunity and others that will give him a tremendous advantage in realizing his screenwriting ambition.

Even though Herman has difficulty acknowledging his family's advantaging circumstances, he believes, "I have a firm grasp on the concept [of privilege]." According to him,

> A person's social class doesn't define them at all so that applies to privilege as well. Your privilege doesn't say much about who you are as a person. Instead, it reveals one of two things about you. There are essentially two different kinds of privilege that someone can have and these are ways to distinguish a person's privilege. The first is economic privilege, which is determined by affluence. Then there are also those who are more socially privileged with a wider social network. A person with privilege is either monetarily wealthy or socially wealthy. And some people, very few people, have both.

As someone who does not place significance on social interactions and relationships, Herman believes that economic privilege is more valuable to a person than the social form. He explains, "Economics impact your existence more. Admittedly, I've mostly only encountered those who are economically privileged so I've seen how that benefits a person. I can notice someone who's economically fortunate. They tend to have a better education and you just know they're privileged." He insists, however, "I mean it definitely registers that a person is economically privileged, but I don't let that have too great of an influence on my preconceived notions of that person." Although Herman admits he can distinguish social classes and knows "a person's level of education by just speaking to that person," he believes, "These factors don't necessarily reveal who that person is, so I don't interact with them differently than I would anyone else." For him, "Privilege can result in certain success and happiness, but it has little to do with who you are as a person."

To some extent, Herman acknowledges that advantages make it a lot easier for individuals to accomplish what they want in life, but he quickly points out that "Hard work can change any situation. If you work hard enough, then you can accomplish whatever you want." He emphasizes that hard work is the primary factor in achieving success "for both rich and poor." For example, he claims, "The only reason that I get good grades in school is because I work hard. Nothing else really plays a dominant role in what grades I get. [My grades] reflect only the work that I've put into getting those grades." To emphasize this point further, he says, "There are several classmates who are more intelligent than me, but they don't work as hard as I do. They rely only on their natural abilities, which allow them to be somewhat successful, but they aren't reaching their potential. They aren't as successful as they could be."

Herman partially acknowledges that other factors, such as wealth and educational opportunities, also play a significant role in achieving what one wants out of life. He says that elite preschools, for example, "put kids immediately on the right path to achieving success; their futures are like determined at 4 years old because their parents have the money to pay for them to attend a very good preschool." He continues,

> It's compounding privilege in a way, so if you go to a good preschool you'll go to a better kindergarten and then a better first grade. This then compounds into your kid becoming president or a doctor or what have you. I think small privileges, like going to a top preschool, can have a snowball effect and tremendously shape someone's future.

Although Herman initially had difficulty applying this example to his own life, he acknowledges, after further consideration, "I can see a little of this example reflected in my own life. The educational experiences allotted to me would most likely be unavailable in a lower social class. My education has had, and continues to have, a tremendous impact and influence on me and my life." Once he makes his understandings of privilege more personal, however, he becomes confused. With frustration, he complains, "I feel like I'm contradicting myself somewhere here. I'm not sure if I'm expressing my ideas clearly enough." When discussions about privilege and social class turn personal, Herman struggles to stay on script. Realizing he may have contradicted himself by going off script, he reemphasizes his earlier point that "hard work trumps everything else; how wealthy you are and going to a good school helps, but hard work is absolutely necessary for achieving success."

Intellectualizing privilege is something Herman has learned to do and can do readily. Being asked to identify with privilege, however, brings his advantages to the forefront, making him feel uneasy and, at times, frustrated and confused. Still sorting out his social class identity, his script for talking about his advantages in schooling and life is very much under construction. Through the contradictions, his present script reveals too much about his conflicted understandings of his privileged position. He has yet to find "the right words for describing my social class and how it impacts my life." Although lost for words, he is clear about wanting to distinguish himself from the affluent majority of his immediate world to avoid fully acknowledging the advantages associated with that identification. Staying on neutral ground allows him to acknowledge his advantages partially while simultaneously diminishing their importance.

NOTES

1. As indicated later in this chapter, his reluctance to share personal information made him a challenging participant during this research project. Over the course of the interviews, however, we discovered that Herman would eventually reveal more personal information the longer he talked about a particular topic. Because of this, we had longer interviews and more exchanges with him than with the other participants in this study.

2. With a 45 percent acceptance rate, Chesthill is one of the most selective private high schools in the state.
3. Of this total enrollment, 18 percent are students of color and 25 percent are international students, while 33 percent receive some level of financial aid.
4. Herman's contradictory statements about the level of competition at Chesthill may stem from confusion due to the contradictions that are often a part of the culture at elite schools. Howard (2008) found in his study of elite schools that contradictions often arise in what schools say they want their students to learn and what they actually teach them. Like most other elite schools, Chesthill claims to place significance on cooperation and community. Instead of promoting cooperation and community, however, Howard found that elite schools' competitive environments often promote the opposite and provide little room to uphold the values that the schools purportedly are fostering. From what Herman shared about the culture at Chesthill, he and his classmates similarly are receiving mixed messages about how they actually should be interacting with each other. See also Howard, 2009.
5. In the process of constructing the portraits, we were in frequent communication with the participants. Some of them wrote stories in an email. Instead of retelling what they wrote to us, we decided to include their stories in their own words. At the beginning of this section and several sections throughout the book, these stories written by the participants themselves are italicized.
6. We include the tuition for boarding students because it is unclear whether Herman is a day or boarding student. Throughout the interviews, he claimed to be a day student, but then he shared an article with us about how he had won a screenwriting competition. That article identified him as a boarding student. When we asked for clarification, he did not directly address the inconsistency. He responded, "I'm not sure why that's there." After that exchange, he no longer identified as a day student, as he had up to that point.
7. Before the research project, Herman, like all the participants, was asked specific questions about his parents' occupations and educational levels to determine his family's economic status and eligibility to participate in this study. He realized after making this statement that his claim about receiving financial aid would be too unbelievable to us because we knew details about his family's financial circumstances. His claim gives some indication of how he wants others to perceive him.
8. See Johnson (2001) for a discussion on how privilege is formed from standards of comparison, or, in other words, reference groups.
9. Brantlinger (2003) finds in her study of affluent mothers that affluent people locate themselves within the middle-class boundaries to distinguish themselves from the rich and avoid the upper-class category and the unflattering images associated with that category. Brantlinger argues that the middle-class category is a positive collective with which to identify. The mothers identified in the middle to distance themselves not only from the upper class but also the lower class, allowing them to uphold a positive self-image and to rationalize their advantages. See also Brantlinger (1993, 1999) for how the rich and poor are commonly portrayed.
10. By emphasizing his parents' attitude instead of their resources, Herman is echoing the popular understanding of social class in the United States, which is conceived in stylistic as opposed to structural terms (Rouse, 1995). Davidson (2011) argues that the dominant "commonsensical understanding" of social class is defined "in terms of markers of personal style, desires, and attitudes" (p. 11). Using this understanding, Herman frames his advantages simply as a matter of "personal choice" (see also Howard, 2010).

4 Kayla
Dribbling toward the Goal

with Adrienne Bowles, Jenifer Goldman,
Celeste Lattanzi, Kate O'Callaghan,
and Morgan Rublee

I just want to find something that I love to do and still be able to have success.

When the end-of-the-day bell rings, seventeen-year-old Kayla closes her books, hurries to the locker room, and joins her teammates to get ready for the soccer match against their rival school. She puts on her bright red-and-white uniform, straps on her shin guards, pulls up her socks, and laces up her cleats. Once everyone gears up, Kayla and the other players take to the field for warm-ups and then follow a familiar pregame ritual to sharpen themselves, mentally and physically, for the competition. After a half hour of stretching, passing balls back and forth, and encouraging each other with praises, fist bumps, and high fives, the entire team feels confident and energetic. After the referee blows his whistle to signal that the game will start in a minute, Kayla and her teammates run toward their bench for a quick message from their coach, then huddle together and break with a loud cheer.

The opposing team wins the coin toss and gets to take the kickoff. Kayla takes her position at center midfield and anxiously waits for the referee to blow his whistle. Once the ball is kicked, she does not stop moving while she plays both offense and defense. She endlessly runs up and down the field, helping the defense gain possession of the ball and then moving it up for the forwards to take a shot. For the entire game, she has little time to catch her breath, frequently controlling the play in the most crowded area of the field. Always moving, looking for opportunities to pass or to become open for her teammates, her center-midfield position requires a strong sense of confidence and calm and a willingness to be the hardest worker on the team.

After eighty minutes of play, the buzzer sounds to signify that the game has ended. Kayla steps off of the field and grabs her water bottle before shaking hands with the opposing team and listening to her coach's post-game speech. Although the game has ended, she knows that her hard work is far from over. She will need to put forth the same effort and dedication that she demonstrated on the soccer field toward her schoolwork later this evening. As on most evenings, she will spend hours studying and doing homework to maintain her nearly perfect GPA. With her academic responsibilities and soccer obligations, she has little time for anything else, especially socializing with her friends.

Although her friends "don't expect to hang out a lot" and are understanding of her demanding schedule, she finds not having time for them "frustrating" and "really difficult to deal with" at times. When Kayla is traveling to a tournament or spending an afternoon at practice or an evening doing homework, she occasionally feels as though she were missing out, and she wishes that things could be different. Even though her love of soccer and her determination to maintain a strong GPA eventually repress these feelings, "I still feel like it kind of sucks to always be so busy." She goes on to say, "I just wish that I could do all of it—play soccer and do what I need to do for school and be with my friends and do what they're doing," but she knows that achieving this balance in her life, at least for the moment, "is fairly unrealistic." Not willing to slow down or redirect her priorities, she decides to focus on the positive aspects of having so many responsibilities rather than the negative ones.

Although Kayla finds herself at times "stressed out" and "on the verge of a breakdown" from all the commitments consuming her life, she firmly believes, "It's all worth it 'cause all of it's going to help me achieve my goals." She has not figured out what she wants to study in college or her career aspirations, but she knows, with absolute certainty, that she is heading in the right direction to achieve success. She holds firmly to the philosophy that "if you just get the work done, then it will be easier in the end." Right now, the end does not seem nearly close enough amid preparing for the college admission process; Kayla thinks, "I have so much more to do before I'm ready to apply to colleges."

For the most part, Kayla confidently believes that she will get into one of her first-choice schools, which are also the top-ranked universities in the U.S., with her high GPA, top scores on college entrance exams, and achievements in soccer. "In the grand scheme of things, I guess I don't have too many things to worry about," she states confidently. Given her family's privileged financial circumstances, "I don't have to worry about things like tuition. [My parents] tell me that I just need to work really hard and get into a top school and don't even think about the tuition." She feels both "fortunate and somewhat guilty" that she does not need "to stress or even think about the financial stuff about college like so many other kids have to." She explains,

> Thinking about the fact that I don't have to worry about [the costs associated with college attendance] makes me feel like I don't give back enough, just like in general. I'm taking this way too much for granted

and don't have real worries. So many people have so many bigger concerns and all I really have is a stupid little test at school or getting into the college that I want.

Not wanting to take her advantages for granted, Kayla believes, "I really have to work hard so that I'm not taking any shortcuts. I'm going to have to work to reach my goals; it's not going to be handed to me." Her feelings of guilt about her advantages quickly disappear when she focuses on the amount of effort and work that lies immediately ahead of her in gaining admission to a top-tier college. "I guess everybody's problems are unique to their situation," she concludes.

In thinking about the fast-approaching deadline for submitting college applications, "my only real concern has to do with me not being more involved in extracurricular activities and just playing a sport." Because her academic and soccer obligations have prevented her from being involved in other activities, "I worry a little that I won't have enough on my [college] applications that will make me stand out and be really competitive. I know I need to do more." In comparing herself with her peers, she believes, "A lot of them have so much on their college applications and have been involved in so many different things and have a huge range of experiences and activities; I feel like they have way more than me." Part of her "regrets being so involved in soccer with all the time commitment it takes," whereas another part of her is "satisfied with my decision to play soccer so that I was able to do what I love doing." If she "could go back in time," then she would "probably do things a little differently and not focus on soccer as much so I could've done other things." She would, at least partially, give up what she finds most enjoyable in her life to be "more competitive on college applications."

Unable to undo the past, Kayla looks to the future with plans to add more extracurricular activities to her already overwhelming schedule so that it will "boost my college applications." Even though she would cut back on soccer if she had the chance to go back in time, she is unwilling to give soccer up at the present or in the future. "I just can't stop playing at this point," she explains, "I have to find a way to add more to what I'm already doing at least until I know [what college] I'm going to." With next year being her final year of high school, she also hopes "to enjoy the time I have with my friends and my senior year before we all go off to different places and really make it last." But she knows "deep down inside [that] it's probably unlikely anything's going to change and that I'll get to hang out with friends any more [than I do right now], especially doing more extracurriculars." Kayla knows that she will ultimately "choose work over fun," believing that "fun will probably come later after I get to the point that I need to get to; for now, it's mostly about doing work so that it'll all pay off later."

Kayla wants to get involved in more extracurricular activities not just because she wants to flesh out her college application. Most importantly, "I really would like to be involved in something where I could give back in some way, and to do more around the community." For several years, she has been sporadically involved in the local chapter of the National Charity League (NCL), a mother-daughter philanthropic organization committed to community service, leadership development, and cultural experiences, with her mother and two older sisters. "My mom is really big person in the organization, so we try and do stuff like that together as much as I can," she reports, "But I don't get to [volunteer] at NCL as much as I would like to." Her mother, more so than her father, has emphasized the importance of service throughout her life. Kayla has taken her mother's lesson about "giving back" to heart and would like to get more involved in NCL and other service and philanthropic community organizations. Although she would like to do more service and other activities, "I just can't do anything else more than what I'm doing; I just don't have enough spare time and need to keep focused on what's really important right now." Because she has not been able to identify "the perfect extracurriculars," ones that will "look good [on college applications], fit into my schedule, and [be] something I really want to do," she plans to settle on activities "that don't take up too much time but still look good."

In addition to adding extracurricular activities that will benefit her in the college admissions process, Kayla plans on increasing her nearly perfect GPA by the time she applies to colleges. Earning good grades has always been important to her, but in the past year or so, "[getting good grades] has kinda turned into an obsession." Although Kayla believes that "grades are not a good representation of who someone is at all," she still plans "to do what it will take [and] sacrifice my social life and free time" to achieve higher grades and become the top student in her class. She realizes that this will not be an easy goal to achieve. Attending one of the top public high schools in the nation,[1] where "everything revolves around getting good grades, getting into a top college, being the best, and just working hard," several of her peers hold similar aspirations, vying for the top rank in their class and striving to earn an more than perfect GPA.[2]

Located in an affluent city in Southern California, her high school, Sprucewood, offers a de facto private-school education that prepares students to become competitive players in the college admissions game.[3] Most members of its largely affluent student body[4] come from families with enough resources to supplement their children's Sprucewood education and thus to help them become even more competitive. They have taken preparation courses to get top scores on college admissions exams, received private tutoring and individualized instruction to maintain high grades, traveled extensively for cultural awareness and educational enrichment, attended summer programs, and participated in extracurricular activities. Kayla explains, "Everybody comes from families that give their kids whatever they need to get the best grades, the best test scores, and just be the best."

Kayla knows that becoming the top in anything, especially in academics, within this ambitious, high-achieving group will be a challenge. Driven by the same competitive spirit that she demonstrates on the playing field, she believes, however, that she can accomplish whatever she sets her mind to through hard work and determination. As she explains, "I don't think things come easy in general, so this is no different. If you want to be successful now so you can be successful later in life, then you're going to need to work hard." Defining success, at least for the moment, as acceptance into a top college,[5] she plans to spend her remaining time in high school striving to outdo her peers academically. "It's the only way that I can stand out on college applications; I have to be at the top of my class and have the highest GPA," she reiterates.

IN THE MIDDLE OF A TUG OF WAR

Many changes occurred in Kayla's life when her parents divorced during her middle school years. As in her position on the soccer field, she found herself in the middle between her parents. "I became sort of like the link between the both sides of our family. [My parents] didn't really talk with each other, so I became like the messenger between them and was like the mediator between them," she explains. Even when they were married, "my mom and dad didn't ever communicate too well because they argued and fought a lot." After the divorce, her parents nearly stopped talking to each other altogether. "They speak to one another when it's absolutely necessary," she reports. For the most part, Kayla manages her in-the-middle position well by avoiding certain topics and doing what each parent expects her to do.

Although she lives under the same roof as her father, Kayla admits that she does not see him very often. As she explains, "My dad is always out, he travels a lot, and he works a lot. When he has free time he likes playing tennis with his friends, but that isn't too often. Most of the time he is working or just out doing something for his company." Kayla and her father live two parallel lives, rarely seeing each other. She claims that this is not something new because "growing up, I was mostly just taken care of by my nanny and my dad was never around that much." She goes on to say, "Nothing has really changed as I've gotten older. He's always busy doing one thing and I'm always busy doing something else." Even though Kayla's father is often absent, he still manages to show his support and love for her. She explains, "My relationship with my dad is very loving and honest. He isn't around a lot, but he never ceases to show his love and support and affection for me." Without doubts, Kayla knows "my dad will be there when I need him to be and he always seems to be there at the exact moment when I need him the most."

Even though Kayla lives with her dad, she has a much closer personal relationship with her mother. She finds her mother's "laid-back and easygoing" personality comforting and "less intense and not as intimidating as my dad." Because her mother has a "calming presence," Kayla makes a point to see her mother as much as possible. As she explains, "I guess I'm more like my dad and stressed out all the time. Being around my mom makes me calmer, destresses me. Sometimes I just go over to her place and hang out so I can relax and take a break from things."

She ends up seeing her mother more than her father because "she isn't as busy as my dad so our schedules match up better." Although her mother keeps a busy social calendar and spends a considerable amount of time engaged in physical activities and her artwork, she makes Kayla and her two sisters top priorities in her life. As she explains, "My mom will drop everything if we call her and tell her that we need to see her. She is always available for us, no matter what." According to Kayla, her mother is so available because "she doesn't really have an official job. So what she does spend her time doing isn't as important as we are to her."

Kayla heavily relies on her mother for advice and comfort, describing their relationship more as a friendship than "your typical mother-daughter relationship." She explains,

> My mom and I are closer than most moms and daughters. She's more of a friend than my mom, just because I can tell her anything and not expect to get in trouble or anything. She is more there to help me out. And my dad is also really lenient, but I would not say we are close like that. I don't really tell him everything about my problems or anything like that. He is really understanding, but I go to my mom most of the time because she's just better at listening to me and not telling me what I need to do.

Even though she does not often reveal too much about her life to her father, she still relies on him to be there when she needs him to be. She may not look to him for advice, but "I look up to him as the example that I need to follow and have complete respect for what he's accomplished. I've seen in him what it takes achieve the kind of success he has had."

When Kayla's parents married, her mother played a similarly supportive role for her father. As she explains, "My dad visited Taiwan when he was in his twenties and met my mom. Then my mom came back to California with him because that's where my dad was going to college and then got married." Leaving her home "to go with him on the other side of the world," she claims that her mother's life "revolved around my dad and making sure he's successful." Although her parents found little common ground, they agreed that "the success of my dad's company was more important than anything, and whatever it took to make it successful they both were willing to make the sacrifice. Their entire focus was on making the company a success." Shortly before Kayla was born, her father started an import and export business selling plastics to major companies. By the time she entered kindergarten, "his company had grown to be one of the biggest businesses for that industry." Part of what made it become such a successful business so quickly is that "my mom worked with my dad at the business and supported him with whatever he needed." To a certain degree, her father recognizes the important role that her mother previously played in the business, but for the most part, he takes sole credit for "building it up from nothing and making it what it is today." And Kayla agrees that her father deserves most of the credit. "I think my dad just worked really hard at making it a success. He started his business from nothing and I know it wouldn't have been successful without his perseverance and hard work," she believes.

Through her father's example, Kayla has learned that success does not come easy. She credits her father's example with teaching her "to appreciate what I have and know that many others don't have the same as I do." She further explains,

> My dad has this illness that he was born with, and his parents died when he was really young. He didn't have any money growing up and he had to take care of his siblings while still dealing with his illness. It's so inspiring because he's so successful now and I don't even go through a small number of the problems he faced. It is super inspiring, especially since he is so smart and got into such a great college purely on his own.

Kayla is inspired by her father's example of "[overcoming] odds to get what he wanted out of life" and she plans to do the same. Although she will not face the same difficulties he had to face, "I know there'll be obstacles; there are always obstacles that you have to get past to achieve what you want and I believe, like my dad, that I'll get past anything to get where I want."

Kayla lives by her father's example in working toward her ambitious goals. She reports, "My dad really notices how hard I work and how determined I am. He tells me that he sees a lot of himself in me, and hearing him say that always makes me proud." Considering Kayla to be more like him than his other two daughters, her father would like her to eventually take over his business. Kayla agrees that she would be best suited to run the business one day, especially in comparison with her older sisters, who "spend a lot and take my dad's money for granted." She claims to be "more practical than them" and "more willing to work hard at something and more responsible." Even though she and her father consider her to be best suited for the job, "I don't know if that's what I'll actually do or something that I want to do with my life." Although she has thought about this possibility, she feels caught in the middle between following her father's goals for her future and finding her own personal path to success.

Kayla also finds herself in the middle between her parents' differing college expectations for her. "My dad pressures me to work hard and earn top grades. He always says I need to get into a really good college. But my mom has always said I don't need to get good grades and I do not need to go to college to be successful in life," she explains. Her parents' differing expectations stem from their distinct backgrounds. Although both come from working-class families, they took different paths after leaving home to achieve financial success. Kayla's father got into a highly selective college and supported himself throughout his college years. He then worked at several jobs to learn what was necessary for starting his business. In contrast, her mother never attended college but began working at "various day jobs" to support herself. She then married, helped her husband build a successful business, and became wealthy enough to spend her life painting and pursuing other interests full time.

Kayla believes that her parents' different life experiences influence their expectations for her. She says,

> They both draw on their own lives to give me advice and form their expectations that they have for me. And since they are different their expectations are different. I feel like I'm in the middle of this tug-of-war game with my parents: one of them telling me to do one thing to become successful and the other one telling me something totally different.

She finds it difficult to sort out their conflicting messages because "both of them are successful, in different ways, but still successful." At times, she wants to follow her mother's advice in order "to avoid being stressed out my whole life and do something that I really would love doing and trusting that everything will work out in the end." But more often "I think to myself, 'Dad probably has the most realistic advice.' I need to do what I have to do to become successful and not rely on things just working out." At this point, she mostly follows her father's advice and does what she needs to do more than what she wants to do. Respecting how her father became successful more than how her mother did, she believes that she will inevitably follow in her father's footsteps: attend a top college, join the corporate world, and take over his company or start her own.

Although Kayla's parents hold conflicting views on the future path that she should take, they are unified in their expectation that "I'll one day be doing something that makes me really successful." Kayla also holds high expectations for her future and a certainty about her eventual "ultimate success." She struggles to define success on her own terms and has not fully decided whose path to follow. But no matter how she eventually sorts out these uncertainties, she knows that her parents will continue playing an important role in her path to success. "I wouldn't be happy if my parents weren't proud of me and what I was doing," she says. Kayla hopes to embody both parents' perspective so that "I can make both of them proud and not just one of them." But even more importantly, "I want to be able to find something that I love to do so I can be happy and still have financial security."

THE ONLY PLAYER ON THE FIELD

The summer before her junior year, Kayla went on a service trip to Fiji through Rustic Pathways, a program providing travel and service trips for students and families in countries throughout the world. For a little over a week, "I built houses for families in need and was teaching soccer to underprivileged kids." She describes this experience as "unforgettable" and explains,

> I just loved everything about the whole trip. The experience that I received from it was like nothing I had ever experienced before. I love playing soccer and to have the ability to teach all these little kids was amazing. The kids were always excited, even though I only brought one ball to play with because they don't have any equipment. I didn't really like the building houses part of the community service that much because it was very hard work and not something that I was really good at. But overall, the trip was probably the most rewarding thing I have ever done.

Kayla hopes to take another service trip next summer to another "place that I haven't been to before," but she also wants to get a job that summer, which may keep her from traveling. As she explains, "I want to travel more but I also want to get a job so that may take priority. I've always received any money that I need from my dad so it'd be nice to say I make my own money." She plans to spend the summer lifeguarding because this kind of work "will be more valuable than just making money and allow me to become more responsible doing this because it's an actual legitimate job with *real* responsibilities." As for the money she will earn in this job, she plans to "save it because that's what my dad always taught me to do, and then invest it and get interest." Whereas her friends and sisters think about "buying the newest fashion trend" or "blowing money on other useless things," Kayla wants "to do the same thing that I'm going to do when I get older and have a career; I really want to be smart with my money and avoid being wasteful."

Kayla believes her sisters rely too heavily on their father's money, and she is determined to do the opposite. "I see myself as more independent than my sisters and I want to be less dependent on my parents or my dad's financial support as much as they are," she claims. One of the main reasons for her becoming more independent than her older sisters is that she has been left "to do things on my own." She explains, "When [my sisters] lived [at] home my parents were together so they always had my mom around or one of them. But I've lived only with my dad for the past few years and he's always in and out of the house, constantly working. I'm left alone more than them and more on my own." Although Kayla's parents "highly value independence," she claims her sisters never learned to become independent. She believes that her "natural independent personality" and "living arrangements with my dad" helped her learn what her sisters did not.

Similar to her parents' understandings, Kayla defines being independent as "having first the freedom and then the ability to do your own thing and be self-reliant and not dependent on others." She is quick to point out that her version of what it means to be independent also emphasizes responsibility. As she explains,

> I've learned that along with independence come some responsibilities. My parents have always been more lenient than my friends' parents and really relaxed about rules and such. I think that has really helped, because I don't feel the need to be out late, or really do anything I'm not supposed to be doing. I think my parents giving me a lot freedom has been one of the most important things that helped me become more responsible. I don't think there's a real difference between responsibility and independence. You can't have one without the other.

Even though her parents give Kayla a lot of freedom to make her own choices, they still hold high expectations. More specifically, they expect her to complete her homework, maintain a high GPA, get herself to soccer, and avoid engaging in "stupid and dangerous" activities. She abides by their expectations "without them watching my every move," because "I know how to take care of myself and complete my responsibilities without them or anybody else hovering over me constantly and reminding me what I need to be doing." She further states, "It's pretty simple—I know what I need to do for school and soccer and with other things and I do it."

Kayla's parents emphasize the significance of being independent also to prepare her "not to be overly reliant on our privilege and that I need to be independent enough to deal with whatever situations that I encounter in the future." She further explains,

> I grew up with many advantages, and in a privileged home, and because of this my parents want to teach us all to be independent. They do not want us to be dependent on money or on nice things because having those things may not always be the case. You just never know. If you get too dependent on those things, then you won't be able to adjust to the situation if circumstances change.

Because both her parents came from working-class backgrounds, they stress the instability of their privileged circumstances. "My parents say over and over that our current [financial] situation isn't guaranteed to be the same always. They raised me to not depend on people or material things so that I could be more realistic, like understanding the reality of things," she reports. Although Kayla believes she knows the reality "that nothing is really guaranteed," she does not hold her parents' uncertainties about the future. Quite the opposite, in fact, she is certain that she can maintain the same privileged lifestyle to which she is accustomed. "Maybe it's because I wasn't raised like [my parents] so I can't see what they're saying, but I just don't see my financial situation changing that much—other than hopefully improving," she explains.

Instead of absorbing her parents' anxieties about the future, Kayla actually learned to value what she has and not take her advantages for granted from their lesson about the insecurity of their wealth. She credits her parents for helping her develop a "realistic view" of the responsibilities that come with her wealth and the hard work and determination it will take to maintain that wealth. This view, in turn, keeps her mindful of her advantaging circumstances and fuels her drive "to give back." As she explains, "I think knowing that I shouldn't take my privileges for granted and that I need to work hard to keep them has in some ways made me appreciate them more and that has helped me keep in mind that not everybody has the same privileges and in the same situation." Realizing that "there are so many people that face some challenging situations in life that I don't have to deal with," Kayla is both motivated "to help those that are less fortunate" and "to work hard to support the goals that I've set for myself." This realization also includes her understanding that "I need to do everything on my own and not just rely on the privileges I have." At the same time, however, she knows that her parents will always be there to support her emotionally and financially if needed. Determined to be independent, she does not want to rely on them, but "it helps me to be more independent, knowing that I can have their support." She goes on to say, "I just want to know that they'll be there [even though] I'm doing everything on my own."

Kayla strongly feels the need to prove that her accomplishments are attributed to her hard work and are independent from her wealth. Especially in school, she sometimes senses that her peers think she lacks motivation and does not care about her academic success. She explains, "Because I'm an athlete and really into soccer and my dad makes a lot of money, I think a lot of people don't think that I, one, care, or two, am that smart; some people think that I get things handed to me." She also believes that her peers perceive her this way because she is a female. As she explains, "People sometimes think I'm a bimbo or something, that I just care about clothes or I don't know, girly stuff, but I think that their views are stereotypical." She responds to her peers' assumptions by striving even harder to earn exceptional grades not only for her college applications, but also to prove others wrong. She reports, "I make it a point to show people that I am an intelligent person and I do focus on my grades and it is a priority in my life." With her competitive spirit, Kayla feels a sense of accomplishment when she receives a good grade, because "it proves people wrong by showing them that I do care and am as smart, or even smarter, than they are." She claims, however, a more important source of motivation for earning good grades is "proving to myself that I am able to accomplish something on my own because of myself and my hard work." She admits though, "It does feel good proving other people wrong, but that isn't my main motivation; it's just an extra benefit."

PRESSURE SITUATIONS

Kayla kept looking at the large B- written in red ink and circled at the top of her paper. Her seventh-grade teacher had filled her three-page paper with copious comments, but she could not turn her attention away from the letter grade. Eventually she broke her gaze to look around the classroom at her peers. "I noticed that nobody was looking at their papers and they were talking, just waiting for class to start. I figured they must've gotten better grades than me," she recalls. Devastated and feeling like a failure, it took everything she had to hold back tears and contain her emotions. She remembers, "I wasn't going to have an outburst at school so I acted like nothing was wrong and went on with my day."

By the time Kayla arrived home, she was no longer on the verge of tears but still upset. As soon as she walked through the door, her mother sensed her distress and asked her what happened. "I got this bad grade on a paper that I worked hard on and thought I would get an A on. I just don't understand why I didn't," Kayla informed her, and then told her all the details related to receiving a lower-than-expected grade on the assignment. Her mother listened attentively, giving Kayla the space to release her frustration and anger; then she attempted to comfort her by "assuring me that grades don't define a person's success and that I shouldn't stress so much about everything." Kayla was not fully convinced that "grades didn't matter as much I thought they did," but nevertheless appreciated her mother's efforts "to make me feel better about getting a bad grade."

Until a few months ago, her mother regularly deemphasized the importance of grades but instead redirected Kayla's attention toward learning. "Growing up, my mom always told me to focus on what I was learning and not worry about the grades that I was getting. She always told me that my learning was what's important and that grades didn't always accurately reflect that," she reports. At the middle of this school year, however, her mother's carefree attitude about Kayla's grades began to change:

> I just had my academic counseling meeting and this semester is really important, junior year second semester. This semester is supposed to be one of my highest GPAs, and my counselor kept stressing that over and over again to my mom. And my mom usually doesn't worry about my grades, but her opinion changed after that meeting. Now she reminds me about my grades all the time.

Kayla finds her mother's change of heart confusing. As she explains, "On one hand, she tells me that success is about being happy and that I don't need to go to college to be successful or happy. Then she's putting pressure on me to get good grades to get into a good college. It doesn't make sense to me." When Kayla asks her mother for clarification, "she doesn't really give me a good answer. She tells me, 'I just want you to be happy,' and doesn't explain what she's really trying to say to me." Although she is unable to sort out her mother's mixed messages, she now feels an additional source of pressure to gain admission to a top-notch college.

For the most part, both of Kayla's parents did not put much pressure on her about her schoolwork or grades until the meeting with the college counselors. After that, they became more concerned about her performance in school and more active in her college process. Although her parents are not always vocal about their high expectations, she knows what they expect from her. "I know they want me to get all A's and get my GPA up more. They don't say that directly to me, but I just know that's what they're expecting. They're telling me this in more indirect ways, like with their questions and stuff like that," she explains. Her parents' unspoken yet understood expectations are putting a tremendous amount of pressure on her shoulders.

Kayla attempts to relieve some of that pressure by reducing her parents' anxieties about her academic performance. She reports, "When I get a good grade on a test or something, I make sure that I tell them about it and show them my grade. And I don't tell them anything that'll upset them or cause them to worry more." In so doing, she has been successful in reducing her parents' anxieties but unsuccessful in easing the pressure they are placing on her. In fact, "they've increased their expectations lately because they've seen what I'm capable of and want me to achieve at my full potential." Finding it impossible to escape their pressure, she is "trying to deal with all the stress the best that I can so that I can still perform at the level that I need to be at and achieve my goals; I'm keeping focused on the larger picture and the goals that I've set for myself."

Kayla, to some extent, realizes what keeps her parents' pressure inescapable is her need to make them proud, especially her father. As she explains, "I really try to win praise from my dad especially, because it's really hard to please him. I know if I do well in school and get into a good college, he'll be really proud of me." As she strives for her father's approval, he urges her to do more, such as getting involved in more activities and taking extra classes that will make her more competitive in the college admissions process. Kayla believes that her father may also have an ulterior motive for pressuring her to do more. As she explains, "He wants me to do what I need to get into college, but he's also steering me toward certain things that will prepare me to take over his business one day. He tells me these things are good for college, but I know there's more to it." For instance, she claims, "My dad always wants me to take Chinese classes because that's the primary language that his company works around and does business with. He also wants me to join the young entrepreneur group."

Kayla finds her father's "hidden agenda" gratifying yet stressful. On one hand, she is pleased that her father has such confidence in her potential and considers her to be the most promising prospect for taking over the business, but on the other, "it just adds even more pressure on me and even higher expectations." In particular, his expectations place her in "an unwinnable situation." She believes, "If I don't want to take over his company, then I feel like I'm going to let him down, and he won't be proud of me. But if I do what he wants, then I feel like I'll let myself down. There's just no perfect solution to this." She is hopeful that this tension will be resolved during college or, at the latest, before she begins her career. As she explains, "I'm hoping that either my dad changes his plans for me because he figures there's a better path for me to take or I decide [taking over his company] is what I really want to do."

Kayla's future path has no fixed destination ahead. When thinking about the possibility of taking over her father's business, she admits,

> I mean it's something I definitely don't want to do, so I feel like I am letting him down. But it's not something that I'd actually consider, because I know I don't want to do it and I know I wouldn't be happy doing it. I don't think he would even want me to do it even if I agreed, because he knows I would not be happy. But at the same time, this is his expectation of me, and he's not really considering other options for me.

Although she believes that she will not end up taking over the family business, she still plans to pursue a business major, following at least partially in her father's footsteps. Before she figures out a major, though, she believes that she must first focus on earning top grades so that she will gain acceptance into a top-notch college. "Thinking about what I'll be doing after college stresses me out. I know I should just focus on getting into college right now and not think about the far future, but it's difficult when that's what my dad focuses on," she explains.

In addition to the increasing demands placed on her by her parents, especially her father, she is facing mounting pressures at her school, where "all they care about is preparing us to be successful in life, like having a successful occupation and making money, and that means first going to a good college." Since starting high school, her school counselors have been stressing the importance of her academic performance and how it will lead to future success. As she explains, "My counselor really emphasizes how important grades are for achieving your goals and puts a lot of pressure on us to get good grades and do the other things that will make us more competitive [in the college admissions process]." As the time for her to apply for college quickly approaches, Kayla also feels increasing pressures from her teachers and other school officials. "It's like that's all my teachers talk to us about. Everything has to do with getting into a good [college] and what we're not doing but need to be doing to reach our goals," she reports.

Although Kayla confronts various external demands to improve her academic performance, she feels no greater pressure than that which she places on herself. Wanting to work hard enough to deserve her current and predictable success in life, she pushes herself to the limit. She believes, "I just can't stop right now, no matter how much I want to at times; it's too critical right now. This is my last chance to reach the level that I need to be at to reach my goals for college." At times she worries that she pushes herself too much in her pursuit of success, but she refuses to ease the amount of pressure she puts on herself. As she explains, "Sometimes, I have to stop and tell myself that I need to take a break or I'm just going to get too stressed out and crash or something, but I never actually stop because I can't right now." She ultimately decides, "I just have to keep going, because I know that it's going to pay off in the end."

LETTING GO OF THE THINGS SHE LOVES

If I were to take a gap year before going off to college, I would love to start in a place where I would be able to work with kids. Ideally, I would go to Asia, because I've always wanted to learn Mandarin and that's where my mom and her family are from. I would love to go somewhere I could be of use where they need help like teaching in schools, playing sports with kids. I would want to be doing something that would be contributing something beneficial to people, something that was needed that I could do.

After spending a good amount of my trip around there, I would then travel to Europe, probably Spain and Italy, because I have always wanted to go to those countries. Not sure why those places in particular, but it seems like I could do a lot there and experience things that I haven't experienced before. I would buy tickets to the nosebleed section of all the big soccer games and stay in little hotels run by old ladies that have you do chores in return. I would want to have real kinds of experiences and just not just ones that a typical tourist has.

Kayla has thought long and hard about taking a gap year. She would love to travel abroad and have an experience similar to her service trip in Fiji last summer. "The program that I was with this past summer actually offers a gap year that lets you travel and do basically the same thing I did, but for a whole year, and that really interested me and I still think about it," she reports with excitement. Although Kayla is keenly interested in going on a longer trip through this program, she admits, "I probably would never be able to do it." She further explains, "It's something that I would not seriously consider, but it is something that I am seriously interested in." Her parents would not be overly supportive of her taking a year off to travel and volunteer because they have always expected her to attend college right after graduating high school. She claims, "They probably wouldn't understand because it wouldn't make sense to them if I were to take a year off." Her parents believe the most direct path to a career is best for Kayla in achieving her goals. For the most part, she agrees with them. She imagines what her ideal gap year would look like, helping kids and teaching classes, yet, deep down inside, she is fully aware that these dreams will never become reality.

When Kayla catches herself daydreaming about taking a gap year, she snaps back to reality and sets her dreams aside. "I know I need to go to college right after high school, because it is the right thing to do, or what seems like the right thing to do," she explains. She has determined that going directly to college is the "right" path to take, because "that's what my dad and my mom want me to do, because they always talk about how I will do really well in school if I don't take a break." Along with her parents, Kayla worries that taking a gap year "will not only delay me working toward my goals but could also potentially keep me from reaching them, because it could hurt my chances of getting into a good school and then when I do go back, make it a harder adjustment." Her parents have been successful in convincing her not to pursue a gap year, but they are not the only ones influencing her decision.

Kayla's peers, teachers, and other school officials are also playing an important role and, like her parents, "everybody thinks that the best option is to go directly to college and not take time off." In discussing their influence, she further explains, "It's just so odd to me that I never hear about anybody taking a gap year or this even being an option for kids at my school. Nobody else that I go to school with would look at it as a normal thing. It's just not an option [at my school]."[6] Kayla feels obligated to follow the path that her teachers, parents, and peers expect her to take; she will graduate from high school and immediately attend college.

The idea of a gap year is not the only thing that Kayla is letting go of to achieve her goals. When she steps off the soccer field at the end of this season, she may never play again. Although she loves soccer and has been dedicated to the sport, she does not plan on playing during college. As she explains, "I used to want to go to college and play soccer at a Division 1 level, but I have changed my goals and that doesn't fit into my plan any longer." She is also uncertain whether she could compete at the highest level of college soccer, especially at one of the top-ranked schools that she hopes to attend. To develop into a better player and reach her full potential, she would need to dedicate time and effort that she is not willing to divert from her academics. Quitting soccer is a tough pill for her to swallow, but she has her mind set on gaining admissions to a top-notch college and "nothing else is really that important."

Because Kayla has given up the idea of playing soccer in college and possibly even her last year of high school, she instead dreams of eventually working as a physical therapist for a professional soccer team. She believes that this job, or one similar to it, would be a way of combining her love of soccer with her financial and professional goals. She explains,

> I could imagine myself in sports medicine for a really good soccer team, in Europe or somewhere. And being a physical therapist, I would always be helping the players out with their injuries. So it would feel good to always be helping others and keep involved in soccer at the same time. But I would want to be one only for a famous team, like their main personal therapist. I would need to be working with a famous team to feel like I've reached the level of success that I want to reach in my life.

Working with a "famous" professional soccer team is only another dream and, as she admits, "not something that I will probably ever really do." She will instead likely follow her father's footsteps by getting a business degree and then entering the corporate world. In Kayla's mind, this more likely path to success is "sort of inevitable." As she explores multiple options for her future, she is starting to realize that the path she will take may already be defined.

Kayla is not fully convinced, however, that she has found a clear path toward achieving her goals. During this process of trying to figure out what lies ahead, she is willing to abandon any current commitments that could possibly stand in the way of "ultimate success." When it comes to letting go of what she loves, "I just have to keep reminding myself how badly I want to be successful, and in the long run, these things like soccer and taking a gap year won't really matter but could keep me from getting to where I want." She believes, "These things that I love do not correlate with success and will not bring me success, and so I have to give them up." According to Kayla, being a top-level soccer player or taking a gap year will not get her into a top-notch college and, in fact, may hurt her chances in gaining admission. She admits that these activities "would give me an immediate sense of happiness, but I need more than that, since that happiness would only last for a short time." Kayla believes that an enduring, more complete sense of happiness will only be achieved when she reaches her ambitious goals. "I'm thinking about the long-term benefits and not just in-the-moment ones," she adds.

Kayla compares her process of figuring out her future to being at an intersection controlled by a yield sign. Nothing is stopping her from proceeding through the intersection except herself. No oncoming traffic; no one behind her impatiently urging her to move forward. She is only yielding to the unknown with the realization that once she begins moving, she will need to decide in which direction she will head. All roads lead her to success, but none of them, at least at the moment, seem to lead her also to something that she will love doing. She is certain that she will eventually know which direction to take. For now, she will continue to yield until she gains a better sense of direction.

NOTES

1. *U.S. News & World Report* ranks Sprucewood High School as one of the top high schools in the nation.
2. In calculating the GPA, Sprucewood students receive a 4.0 when they earn an A in a regular high school course. However, like a growing number of prestigious high schools, Sprucewood assigns weighted grades to courses that are deemed more rigorous and challenging than others such as advanced placement courses and certain honors courses, in which the material is studied more in depth and at a faster pace than in a regular course. Therefore when students receive an A in one of these weighted courses, they receive a 5.0 on a 4.0 scale. Some researchers argue that as more and more college-bound students report GPAs near or above 4.0, high school grades lose some of their value in differentiating students and cause an increased focus on admissions test scores and other information in the college admissions process (e.g., Camara, Kimmel, Scheuneman & Sawtell, 2003). Instead of helping students gain admission to highly selective colleges, some argue that these weighted grades are making college admissions officers pay closer attention to other information in students' applications.
3. A significant portion of the school's funding comes from private donors and organizations. Through donations and fundraising efforts, parents make sure that the school has enough funding to offer their children the kinds of opportunities that will make them competitive in the college admissions game and to maintain Sprucewood's position as one of top high schools in the nation. With resources equal to those of elite private schools, Sprucewood provides students with the kinds of experiences both inside and outside the classroom context that make them competitive in the college admissions process. Sprucewood's national reputation and ranking are also significant in this process. Espenshade and Radford's (2009) research shows that one of the strongest predictors of getting into any college is attending one of the top 72 high schools in the nation. For discussion about playing the admissions game, see, for example, Bound, Hershbein, & Long, 2009.
4. More specifically, only 1 percent of the student body receives free or reduced-cost lunch. Sprucewood is fairly homogenous in regards to race also. The school's racial composition is 67 percent Asian American, 30 percent white, 1 percent Latino/Latina, 0.2 percent African American, and 1.5 percent bi- or multiracial.
5. Kayla believes that gaining admissions to a top-rated college is her next step for achieving financial and professional success later in life. She shares the opinion of most Americans that "winning admission to an elite [college or university] is imagined to be a golden passport to success [and] failing to do so is seen as a major life setback" (Easterbrook, 2004, p. 128). The common belief is that gaining entrance into a high-status, highly selective college is nearly essential for entry into high-status graduate programs and/or into careers providing wealth and power. However, the findings of Dale and Krueger's (2002) study challenge the notion that elite-college attendance is essential to success later in life. They found that it was ultimately the student, not the school, who was responsible for individual success. Regardless, there are other reasons that affluent students like Kayla want to attend elite colleges such as the high status and prestige that comes with attendance. As Khan (2010) points out, "To say

'I graduated from Harvard' impresses, regardless of how one ever did at that school" (p. 99).

6. Gap years have long been common in Europe and Australia, but organized programs have gained traction in the U.S. only in the past few years. Most common gap-year activities include doing volunteer work, taking classes, working for pay, traveling, and engaging in outdoor adventures. Whereas many students take a year off to earn money for tuition, most affluent students are involved in programs that offer international travel or service work (Shellenbarger, 2010; Sparks, 2010). However, many competitive high schools like Sprucewood still emphasize that the best option after high school is going directly to college. Furthermore, even the strongest advocates of gap-year experiences urge students to gain admission to college first and then ask to defer enrollment for a year (Haigler & Nelson, 2005). For affluent students in the U.S., going directly to college is still the most common pathway.

5 Marcus
On His Own

with Courtney Erskine, Cynthia Garvin,
Molly Hodson, Peggy Meyer, and
Hannah O'Brien

When it comes down to it, just myself will help me get over obstacles in life.

In most situations, Marcus is a young man of few words. But when he speaks, he does so in a deliberate manner that is beyond his nineteen years. When posed a question, he does not hesitate to ask for clarity. He sometimes requests that you repeat or rephrase your inquiry to make certain that he fully understands what he is being asked. Once assured that he does indeed understand, he pauses to give it thought and formulate his answer before articulating his ideas in a concise and confident manner. His ability to communicate with others effectively, he will tell you, is one of the most valuable skills he took away from his years at Parkridge Day School, a co-ed, private school fifteen minutes away from his family's home in a small, affluent suburb in Massachusetts.

Parkridge enrolls both boarding and day students. With his family living so close to the school, Marcus was a day student. He attended his prep school over the local public high school initially because he felt that "it would be a much better experience overall." He believed that Parkridge would provide the best environment for him to develop not only academically but also socially because of its diverse student body.[1] Located in an affluent white suburb, the student body at the local public high school was almost entirely white. Up to that point, Marcus had spent his entire academic career at predominantly white schools. He no longer wanted to be at a school where he would have been one of the very few students of color; he believed that he would "develop overall and become a better person" as part of Parkridge's more diverse community. Although he wanted a more heterogeneous school, football was the main reason he decided not to attend the local public high school. Marcus found it unacceptable that the school did not have a football team. When it came time to decide where to go for high school, "my heart was set on just one school" because of Parkridge's "powerhouse football program."

Marcus remembers how he was encouraged to develop strong social and verbal skills during his time at Parkridge. At the start of freshman year, speaking in front of large groups of people made him "incredibly nervous." He quickly discovered that he needed to get over this because his teachers required students to speak in public frequently. It was a gradual process for him to become more comfortable speaking in front of people. He recounts the small steps he took; first, he practiced speaking in class; then, slowly, Marcus felt that he "could present to my whole grade, then the whole school [and] eventually alumni of the school and donors." Learning to communicate effectively is a skill that he has come to value more and more since graduation. He believes that it will be especially beneficial in the future, particularly when the time comes for him to enter the working world after college and establish a career in business or finance. He believes, "I probably wouldn't have developed my public speaking abilities nearly as much as I did if I had gone to another school, like [the local public school]."

Looking back, Marcus firmly believes he received a better education by attending a private school. His school "wasn't like a standard classroom like you'd have at a public school or even in college." At his prep school, he felt that he "couldn't just sit in the back corner, not say a word, keep getting hundreds on tests, and get a 4.0." Marcus could not coast on intelligence alone, as he believes students can sometimes do in public schools. Instead, Parkridge emphasized interactive and interpersonal learning over simple rote memorization. His teachers never gave lectures but instead focused on "student-centered learning that was based mainly on discussions." He recalls that he and his classmates often sat in circles to encourage student-led dialogue and debate. Because of the small class sizes, he believes they were "kind of forced" to participate and to offer their thoughts, opinions, or skepticisms. But at the same time, students were given a lot of freedom in their learning. For Marcus, this teaching style had the perfect balance between "forcing you to become a better student and person and giving you the room to make your own decisions and have a say in what you're learning."

Marcus also emphasizes how being exposed to the diversity within Parkridge's student body broadened his learning experience. While there, he enjoyed being surrounded by people who hailed from all parts of the United States as well as from every corner of the globe. Because of this diversity, he could interact with peers from various countries across Asia and Europe. These sorts of interactions had significant influence on his overall learning. His diverse peer group provided "an international aspect," which contributed to a multicultural outlook that he might not have developed otherwise. Although Parkridge's student body was diverse and students were encouraged to interact regardless of differences, Marcus reports that the "typical cliché cliques existed."

Students at Parkridge primarily divided into four social groups: jocks, geeks, drama kids, and artists. Some students managed to cross group borders to socialize with peers from more than one group; but for the most part the social interactions between groups were limited. In discussing his own social group, Marcus makes it clear that he belonged exclusively with the jocks. Although he had many other activities and accomplishments—he frequently appeared on the academic honor roll, participated in Parkridge's dance program, regularly performed community service both locally and in Central America, and appeared in several of his school's theater productions—being an athlete defined Marcus's identity. He was a multiseason athlete, playing basketball in the winter and baseball in the spring, but his real passion was football. He was an accomplished football player throughout his four years at Parkridge, but his love for the sport emerged years before he actually began playing. From a young age he grew up watching his father coach and his older brothers play. For as long as he can remember, his family has lived and breathed football. Marcus believes that it is only natural he has no greater passion than he does for the sport and the reason it is a big part of who he is.

MEANINGFUL RELATIONSHIPS

Parkridge is fond of its traditions and homecoming is one of the most cherished. Homecoming week is filled with pep rallies, the return of alumni to campus, performances, and a formal dance. It ends with the main attraction—a football game against their biggest rival. The school spends a significant amount of time during the week "getting pumped up and psyched [for the game]." Football practices are grueling and longer that week. Parents, mostly football players' mothers, hold socials and fundraisers. The entire community participates in festivities that honor the school's history, including competitions to see who has the most school spirit. After a long week of rallying together, socializing, and cheering on the football team, the night of the big game arrives. And it ends as everyone in school community had hoped. In front of a packed stadium, Parkridge "destroy[s] the other team and [comes] out with a great victory." Filled with excitement, students head to a formal dance, what is considered "fall prom," to celebrate their victory. Win or lose, the dance is held each year after the game, as it is a part of the school's tradition, but as Marcus explains, "fall prom is so much better after a victory because you're in the mood to have a good time. Nobody is in a good mood [at the dance] if we lose." Because they win, "it is the perfect night."

Early the next morning, Marcus receives a phone call letting him know that two of his teammates were involved in a severe car accident after the dance. Not many details are provided; he is simply informed, "It was a really bad wreck." Marcus and his classmates are left in the dark until they return to school the next day, when their headmaster announces that one of the students involved in the accident has died and the other is in critical condition.

The death of the boy sparks an outpouring of grief from the student body, but his teammates are especially affected. School officials decide to cancel classes for the rest of the day. Concerned about the well-being of the other football players, Marcus's coach calls the team together to give them the opportunity to share their feelings and thoughts about the tragedy.

Andy, Marcus's best friend, stands up first and tearfully tells the team, "I just want to let all of you know that I love every single one of you. This really puts our lives into perspective about how life is short. I have all of your backs if you guys need anything."[2] Too grief-stricken, Marcus remains silent. He wants to echo Andy's remarks and give his teammates advice. "You guys are family—each one of you. It's important that we stick together. We need to depend on each other to get through this," he thinks but unable to say aloud. For nearly two hours, the players take turns expressing grief for the loss of a fellow teammate. For Marcus, this meeting marks "the beginning of making this horrible incident [into] something that brought us closer together."

Even though it has been over three years, Marcus gets emotional in sharing what happened that homecoming weekend. He is unable to maintain his usual composure, which often masks what he is truly feeling inside. His uncontrollable emotional response reveals just how meaningful he finds his relationships with teammates. In high school, when he was not in class or doing homework, Marcus spent most of his time with fellow football players. He was friendly with his baseball and basketball teammates, a few international students from Germany, as well as one or two "random friends involved in student government." However, his core group of friends consisted solely of his football teammates. Because most of them were boarding students, they often hung out at Marcus's house on the weekends to watch movies, sleep over, and enjoy his mother's home cooking. They enjoyed spending time with each other even "when we weren't doing anything too specific." Contrary to his usual, reserved self, Marcus was "very open with [these] friends" and revealed "personal stuff about school and sports and just life in general that no one else really knew about." These relationships continue to be "way beyond your typical friends." He considers them to be "more like brothers."[3]

Marcus continues to talk to several of them every day, despite the fact that they attend different colleges across the country. As he explains, "I just couldn't imagine them not being in my life. We developed a strong bond. It doesn't matter that we don't live close to each other." Although Marcus describes himself as very loyal to his friends, he admits, "I'm meaner to these guys than to other people, in the way that only brothers can be." For instance, he describes his relationship with his best friend, Andy, by saying,

> He used to spend months at a time at my house. He's gone on vacation with my family and me and stuff like that. He's basically part of the family. We always joke with each other and stuff like that, we go back

and forth a lot, we fight a lot and then you know, at the same time, we're best friends and we look after each other. He's always going to be there for me and I'll be there for him.

The brotherhood between him and his teammates played a significant part in his overall educational experience at his prep school. They pushed him to be not only a better athlete but also a better person.

Although not as significant as the brotherhood with his teammates, Marcus also built meaningful relationships with many of his Parkridge teachers. With a teacher-to-student ratio of one to five, class sizes were small enough to encourage close relationships between faculty and students. Marcus believes, however, that it was his teachers' availability outside the regular school day that helped foster these relationships. Because most teachers live on campus, act as "dorm parents" in student housing, eat meals in the same dining halls, and serve as coaches and mentors, Marcus and his classmates had multiple opportunities to interact with teachers outside the classroom. Even as a day student, he frequently spent time with teachers outside classes, and these interactions allowed him to establish "long-lasting relationships" with them. Although he is about to finish his first year at college, Marcus still regularly keeps in touch with several of his former teachers because their relationships stretch far beyond school walls.

Through his meaningful relationships with teachers and teammates, Marcus developed particular values that he believes "have been incredibly helpful in working toward my [academic and life] goals." When asked whether or not competition is one of these values, he initially claims, "it wasn't something that defined [these relationships]," because the overall environment at Parkridge does not "particularly emphasize competition." Upon further reflection, he recalls people "trying to be always right, raising their voices in class discussions and debates, just trying to stand out above everybody else." He also remembers that "it was pretty competitive when it came to things like SAT scores and GPAs. Everyone wanted to stand on stage and receive their pin for getting high honors and stuff like that." Because his friends were athletes, he believes that they were likely more competitive than other Parkridge students. No matter what they did together, "whether it was taking a test or playing a video game," they vied for first place. These competitive interactions, Marcus explains, motivated him "to strive to do better than I would've without [those interactions]."

These relationships also helped Marcus to develop and value a sense of accountability. His teachers stressed how important it was for him to take responsibility for the quality of his education and to be aware of his actions and decisions so that he may achieve success. They not only gave him freedom to make choices about his learning but also directed him "down the right path to success in my academics." They emphasized that academic freedom must be accompanied by responsibility. Above all else, they effectively taught him and his classmates this lesson by "treating each person as an individual." What made sense for one student did not always make sense for another. He reports that his teachers gave him a fair amount of freedom to make choices because he demonstrated "a high level of responsibility."

Marcus describes how faculty members "definitely had different expectations for different students based on their ability." Whereas he might not have been "one of the top two students," he was "definitely up there." Because teachers considered him a high achiever, he claims that they graded his work "tougher than other people's work [and] made me work harder to earn my grades." He recalls an experience illustrating their high expectations:

> In my sophomore year history class I wrote a paper I worked on for hours and hours and hours, and I ended up getting like a B- on it. I went to see [the teacher] and he was like, 'You know you are one of the best students in this class, you can do a lot better than this. Yeah sure, it could be a B+ paper but I gave you a B- because I think you shouldn't just do well compared to other people, but do the best that you can personally.'

Taking his teacher's advice to heart, Marcus opted for a particularly full class schedule, adding several more advanced classes each semester. He kept his teacher's words in mind as he overcame some challenges that semester. In particular, he experienced academic difficulties in honors Spanish, which he remembers as "a really tough course with a tough teacher who gave unfair work." He decided that "instead of just moaning and complaining about how unfair things were, I made it a point to see [the teacher] three times a week and have lunch with him and just review every single thing of the entire trimester." Marcus made the decision "to uphold higher standards even when I was facing these problems."

Although Marcus gained a considerable amount from his teachers, he feels that Parkridge's "top-notch" education is what propelled him along a path toward a successful future. He likens the quality of his education to that of "a high-end steak restaurant," where "you're getting a top-quality product, good service, and leave full." Parkridge challenged him in ways that "no other school could have." Although he found his academic environment demanding, he reports that he never felt overwhelmed, because he "manages time well [and] pick things up quickly." Furthermore, despite his extensive responsibilities as a student, athlete, tour guide, and student body president, Marcus claims that he remained unfazed by his packed schedule because he preferred it to a lighter one. He likes being always on the go.

Even in the summertime, Marcus's schedule was full. He held a landscaping job in the summers, not necessarily to make money but because it kept him busy. As he explains, "I don't like sitting still a lot because I get really bored quickly." He made every effort "to starve off boredom" even if it meant doing something that was "pretty brutal, a lot of work and very little pay," as he considered his landscaping job to be. In this job, he came to realize "how fortunate I was." His work experiences also reinforced the message that he has heard his entire life from multiple sources: "You can overcome challenges by working hard." As he explains, "It was tough but I managed to do it because I worked hard at it. Not because of anybody else, but because I worked hard at it. It definitely made me a harder worker and realize even more how important working hard is." When looking ahead to consider what it will take for him to achieve his life and career goals, a similar attitude emerges. He believes that down the road, "if I had any disadvantages, I would do something to make it an advantage, or not make it a disadvantage. I really don't let anything hold me back whatsoever." As he found ways "to power through difficult classes" at Parkridge and be successful in his landscaping job, he believes that he will overcome whatever obstacles he may encounter along his path to success. He just has to keep in mind what he learned during his time at prep school—being accountable, responsible, a hard worker, and proactive will lead him to success.

STAYING BUSY

Marcus is currently in his first year of studying business at a small elite university in New England. He finds his university to be "a pretty tough school, especially in terms of workload." He often feels like he is "studying all the time" and needs to give up hours he would normally put into extracurricular activities in order to focus on schoolwork. Because these activities, especially sports, have been an important part of his life up to this point, he feels very unsettled in his new college life. So far, Marcus "definitely like[s] high school more than college" and would much rather discuss his fond memories of Parkridge than talk about what he does not like about his current academic situation. He misses the scaled-down size of Parkridge, where he saw "the same people every day" and was able "to build much stronger relationships" with his peers and teachers. At his university, "everyone is doing their own thing, has their own extracurriculars and activities and things like that." Due to an injury, he is not currently on the university's football team, making him feel especially disconnected from the community. Not playing a sport makes him feel "so unlike my usual self." He jokingly remarks, "I break a sweat when playing any kind of sport now. I really have gotten out of shape." With his athletic build, it is hard to imagine that Marcus is that far gone, but his comments are more a reflection of his feeling "sort of lost" in his new academic environment.

Part of what makes him feel out of place at his university is that he is "not too big of a partier," which forces him to lead a very "independent social life." Because he avoids large social functions and does not drink alcohol or do drugs, he has become a loner. Peer pressure to participate in these sorts of activities was something he first encountered at Parkridge, but he "never really fell for it." In college, he has not experienced nearly the same pressure that he did in high school. However, not caving to these pressures comes at a social price. He only gets to meet people by making "small talk in class [and other situations] like that." This provides little opportunity for him to make meaningful connections with others.

Instead of hanging out with peers, Marcus spends most weekends catching up on homework and working at his internship. He currently works at a computer software company located near his school. At the company, his primary responsibilities are to gather feedback on products and to make sales. During his first semester at college, he set up this internship by "approaching my neighbor because he works at the company," who then "put me in touch with the recruiter." The original plan was for Marcus to begin working full time the next summer, but "[the company] wanted me to start early, so I worked my entire spring break there, and now I work there about once a week for eight hours."

Being in a professional setting allows him to utilize the knowledge and skills that he has gained through his education. This work experience also gives Marcus the opportunity to think harder about his priorities, allowing him "to nail down my plans for the future." Since attending college, it has become increasingly clear to Marcus what he wants to achieve in life. As he explains, "I want to afford a nice house, a nice car, take care of my family, make sure my kids go to good schools, you know, that they are able to graduate college without debt, things like that." For him, "money is definitely something that motivates what I do."

In working toward his dreams of making a lot of money one day, Marcus devotes a portion of his free time to trading stocks online and developing a football recruitment website for high school athletes hoping to play in college. Even though he began working on the website in his junior year of high school, he did not really devote much time to its development until he entered college. Developing the website is a particularly exciting endeavor for Marcus because it affords him the opportunity to stay tied to Parkridge and football, albeit in a different way. In fact, he believes that his prep school connections—"in particular the ones in [Parkridge's] powerhouse football program"—will be vital to the completion and success of the project. He plans to rely on this social network[4] to gain access to top recruiters and to help spread the word about the project to athletes. He has already begun utilizing these links, and "it's paying off." Over the past year, he has been connected to several top recruiters who have provided him with "positive and valuable feedback." These networks, Marcus predicts, will continue to be significant in achieving his goals for the project.

Working as an intern, day trader, and website developer takes up most of Marcus's free time, making it nearly impossible for him to do much else. But Marcus enjoys staying busy and particularly enjoys being engaged in work that brings him closer to his goals. He is confident that the work experience he is gaining from this internship will one day lead him to a lucrative job. He is equally certain that his website and stock market investments will be profitable. He has no doubt that the work he is doing now will pay off in the end. Admittedly Marcus's dream of turning a profit is a driving force behind these endeavors; however, it is not the only reason he keeps his schedule so packed. In truth, Marcus is lonely. He is "not having a lot of fun" at his university. Finding his courses "boring and not very engaging" and filled with "mindless busy work," these side projects give him respite from his lackluster present-day life and allow him to maintain ties to his much more enjoyable past. Keeping in frequent contact with teammates, staying connected to former teachers, and utilizing social networks allow Marcus to maintain a connection to his former life as a part of Parkridge's community.

INVALUABLE LESSONS

Marcus sits in the living room of his family's home talking with his parents and brothers. Home is the place he finds most comforting and familiar. Whereas often quiet and reserved, Marcus is more open and animated around his family. He especially enjoys telling them stories "about what went on during the day" that are usually "nothing too serious." His stories typically have one main purpose—making his family laugh about "stupid stuff" that he has witnessed in his daily life. On this particular occasion, he is telling them about an argument between a professor and one of his classmates. He recounts every detail of the incident, embellishing a few to make the story more entertaining. They hang on his every word and find his story quite entertaining. Marcus accomplishes what he set out to do. When he finishes, everyone's attention quickly shifts to his father, who takes the opportunity to surface a lesson Marcus "should've learned from this incident" about maintaining respectful relationships with his professors. "No matter what the story is about," Marcus explains, his family, and especially his father, "will find some way to give me their feedback or advice."

Marcus has lived in the same house most of his life with both parents and, until they left for college, his two older brothers. For the past several years, he has rarely seen his brothers, but they have "managed to remain tight" with one another. His oldest brother is twenty-four and currently lives in Lebanon, where he attends graduate school. His middle brother is twenty-one and studying at a private university in New England, a bit farther from home than where Marcus attends school. Both his older brothers also attended Parkridge and share many of the same hobbies and interests. They all lead active lives and enjoy playing, discussing, and watching sports. When they are together, they like to "play basketball and lift [weights] together and just do active things." Although they are "not particularly competitive with each other," they often engage in competitive activities during their time together because, as Marcus explains, "we're all pretty competitive in general."

His parents married not long after his mother immigrated to the United States from Lebanon, where most members of her side of the family continue to reside. When his parents married, his mother worked in a bank, but she eventually left the working world to focus on her family. She has been a "stay-at-home mom and wife" for as long as Marcus can remember. His father is of Native American descent and was adopted by a white military couple at a young age. He spent most of his childhood moving from one part of the world to another. His adoptive family eventually settled in the New England region, where he has been ever since and plans to remain. For the past twenty years, Marcus's father has worked as a defense contractor; he travels often for his job, mostly going back and forth to the Middle East. However, he makes it a point to spend as much time with family as possible—even if that means that they travel with him on business trips. One of the main ways that Marcus's family spends time together is through sports and other physical activities. They also are all passionate sports fans and enjoy watching professional baseball, basketball, football, and hockey games together.

Marcus considers his family relationships to be very close, particularly so with his father, whom he talks "to every day except when he's traveling, but even then it's pretty frequent." Growing up, he remembers, "My dad would always play sports with me. He always had time for me no matter how busy he was." Although not quite as close with his mother, Marcus comments that she also "played a very big role in my life and [was] always there for me. I feel I can go to her when I need to." When he lived at home, both parents were "extremely involved" in his life and, to a certain extent, find ways to remain so even now while he is away at college. Wishing that they were not quite as involved, he sometimes avoids sharing "every detail of my life with them," particularly when it comes to things like "my grades in college and setting up my internship." He also wants to dodge their potential "harsh criticism" when he is not completely sure they will approve of his decisions and actions.

Marcus believes that his parents, at times, can be "pretty strict" and do not give him enough "space to make my own decisions." This was especially the case earlier in his life. He recounts a time when he was around eight years old:

> I was in the mall with my brother and my dad. And me and [my brother] kept arguing and we started yelling at each other, fighting, and some people heard us. My dad wanted to teach us a lesson, so he had us just start doing push-ups in the mall in front of hundreds of people, and it was so embarrassing. And that was it. He basically just said, 'Don't act like a punk. Represent yourself. Be respectful. Don't embarrass yourself. Don't embarrass your family.'

Marcus recalls his mother holding him to similar high standards. For example, during his senior year of high school:

> I got a C+, the only C I've ever gotten in my life, and it was just a tough honors course and my mom really got on me about it, she told me something like, 'That's ridiculous, there's no way you should get a C+ in this class,' *blah, blah, blah*. So the next trimester I had to kind of prove to her that I'd learned from this experience.

He further explains that his parents "didn't really let me go out much," and when he was allowed out, he had to adhere to a strict curfew. Although he did not "enjoy their restrictions," his parents taught him "invaluable lessons that have really paid off." He explains, "I think overall they did a pretty good job raising me. They always raised me to be very personable, very talkative, always be polite, mind your manners everywhere you go, no matter where you are, and things like that."

Marcus emphasizes that his parents supplemented their "tough love approach" with an "unbelievable amount of support." For instance, when he was having difficulty with his Spanish honors course in high school, his father gave him the support he needed to get through this difficult time:

> He just told me, 'Life isn't easy, and if you have classes like that, you can't just accept that it's tough, you need to go out there and work harder. That's the way it works. So instead of just taking a C and getting A's in all the rest of your classes, go see the teacher and put in extra time.' He pointed me in the right direction when I didn't know what to do about the situation.

Marcus feels "thankful for my parents and everything that they've taught me growing up, and you know, how to act, and keeping me in check and teaching me about morals and values and integrity and things like that." He considers himself "more privileged than others" for having such good teachers as parents.

UNRECOGNIZABLE PRIVILEGE

Marcus started becoming aware of his family's social class status about ten years ago. Around that time, his father moved up quickly in his career and he recognized that they were more financially stable and no longer "part of the lower class." It took a few more years before Marcus came to the realization that his family "had entered the upper class." Marcus pinpoints the exact moment when he made this discovery:

> I'd say it must have been seventh or eighth grade, I was coming back from basketball practice. My dad picked me up, and I was walking outside, and I saw a real nice, brand new Mercedes sports car. And my dad was like, 'That's ours,' and I was like, 'Oh, wow.' It was a real shock

to me. I'd never seen a car like that before, so it was probably the first time I realized our social class.

At that moment, he became aware that his family had "finally made it financially." He had never thought much about his family's socioeconomic status until then. To some degree, he knew his family did not enjoy the "financial stability that others had," but they had what they needed. He claims, "Money didn't really matter that much back then." However, it has become increasingly important to Marcus since the day his father picked him up in a brand new Mercedes Benz. During his trips to Lebanon, for instance, he recognizes that money had become a major motivating factor in his life. As he explains, "It's a very materialistic country. You see a lot of exotic cars, exotic yachts. That always keeps me motivated. When I'm older, I don't want to be the guy that can't afford that."

Although he expresses a great desire to be "financially well off" in discussing his future goals, he puts forth a far more moralistic viewpoint about what is really important to him in life. Status and money are not nearly as important to him as some other aspects of life. As he explains, "My parents always tell me three things—faith, family, health—come first in life. Those things are more important than how much money you have or don't have." He goes on to say, "Some people may be unhappy without money, but it makes no difference to my family." He feels like his family never placed "any sort of big emphasis on material things" and always encouraged him "to count my blessings." For instance, Marcus claims that even though his family is wealthy, "we're still grounded." As he explains,

> [My parents] never buy me luxury items. They never buy me anything I don't need. Everything they've bought me was something really important to me, or something I needed, or something like, you know, football equipment or something like that. It wasn't like, 'Oh, I really want this nice sweater.' They wouldn't just randomly get that for me.

Because his parents "made sure never to spoil me," he feels that he has learned to be grateful for how fortunate he is in life. He believes that his parents raised him to appreciate his situation, whatever it may be, and to always do the best he can with what he has.

At the same time, Marcus is driven to maintain his advantaged economic standing. He wants to do whatever it takes to avoid sliding back into the "lower class." In discussing his economic privilege, he repeatedly points out, "I wasn't always this fortunate in life. When I was younger, we were a lower-class family." Although his family has lived in the same affluent suburb and in the same "decent-sized house" his entire life, he and his brothers mostly attended elite private schools during their educational careers, and his father has been in the same line of work since Marcus was a baby, he believes that his family was firmly situated in "the lower class" until just before he entered high school.[5] Whatever his family's social class might have actually been during these years is irrelevant because he perceives that they were economically disadvantaged. Because he feels that he knows what life is like on both ends of the social class spectrum, he claims, "It's definitely motivated me. I don't want to go back to being anything other than upper class once I finish school; it's completely unacceptable."

Marcus cites his father's career and financial achievements as a major source of inspiration for working toward his goals. His father's success is especially motivating because "he made it completely on his own." Given that his father never attended college and did not come from an affluent background, Marcus believes he has no choice but to meet or exceed his father's achievements:

> I've grown up with a thousand more opportunities than [my dad] had, and it makes me think that there's no excuse to be just as financially successful as he is when I'm older. You know, I should be more successful than he is. So he definitely inspires me, you know, makes me want to work hard at school, even though I don't like it, so it will pay off one day in the future.

He sees his father's climb up the economic ladder as "epitomizing the American Dream," because he achieved success "by working hard and making the right career decisions." According to Marcus, no one made his father's success a reality other than himself. Following his father's example, Marcus emphasizes that hard work and making "sound decisions about my future" will also be key factors in his eventual success.

In looking ahead, he believes that it will not be easy for him to achieve the level of wealth and success he wants. As he explains,

> Oh, it will definitely be difficult. Working at a hedge fund or owning your own company or my website. I mean if it was easy, everyone would do it. I mean it's doable of course, but it's going to take a lot of hard work. It's definitely going to be a lot harder than I think, but it's definitely doable. I mean, anything's possible.

Although he will inevitably face some challenging obstacles, and some he cannot even imagine at present, he does not see anything that could possibly stop him from getting what he wants out of life. To a certain extent, he recognizes that his advantages in life and schooling make it more likely that he will overcome these impending challenges than it is for others without such advantages. He realizes, for instance, that not too many people are able to obtain the "top-notch" education he has received by attending a prep school—where tuition for day students is over $40,000—and a private university that costs $53,000 per year. He partially acknowledges that his educational experiences and advantaged life circumstances make him "better prepared to tackle the challenges thrown at you [in life]" and have put him "ahead of the game."

Marcus insists, however, that he does not simply rely on his family's wealth but instead "put[s] in the work it takes to become successful." Because of this, he tells himself that "my advantages don't define who I am, but my work ethic does." Similarly, he is defined by "how I interact with people from all walks of life." He credits his parents for teaching him not to judge people on how much they have or do not have but instead to judge them on their character. This valuable lesson came through his parents having "a lot of friends who are the lowest of the low and the highest of the high, some of them even billionaires. It didn't matter how much money people had; what counted was that they were good people." Trying to follow their example, he says that the majority of his Parkridge friends received financial aid and that they were "from a lower class." In fact, he asserts, "I don't even think I have any friends that are from the upper class." He also claims, "I haven't even dated girls in the upper class. They've mostly been in the middle class." Marcus believes that "a person's social class status has never been an issue" in his relationships. Instead, he wants "people who are upstanding and have the same values as me."

Judging people by their character and not their status, Marcus firmly believes that he does not "even notice social class differences" most of the time. He reports that it was not until his sophomore year of high school that he even began noticing any class differences among his peers. Most often, the clothing some of his peers wore to school indicated these differences. He remembers,

> At school I used to always just dress in, I mean, pretty low-end clothes, just because I never, I don't really dress in very nice clothes. Then I'd see the international kids and they would always be dressed the nicest out of anyone in the school. That's when I really started realizing, you know, wow, a lot of people are real materialistic and, you know, want to wear real nice, fancy clothes and stuff like that, but I never really fell for that kind of stuff.

Marcus points out that a class marker, like clothing, reveals people's values more than their actual economic and social position. His own appearance, for example, is a testament to this belief. As he explains, "[Because] materialistic things have very little influence on my life, and I am not pretentious like some people. Most people I'm with would never ever guess my social class just based on how I conduct myself, the people I talk to and hang out with, how I dress."

Marcus claims that what he values in life "didn't change when we became more financially well off." He goes on to say, "I've just always been myself, [both] when we were in the lower class and when we were in the upper class." Significantly downplaying the role of his family's wealth in shaping his values, he insists that he "would have turned out much the same if we were still in the lower class." According to Marcus, the lessons and values he learned through his relationships with family, friends, and Parkridge teachers are really "the only things that have influenced me." He maintains that his family's wealth has little to do with what he values in life and who he has become.

Believing his family's wealth is "pretty insignificant" in his life, Marcus claims that his privileged class status is not apparent to most people. He quickly points out that he does not "try to hide how well off we are but still people just can't really tell by what I do and how I look like." He feels that his class privilege really only becomes noticeable when he is around his father, who is "a pretty extravagant spender and really likes buying nice cars and things like that." Marcus comments that when he is with his father, "generally people figure out how well off I am. Like, we go to a sporting event and I'm in really good seats or I'm at an NBA game and I'm on the court, little things like that. It just is obvious that we're rich, where you can see the kind of social class we're in." During these moments, Marcus reports that people "react to me differently than usual. They see me as someone with money and are motivated to connect to us because of our money." However, when he is on his own, and particularly not around his father, he firmly believes that his privilege is never apparent.

MAKING IT TO THE TOP

Even though Marcus's parents push him to do well in school, he says that they ultimately leave it up to him to be responsible for his own choices and actions. They stress that working hard is "for your own good" and "getting a good education is only going to help you in the long run; it's not going to help us if you do well." They have instilled in him the thinking that "you're on your own" and "what you put in is what you're gonna get out, that's your choice." For the most part, they trust him to make his own decisions in his life "as long as I'm working hard and never settling for second best." Although Marcus feels some pressure from his parents, he believes that no one puts more pressure on him than himself. He feels that his attitudes, choices, and actions are what lie behind the success he has achieved so far in his life and that they will continue to be key in getting what he wants out of life. The way he approaches his college education exemplifies this attitude:

> I strive for perfection in every single class I go into. I mean, sometimes the teacher will say, 'What's your goal?' And my goal is to get a 4.0 in every class. I want to be perfect in every single class I can and be like a sponge and suck in as much information as I can. Perfection will always be my goal.

Sitting in the front row in every class and hiring a tutor when he is struggling with a subject are just two actions that demonstrate how "I'm taking responsibility for what I need to be to secure my success later on." He believes that he is making the "right decisions and doing what I need to be doing to achieve my goals."

Marcus recognizes that many of his peers also work hard, make good decisions, and are motivated, but claims that:

> I'm more motivated than most people in general. I'm willing to work harder than most people. I want to be very successful when I'm older. I want to be a thousand times more successful [than] my father is now or anyone in the world for that matter. I put a lot more pressure on myself than most people in general. I feel like most people would say, 'Oh, as long as I'm happy I don't care what amount of money I'm making.' If I really liked my job and I was making like $50,000 a year, I wouldn't be satisfied yet. I just put a lot of pressure on myself to be more successful than that. Not because I'm super money hungry. I guess just for my own self, for my own personal beliefs. I always want more; I'm never satisfied with what I have and where I'm at.

He constantly pushes himself to do more and be better. Next year, for instance, Marcus plans "on stepping up my academic load even more" by taking one class over the standard limit. He also wants to take economics classes at another college "to get ahead of speed" because he is "trying to graduate [from college] in three years instead of four." He also intends to devote more time to trading stocks and developing his website so that he can generate his own income and consequently become more self-sufficient. But what drives him to work even harder this next school year, beyond the aforementioned reasons, is his insatiable appetite to be more successful than he is at this moment. He is never satisfied with what he has accomplished because "there's always more to strive for."

Marcus, however, thinks that he is headed in the right direction. He realizes that he may not follow the exact path he has in mind right now, but he truly believes that "all roads will lead me to success." For example, if his website does not take off, he plans to work on Wall Street after graduation and then eventually to own a hedge fund or become the CEO of a large corporation. Marcus knows that no matter what happens, it will all work out for him in the end:

> I have a lot of confidence in myself. I've always had a lot of self-confidence. I really think one day I can make it to the top. I've never really felt like, 'What if I can't make it there?' That doesn't come into my mind. It's not an option for me to not achieve everything I want. I have a pretty strong mindset when it comes to that kind of stuff.

It is not a matter of whether he will be successful but when and where he will achieve his success.

Marcus is eager to reach his certain destination in life. Although he occasionally entertains the possibility of attending an Ivy League School for graduate studies, he wants to enter the workforce full-time and begin making money as soon as possible. He explains why he is impatient to start working:

> My father always tells me 'Trust me, school is a thousand times better than work. You don't want to be in a rush to work,' but I generally just kind of disagree with him. Like when my dad buys a new car, I just want to start working so I can buy my own car. I'm ready to be successful enough to buy what I want and do what I want.

His eagerness to start his career comes in part from his intense desire to be more independent from his parents—especially his father.

Marcus admits that he has "an extremely complicated relationship" with his father. On one hand, he gives his father credit "for raising me to be the person I am today" and greatly values their "close and supportive relationship." He also believes, "My dad has been a huge influence on my life. I can't imagine what I would be like now if it wasn't for him." On the other hand, Marcus spends a considerable amount of his time and energy seeking to separate himself from his father. He no longer wishes to be in his father's shadow; he wants to be his own person. Attempting to carve out his own identity, he makes great efforts to avoid "acting like my dad" and tries to avoid being as materialistic or displaying wealth as much as his father. He feels "incredibly uncomfortable" and "embarrassed" by his father's conspicuous displays of their wealth.

He recalls a time during high school when his father donated "a large sum of money" to Parkridge's football program. Not only did he not like the fact that this donation made everyone aware of his family's wealth, but it also jeopardized his legitimacy as a football player. Marcus worried that others would think that his position and status on the team had more to do with his father's donation than his hard work and efforts. This incident made it very clear to him that he never wants "to show off how rich you are" because he does not want people to question whether he deserves what he has achieved. It is incredibly important for him to be recognized by others for his merits rather than his wealth. This is part of the reason that he has no plans to follow his father's career path, even though his father "definitely brought it up to me and definitely made it certain that it was definitely a possibility if I wanted to." When this possibility is brought up, Marcus simply responds, "I'm all set." He wants to blaze his own trail to success and plans to avoid taking "any shortcuts in becoming successful," like leaving it up to his father to plan out his future.

Marcus pursues success as a means of gaining independence from his father's wealth and career achievements to establish his worthiness of success even further. He insists, "No one has been responsible for what I've accomplished or will accomplish other than myself." He does not like to admit that his life and schooling advantages have put him "ahead of the game" or that he has received help from others in pursuing his dreams. For example, he does not readily reveal how much assistance he has received from others in developing his website; in fact, he normally frames it as a solo project. Eventually, though, he shares, in passing, that his father fronted him half of the money necessary to launch the site. He then emphasizes that this is only a loan and he plans to pay back "every dime my dad gave me [for the start-up]." When pressed further, he confesses that he has a business partner who is "a buddy of mine who actually graduated college last year and now lives in Las Vegas." His partner contributed almost the other entire half needed to launch the site. After revealing this information, he quickly points out, "Even though we keep in touch all the time, it's not like a 50/50 thing. I'm the majority owner of it. I do most of it." Feeling guilty for taking too much credit, he eventually claims, "[My business partner] definitely helps me out a lot. He's pretty important to the project."

Marcus dislikes the fact that he needs others at this juncture in his life as he struggles to assert his independence. Attempting to be fiercely independent, it is difficult for him to admit that he needs to rely on others for assistance and feels ashamed that he cannot make it on his own. He is often reluctant to divulge just how much help he receives from others, but at the same time, he appreciates the support he receives from his friends, teachers, and family. He is "incredibly grateful" for their financial and emotional support, their guidance, and the important life lessons they have taught him. It takes him a while but he eventually acknowledges that he cannot achieve what he wants in life on his own. He must rely on others. After he makes this confession, he quickly redirects the focus back on a belief that he holds firmly: "When it comes down to it, I'm the only person responsible for what I accomplish and how successful I'll be." In the end, he always manages to reaffirm that he is on his own.

NOTES

1. Students of color make up 13 percent of the student body at Parkridge. International students make up 14 percent. This is significantly more diverse than the student body of the local public high school, in which 97 percent of the students are white.
2. Marcus reports that Andy's statement was too meaningful not to be remembered exactly as he told it to his teammates. He is certain that he is quoting his friend verbatim.
3. Marcus is describing the kinds of intimate connections commonly established on male sport teams and that several researchers have noted. Pollack (1998), for instance, argues that sports are one of the most important activities through which adolescent males not only genuinely express themselves but also establish intimate relationships with others. Marcus's narrative about his "brotherhood" with fellow teammates supports this assertion. However, Kimmel (2008) argues that these intimate relationships (or brotherhoods) are

not all positive, since they tend to reinforce a particular gender storyline for males that reinforces hypermasculine and misogynistic behaviors. Although disagreements exist about whether these relationships are positive for male adolescent development, there is a fair amount of agreement in this body of work about their importance.

4. Although Marcus claims throughout his narrative that he wants to make it on his own, he fully intends to use his social networks, or what sociologists commonly refer to as *social capital*, to make his project successful. Bourdieu (1986) argues that social capital is "the aggregate of the actual or potential resources which are linked to possession of a durable network of more or less institutionalized relationships of mutual acquaintance and recognition" (p. 248). He further explains that social capital is "made up of social obligations ('connections'), which is convertible, in certain conditions, into economic capital and may be institutionalized in the form of a title of nobility" (p. 243). Although different scholars offer a range of definitions that emphasize certain aspects of social capital over others, they tend to share the core idea that social networks have value. Some social networks, especially those available to privileged individuals, have greater value than other ones. Although Marcus has access to various social networks through family, school, community, and so on, he finds the ones at Parkridge most valuable in making his venture profitable. For research on the valuable social connections offered at elite schools like Parkridge, see, for example, Baltzell, 1989; Cookson & Persell, 1985; Domhoff, 1998; Khan, 2011; Useem & Karabel, 1986.

5. We are pointing out these contradictions by using only the information Marcus gave us about his childhood. From this information, we conclude that it is very unlikely that his family would ever have been considered economically disadvantaged by most standards. However, the important point here is not his family's actual economic status at this point in his life but instead what he understands it to be. These contradictions reveal some of the tensions that exist in his self-understandings.

6 Sarah
Alone in the Crowd

*with Ian Borthwick, Annie Chen,
Kelsey Cromie, Andrew Rhoads,
and Hillary Rowse*

*My school doesn't really have a sense of community. You find your group
and stay in it. You're not really connected to the overall community.*

Students are sitting anxiously at their desks, reviewing study notes to do
some last-minute cramming for their Advanced Placement (AP) calculus
test. Except for papers shuffling, not a sound can be heard. The teacher
breaks the silence when she walks in the room. "Clear your desks. I don't
want anything out except something to write with," she instructs. Without
hesitation, the students do as they are told. The teacher walks around the
room to put the exam face down on each student's desk. "Don't turn the
test over until I tell you do so," she warns. When the teacher gets to sixteen-
year-old Sarah's desk, she says in a quiet voice, "Take yours to the small
room today. Ms. Durst is doing something else right now."

Sarah walks to the closet-sized room just a few doors down from the
classroom where she takes her exams for most classes when other teachers
are not available to proctor her exam. She receives accommodations for her
learning disability as mandated by her individualized education program
(IEP). As she explains, "My IEP ensures that I take tests in a quiet environment and I get the use of a word processor. I also get extended time on
writing assignments, like tests and essays." Sarah is the only student out
of the 220 enrolled in the prestigious Science and Math Magnet Program
(SMMP) who receives accommodations. She reports, "I'm certain that I'm
the only student who has ever gotten into [SMMP] with a learning disability. Magnet students don't usually have any problems in school, so I'm
odd in that way." She claims that her classmates rarely notice her receiving
accommodations. As she explains, "They don't pay attention to me leaving
class during tests and probably aren't even aware of the other accommodations for me. None of them know exactly what an IEP is or why I have to
leave. It's just not a big deal."

Sarah enters the familiar testing room that has only a desk and chair;
there is nothing to distract her on the neutral-colored walls. When she shuts

the door, none of the background noise of the hallways can be heard. She enters her own little world. While taking the exam, she uses the test-taking strategies that she has learned over the years; she writes reminders in the margins, surveys the entire exam before answering any questions, answers the easiest questions first to help herself remain calm, and tackles the difficult ones at the end. There is only one question that she finds confusing, and she keeps glancing at her watch to make sure that she has plenty of time to complete it. As she begins working on this difficult question, Ms. Burgin, the learning specialist who works with Sarah most often, interrupts to ask if she needs assistance, such as clarifying directions and/or reading questions aloud. Sarah turns down the offer and redirects her focus back to figuring out this last question. She finishes a couple minutes early and returns to the classroom.

When class ends, Sarah heads to one of the few classes she has outside the magnet program and then attends two more classes focused on math and science before lunch. Hungry after a long morning of classes, she heads to the cafeteria for a quick bite to eat. Amid the clamor of plates, loud chatter, and hundreds of students moving around the cafeteria, she sees the Latino/Latina students in the back corner, sitting around a table by the door that leads out into the courtyard. When the weather is nice these students "congregate outside." The African American students are seated at the neighboring table. Near the entrance of the cafeteria, Sarah spots the "quote-unquote popular kids" snickering and judging everyone who walks by them. To their left are "the band kids, then the stoners, then the sort of all-purpose nerds, and then the magnets." She makes her way toward the magnet table, ignoring everyone else. On occasion, when she needs a break from being around other SMMP students, she joins the all-purpose nerds.

After lunch, she and others at the magnet table attend mostly science classes and school ends with an hour and half of labs. Sarah's day is far from over when the final school bell rings. She heads immediately to her extracurricular activities, attending a Gay Straight Alliance meeting, fulfilling responsibilities as president of the Student Technology Leadership Club, and going to swim practice. These afterschool activities give Sarah a much-needed break from the stress of her classes. She claims that these nonacademic moments in her day help to balance her daily life. After nearly twelve hours since her day began, her father picks her up from school. Driving home, they pass run-down sections of the city filled with dilapidated buildings on their way to one of the most affluent neighborhoods. Once at home, she spends an hour with her neighborhood friends playing *Dungeons and Dragons* before eating dinner with her parents. After dinner, the break from academics is over. As on most evenings, she spends the next several hours doing homework. She finally goes to bed at midnight, only to wake up in six hours to repeat this demanding cycle.

This is what everyday life is like for Sarah, as a student enrolled in the elite SMMP program at her neighborhood public secondary school, Anderson

High School. Within this web of advanced classes, extracurricular activities, *Dungeons and Dragons*, and family dinners lies a driven student who is well on her way toward a bright future. In a couple of years, Sarah will likely leave her SMMP days behind to attend an elite university. During her college years, it is almost certain that she will maintain the same pace to which she is accustomed. It is also likely that she will reach her goal of earning a Ph.D. in chemical engineering. She has a very clear path laid out before her, and there is a little doubt that Sarah will reach her goals in life. She is determined to not let anything stand in the way of achieving these ambitious goals. To some extent, she realizes there will not be much standing in her way. She is aware that her life and schooling advantages make anything possible, but she wants to work hard enough to deserve her predictable success in life.

Despite her intrinsic desire to understand how things work, leading her down a path toward a career in chemical engineering, she has trouble figuring out how to relate to people who differ from her. She describes her family and close friends as upper middle class. She spends nearly all of her time with people very like herself. Growing up in an affluent neighborhood within a midsize city in Kentucky isolates Sarah from the extreme poverty that exists in her backyard. Prior to entering high school, she was far removed from the realities of living in one of the poorest states in America. It was not until she left her private school to attend SMMP that she even began to recognize the social class differences that exist around her. Although the student body at Anderson is fairly diverse when it comes to social class, being a magnet student keeps Sarah almost entirely separated from the nearly two thousand "general students" enrolled at her high school. With a relatively low number of students from economically disadvantaged backgrounds, SMMP is a program primarily for students very much like Sarah. Lunchtime is one the few moments in the day when she has any interactions with general students. And even then, she socializes almost exclusively with other magnet students. Even though people different from herself surround Sarah, she remains isolated from difference.

ELITE CONTEXTS

Sarah invites David, one of the other leaders of the Student Technology Leadership Club, over to her house to finalize plans for an upcoming event. While giving him directions, she tells him that her house is "the small one on the block, with the red door." He's pretty familiar with the neighborhood because most of his classmates live in Sarah's neighborhood or nearby. She is confident that he will have no problem finding his way to her house. He arrives on time. Fortunately she gave him her house number, or he would have been hunting for a "small" house without much luck. When he arrives to her house, he jokingly comments, "Maybe for you it's small, but this isn't really that small." Sarah does not really know how to respond other than with an embarrassed laugh.

For Sarah, this incident creates another "awkward moment" with David, one of the relatively few SMMP students from a low-income family. David is the closest association Sarah has with a person from a different social class. She makes every attempt to interact with David as she does with her other friends but finds it difficult to do so. She makes "offhand comments" around him from time to time that reveal their social class differences. She tries her best to avoid creating these "awkward moments" between them, but it is nearly inevitable that she will say the wrong thing. Because Sarah spends most of her life surrounded by people much like herself, her interactions with David remind her that not everyone enjoys the same advantages in life. These reminders of her privilege are relatively rare given that the realities of the economically disadvantaged are mostly far removed from her daily life.

Although Kentucky is the third-poorest state in the nation, Sarah lives in one of its wealthiest cities. It is often described as having "a fortified economy" because of its "diverse, balanced business base" and strong "manufacturing, technology and entrepreneurial support."[1] It is one of the "most educated cities" in the U.S., with one of the lowest unemployment rates. And within this economically prosperous city, Sarah lives in one of the most affluent neighborhoods. She describes her neighborhood as an "upper-middle-class part of town . . . [with] houses definitely on the high end of home value for this city." The value of the average house in her neighborhood is well above that of houses in most other parts of the city. Her community is prime real estate—close enough to all that the city has to offer but removed from the hustle and bustle of urban life. Many of the families living in her neighborhood are involved in the horse industry, which contributes significantly to the city's cultural and economic vitality.

Although the public schools in her community are highly regarded, Sarah, like many children in her neighborhood, attended Taylor School, a private nonsectarian, coeducational school, from kindergarten through eighth grade. Taylor School enrolls about five hundred and forty students in preschool through middle school. With tuition at approximately $19,000 per year, it is the city's most expensive private school. Families typically choose Taylor for its smallness[2] and its record of success in helping students gain admission to competitive and prestigious high schools. When Taylor students complete eighth grade, 49 percent typically go on to local parochial and private high schools, 25 percent to local competitive magnet programs, 14 percent to boarding schools, and 12 percent to local public high schools.

Sarah's parents primarily selected Taylor because it offers a special program for students with language-based learning differences at an additional cost of $7,000 per year. Because Sarah has dyslexia, her parents wanted to find an educational program that would not only meet her educational needs but also fully prepare her for an academically rigorous high school. After extensive research of the local elementary schools, they determined that Taylor's program was their best option. It utilizes alternative teaching methods to create the kind of learning environment that aims to eliminate the major obstacles to learning that students like Sarah would face in traditional learning contexts. The teacher-to-student ratio is one to four, which allows for more individualized instruction than the regular program offered at Taylor and certainly at the local public elementary and middle schools. Sarah believes that this level of individualized attention during her elementary and middle school years offered her incredibly valuable learning experiences. She believes that it not only allowed her to overcome some of the difficulties she faced in her learning but also equipped her with the skills and knowledge to be successful in a highly competitive high school.

Sarah now attends SMMP, a highly selective magnet program. SMMP's admission process is fairly straightforward. Each year, forty students are selected from the nearly three thousand incoming high school freshmen in the city to participate in SMMP. Students are selected based on their scores on a logic and reasoning test and an algebra exam. The program selects students from the field of the top sixty. It is unclear how forty students are chosen from that pool of sixty; students and their families are not privy to this step of the admission process. The other top scorers who do not make it in the first round are put on a waiting list. Although it is natural for some students to turn down admission to the program because of extenuating circumstances, rarely do more than a couple of students from the waiting list matriculate into the program. Most accepted students and their parents have had their minds set on attending SMMP for years; they are not going to pass up the opportunity to attend.

Those who actually end up making it into the program typically have the financial means to be placed at an advantage in the admission process. Most students enter SMMP from private and parochial middle schools. Like many of her classmates, Sarah took a number of advanced math and science classes during middle school that were not offered at the local public schools. She also attended summer programs and participated in co-curricular activities intended to supplement Taylor's math and science curriculum.[3] Throughout her elementary and middle school years, she also received private tutoring and individualized instruction in these areas. Shortly after starting middle school, she began taking college entrance exams, like the ACT, and other standardized tests not only to evaluate her learning in these areas but also to improve her test-taking skills. By the time she took the admissions tests for SMMP, she had a level of preparation that would be unimaginable to the vast majority of others vying for a spot. To some extent, Sarah acknowledges the advantages she had going into the admission process. But above all, she attributes her success in getting into

SMMP to her own merits and the choices her parents made that allowed her to be academically competitive.

FAMILY IMPRINT

It is family night at Sarah's house and watching *Star Trek I* is on the agenda. Her mom "thinks all sci-fi is dreadful," but Sarah and her father love these kinds of movies, so she is outvoted. This is usually what happens in choosing their activities for family night because her mom is "compromising to a fault." Not that far into the movie, it comes as no surprise that her mom is clearly bored and not paying that much attention to the movie. She, however, makes every effort to appear as if her mind were not wandering elsewhere. Her dad finds it hard to stay awake. He's drifting off to sleep but "valiantly trying to keep alert enough for it to qualify as 'family time.'" Sarah finds the movie disappointing but "couldn't admit that something so geeky could really be this bad." She feels the need to "appreciate it," simply because it's sci-fi, but eventually faces the reality that she really doesn't like the movie—no matter how geeky it is. All three find the movie just awful but sit through it anyway because it's family night.

Sarah's family does not have much time to spend together, so family nights are "sacred." Her parents seem to thrive on a busy schedule that leaves little downtime. Much like Sarah, they are constantly on the go from the moment they wake up until they fall back into bed. Both have demanding jobs—one as a high-level professional and the other as the owner of a small business. "My mother works for the state government as a librarian for a lot of counties, to make sure that they all follow the library laws. My dad has always worked in retail in gun stores but has [had] his own store since about 2005," she explains. They are also actively involved in their community and have all of the responsibilities of being parents and managing a home. Even though their schedules are demanding, Sarah's parents have always put an emphasis on leisure time—the need to take a break and do something enjoyable. And her family finds nothing more gratifying than spending time together.

Sarah claims that no matter what, "every night we eat dinner together" and schedule family night "as often as we can." Over dinner, they talk about some of what makes their lives so busy. Her parents discuss what they accomplished at work and what is still waiting for them the next day. Sarah recaps her exhausting day at school and what is going on in her life. But most of their dinner conversations are not about their stresses and responsibilities. A scrapbook enthusiast, her mother talks about her latest project. A lifelong student of history, her father shares something he has learned recently from his latest research. They especially take pleasure in lively discussions about politics. Her parents are on opposite sides of the political spectrum and Sarah is somewhere in the middle. They rarely share similar perspectives on issues but enjoy engaging each other in heated (but friendly) debate. Their dinner conversations often spill over to their activities during family night.

Sarah describes her family relationships as tight-knit and quite meaningful in her life, even though these relationships are mainly limited to her parents. As an only child, she doesn't feel that she has missed out on anything by not having a sibling. "I have several close friends who live near me, so I feel that I get the good aspects of having siblings without any of the bad," she claims. Even though she has extended family living close by (including her grandparents), she only sees them every once in a while. When asked why she doesn't have close relationships with them, Sarah simply responds, "They are not a part of our nuclear family." As she reflects further, she realizes the reasons for their detached relationships are not so simple. Although these reasons are too complicated for her to fully understand (and therefore nearly impossible to explain), she believes it has something to do with her parents' drastically different class backgrounds. She explains, "Dad's side has always been in one specific social class, upper middle class," and "my mother's side was always in a lower class."[4] She doesn't know exactly why but believes that these class differences have partly caused their strained interactions with extended family members, including those on her dad's side whose economic circumstances are similar to those of her immediate family. Whatever the reasons, she and her parents are fairly isolated from the rest of the family.

Although her parents come from different class backgrounds, they present a unified front to promote a distinctively middle-class parenting style, or what Annette Lareau calls *concerted cultivation*.[5] They actively foster Sarah's talents and skills by enrolling her in various organized activities, reasoning with her, encouraging her to make choices, and closely monitoring her experiences in school. Their focus is squarely on her individual development and making sure that she is on the right track to become successful in life. At this point in Sarah's life, her parents' version of the "right track" is mainly about getting good grades and doing what see needs to be doing to get into a top university. Sarah has set similar goals for herself. "A lot of my standards come from me wanting to get good grades . . . I'm trying to get at least a 3.5 unweighted GPA to qualify for merit-based scholarships . . . I want to get into a good [university]," she says. Although she feels no significant amount of pressure from her parents to follow a particular path, she acknowledges their influence on her decisions. She explains, "My parents don't directly say it; they don't say that I have to get any certain grades. They don't punish me for getting bad grades, but I know that they are proud of me when I get good grades. So that's indirect motivation."

Sarah has some concern about her parents having too much influence on her choices about school and the future. She believes that she needs to become more independent if she is to succeed in life. At present, she is mostly concerned about them giving her enough freedom to make her own decisions and face the consequences of her choices—no matter what they are—so that she will be better prepared for college. In a recent conversation with her parents, she told them that "I'm heading off to college next year and they're not going to be there. I need to become more self-sufficient academically and in other ways too because I'll have to do more things for myself." Although it will be difficult for them to give her more freedom than she already has, Sarah made a convincing argument. Her parents agreed to be supportive in her efforts to become more independent. Sarah's desires to lessen her parents' influence on her choices are more than about making sure she is independent enough to be successful in college and later in life. Above all, she does not want to rely on her parents or, for that matter, anyone else for what she will achieve in life but instead to go forward on her own efforts and merit. She wants to pave her own path to success.

AN ACADEMIC AND SOCIAL ENCLAVE

Magnet programs like SMMP are placed in each of the city's five public high schools purportedly with the intent of improving the district's overall quality of education by ensuring that each school has at least one of these advanced programs. High-achieving students who enroll in these programs are dispersed evenly throughout the district. This plan was intended to promote educational equity and integration across the district. Many affluent parents, however, question whether this was the *real* reason for the equal distribution of magnet programs. A commonly held belief among wealthier parents is that this was a tactic for increasing scores on state-mandated tests at each high school. They believe that the district did this to prevent any of its high schools from being designated as "failing," because magnet students typically outperform their peers on the tests used to evaluate schools' effectiveness. In many ways, these parents feel that their children are being unfairly "used" to increase the district's overall performance. Although this belief is misguided because it does not accurately represent how schools or districts are evaluated for effectiveness,[6] it influences affluent parents' educational choices for their children. More sought-after programs are housed within schools in close proximity to affluent communities. Those located in or even near poor neighborhoods are overlooked—no matter how good the program may be.

With the very narrow focus of SMMP, it does not have the same broad appeal as most of the other magnet programs. Students must have a strong aptitude in math and science and enough interest to have most of what they learn in high school focused on those areas. Despite lacking broad appeal, SMMP is considered the most prestigious educational program in the city. Although location is not the dominant factor in its reputation, it certainly helps that the program is housed at Anderson, a school adjacent to a collection of affluent neighborhoods. One could easily assume that it would not have this reputation if it were located elsewhere. Other factors, however, presumably play more important roles in its reputation, namely its competitive admission process, rigorous curriculum, and track record for sending students to top universities and getting them multiple scholarship offerings.[7] SMMP's prestigious reputation certainly factored into Sarah and her parents' decision. They wanted her to enroll in the best high school program in the city, and SMMP had that reputation. It was more than just reputation that led Sarah to spend years working toward getting into the program and then to go there once she had gained admission. Attending the program nearly guaranteed that Sarah would eventually get into a top university. As she explained, "My parents and I considered [SMMP] the next step in reaching my goal of becoming a chemical engineer."

Anderson is the largest high school in the city, but not by much. Each of the city's public high schools enrolls roughly two thousand students, and Anderson has about twenty-two hundred. Although it is the largest, Anderson is one of the least diverse in the city, with 35 percent students of color,[8] 22 percent economically disadvantaged students,[9] and 4 percent English language learners. This is, however, significantly more diverse than SMMP's student body. Because most enter the program directly from private and parochial schools, the student enrollment in the program is less diverse when it comes to social class and race than the larger student body with one exception: SMMP enrolls a larger percentage of Asian American students. This less diverse student body is just one of the many factors that make SMMP seem very separate from the larger Anderson community.

During the school day, magnet students hardly come in contact with the approximate two thousand other students at Anderson—those whom Sarah refers to as "general students." Although housed in the same building as other classes at Anderson, many facilities are reserved only for the magnet program. It has its own computer lab, reserved for SMMP students only. Most of their classrooms and laboratories are also exclusively for the program. For a significant part of the day, these students are in SMMP-only spaces at Anderson. One of the few times during the day they are around general students is in their humanities courses. Magnet students are required to take advanced courses in English, social studies, and foreign language, which are offered outside the program. These requirements pale in comparison to the number of SMMP classes they must take. They spend a majority of their day with their SMMP peers and teachers, taking courses that "are faster-paced and more challenging than are traditional high school courses . . . and not typically offered at high schools," as stated in the official description of the program.

When SMMP students are not in classes, their time is consumed with fulfilling the other requirements of the program. Each year, they must participate in service projects outside class time. For instance, Sarah describes two recent projects:

> One of our big [service projects] this year is teaching classes to middle schoolers. We have middle schoolers in the county come to our school and we teach them tech skills. And last year, we got a bunch of new computers for our school and we took all the computers that we were replacing and cleaned them out and wiped the hard drives and put open store software and then distributed them to students who didn't have computers in their homes.

SMMP students also are expected to complete a two-year research project with mentors in the science community during their junior and senior years. Over these two years, students must spend 360 hours on their projects. Just before graduating, they present the findings of their projects at a formal research symposium in front of their parents, peers, teachers, and mentors. This extensive research experience and the other requirements are designed to foster competitive students in the fields of mathematics and science, making this an educational program "not for everyone," as Sarah contends. But for her, she says, "It's the perfect place."

Sarah loves school and claims that most of her peers in SMMP feel the same. She believes that the main reason she enjoys school so much is that her classes are "full of fun." She admits, though, that students who "aren't really into [math and science] probably wouldn't find it all that enjoyable." Part of what makes it fun for Sarah is that her SMMP classmates share her passion for learning math and science. She finds it incredibly comforting to be around peers who share her interests and are eager to learn. It is also comforting for Sarah that her teachers make concerted efforts to further encourage their students' passions and eagerness. She believes that they do this most effectively by using various methods such as games, group work, and hands-on activities. She reports that in a recent math class, for example, "We were preparing for the AP calculus exam and we've been taking a series of quizzes on the formulas. We play this game where whoever gets the worst grade has to bring the others a cookie." Like this game, her teachers often use some sort of contest to make learning fun. And what Sarah and her peers enjoy most is a competition that not only clearly identifies a winner but also has some kind of consequence for the loser.

Sarah also enjoys the amount of personal attention she receives from her teachers. She feels that they know her as an individual and what she needs as a learner. This personal attention from teachers came as a pleasant surprise when she entered SMMP coming from a small private school. With classes being larger at SMMP, she expected her teachers not to have the time to focus on her individually, but she receives nearly the same level she got at Taylor. The moment she discovered this about SMMP stands out for her:

> When I was taking my freshman first-level chemistry class, I was having a lot of trouble with the thermodynamics test. So one day after

school, I went in and went over the entire test with my teacher. Basically we just worked the test over and the teacher made sure that I understood it. It stood out to me just because it was so surprising to have so much one-on-one interaction with a teacher, especially because the classes were so big.

This is the first of many examples of Sarah receiving the help she needs from her teachers. She knows that she can rely on them for support and guidance to overcome problems she faces in her learning. This reassurance not only allows her to develop close relationships with her teachers but also to cope better with the academic demands of the program.

Her enjoyment and love for learning virtually disappear when she has to take classes outside the magnet program with the general students. For her humanities courses, Sarah is forced to wade into the relatively strange world that exists just beyond her math and science classrooms. Because these classes are advanced, she is still surrounded by high-achieving students, but she claims that her peers in these classes do not value learning as much as she and the other SMMP students do. Sarah believes that these students are only focused on getting good grades. She explains, "I wish it could be more focused on learning rather than on getting good grades. But unfortunately getting the grades is what is going to help with college admissions, regardless of whether I actually learned from the material." She asserts that such a disregard for learning does not exist within the magnet program. This perception of general students has led her to the conclusion that academic rigor does not exist at Anderson outside SMMP.

Sarah establishes stark contrasts between SMMP and the rest of Anderson: SMMP's teachers are more engaging and supportive and its students are driven and passionate about learning; the rest of Anderson lacks academic rigor, has "teachers who aren't as involved with students, and that's where slackers and stoners tend to be." For Sarah, SMMP provides the ideal environment for learning. She has difficulty finding anything else positive at Anderson. Because of her negative opinions about the rest of Anderson, she finds every opportunity to minimize her time outside SMMP. Like other magnet students, she takes some of her humanities courses online and during the summer. Because magnet students have to take more classes than others at Anderson, she completes some outside regular school hours to free up her regular schedule so she can have more class choices. When given the opportunity, Sarah usually chooses to take more math and science courses. Even with a more flexible schedule, she still must take classes outside the program each semester. She cannot completely avoid the rest of Anderson. When she attends these classes, she undergoes a transformation. Although still high-achieving, she becomes a bored, unengaged, and unmotivated student. She is eager to return to the social and academic enclave of her magnet program.

A PATH TO SUCCESS

During the school year, Sarah's choices about how she spends her time are mostly constrained by SMMP's demanding requirements. Her daily schedule rarely changes. For the most part, Sarah is content with this routine because it allows her to manage her numerous responsibilities "without going crazy." But she looks forward to summertime because it offers more variation in her life. Although her summers are often highly organized, she spends that time engaging in diverse activities. As in previous summers, Sarah will spend this upcoming summer having various experiences that are intended to better prepare her for the future. For as long as she can remember, she has spent her summers going to camps, doing internships, taking additional classes and organized lessons, and engaging in various other enrichment activities. Other than the two weeks her family vacations each July at their beach house, one constant feature remains in Sarah's daily routine during summer: working toward her future success.

"Success is multifaceted, like doing something that makes you happy and also making enough money to support your family. I don't think it's easy, but it's doable," Sarah argues. And the only thing that would make "somebody unsuccessful is just giving up." She is determined never to give up on her aspirations. Sarah believes she is on the right path to a successful future and has no doubt where she is headed—she will eventually have a career in chemical engineering. She has her future all planned out, and deviating from those plans is very unlikely because, as she explains, "I think the field [of chemical engineering] is really interesting and I love science. I think I've always wanted to try and solve problems, and I have always enjoyed chemistry. I took a chemistry class when I was in the eighth grade and I really enjoyed it. That's when I decided I wanted to try and become a chemical engineer." Sarah contends that in five years, "I'll be on my way to graduate school." And in ten years, "I'll be working for a company doing chemical engineering." She speaks about her future with absolute certainty.

To some extent, she knows that her schooling and life advantages make it a lot easier for her to accomplish what she wants in life. She imagines that if she were economically disadvantaged, "It would be more difficult to be successful. I would have to work a lot harder to achieve my goal and have to work a job during high school and in college. It would definitely be more difficult, because I would have so much more to worry about." But Sarah does not see many obstacles standing in her way of pursuing her dreams. In her eyes, the only reason that she would not pursue her future plans is if "I realize that either chemical engineering is too hard or I don't actually like it as much as I think I do."

She does not see her learning disability as an obstacle in achieving what she wants out of life.[10] Although earning degrees in chemical engineering will be challenging, she has no doubt in her eventual success. Instead of being a source of discouragement and hindrance to academic success, she views her learning disability as a source of motivation. She explains,

> I'm dyslexic, and I'm in the magnet program. So it affects the standard that I hold myself to. There was some concern when I started out at [SMMP] that it would be too much work. Some people had their doubts and thought it was too difficult for me. So I feel almost obligated to stick with it to show that just because I'm dyslexic, doesn't mean I can't handle the curriculum.

Research indicates that for most students, having such a significant learning difference would be an enormous obstacle to higher education.[11] Sarah, however, believes that she has "never allowed [my learning disability] to keep me from pursuing what I want." She also recognizes that she has been provided opportunities, like attending an elementary and middle school program especially designed to meet the needs of students with learning disabilities, to overcome the challenges associated with her learning disability that many others do not have.

She never questions whether she will have the opportunities she needs to reach her goals. She explains, "It has never been a question for me, whether I'm going to go to college. And so, achieving my goals of becoming a chemical engineer is much more realized, because I know that I'm going to go to college." She goes on to say,

> My parents are very supportive of all of my academic choices. They want me to do what I want to do with it; that's what they want me to do for my career. And maybe there has never been any doubt that I'm going to go to college. Like, it may not be easy to pay for—I don't think it's easy for anybody—but my parents and I, we're going to make it happen, no matter what.

For Sarah, both her family's good educational choices and their financial means make what she wants to accomplish very likely.

She believes, however, success depends upon factors more than wealth and good decisions. Above all, it takes hard work to get what you want in life. She often points to her maternal grandfather's life as evidence that success is achieved through hard work:

> He did what he wanted. He put himself through graduate school and he got a Ph.D. He was born at a much lower social class than where he is now. He was going to grad school and he had two kids, my mom and my aunt, and he followed his dreams, as cliché as that may sound.

Over the years, she has heard stories about her grandfather ascending the economic ladder. His example has taught her that no one gets what she or he wants out of life without working for it, and a person's position in life is a product of what she or he has done. She has learned that her family's wealth and good choices are not sufficient to guarantee future success. Instead, it will take hard work not only to maintain her privileged circumstances but also to spend her life doing what makes her happy.

Although committed to the idea that hard work leads to success, Sarah acknowledges that her advantages make the path ahead easier for her than for those who are disadvantaged. Right now, she is focusing on what lies immediately ahead of her—getting into a top-rated university. She believes that it will be easier for her to achieve this goal than it would be for a person coming from poverty. In fact, she believes it is difficult for poor people to make it to any college, not to mention a top-rated one. She explains,

> Someone who is not privileged would need to work harder to put themselves through college. It would just be more difficult. Poverty limits a lot of the options they have. Going to college would take a lot of effort, and probably result in a lot of student loans, and that sort of thing. In that scenario, people would choose to pursue other career path. It would be very difficult for people to make it out of poverty. To get out of poverty, working really hard is one aspect, but I think there's also a certain element of luck. Like, ending up in jobs where they can advance.

From Sarah's perspective, poverty is an obstacle to success that can be overcome by hard work and some luck. She adds luck because "life isn't necessarily fair." She goes on to explain,

> I mean, even if it's little small things, there's just no real way to give to every single newborn baby the exact same life, or the exact same set of advantages and disadvantages. I would say that for most people life isn't fair. I would say that life has been fair to me. My life is certainly better than most, than a lot of people's lives.

Sarah speaks about her advantages as being lucky enough to have them and making her life fair. She stops short from connecting the fairness/advantages of her life with the unfairness/disadvantages of others. Instead, she argues that those who are not as lucky contend with unfair circumstances that make being successful more difficult. She makes it clear that anyone can succeed; it is just harder for those without her advantages.

She believes that disadvantaged people often do not even try to overcome the obstacles in their lives because of this unfairness. For instance, she has observed a classmate in her art class not even trying to be successful in school. She finds that "she doesn't always pass her classes, so she isn't passing enough classes right now to graduate. If she doesn't pass seven out of eight of her classes this year, she can't graduate. So she has to work really hard to get her grades up in those classes." Sarah describes this classmate as "probably from lower class, or at least that's the impression I get." Sarah concludes that her classmate is from a disadvantaged background in part because of her lack of effort and low achievement. She finds it difficult to believe someone with the same advantages that she has would do so poorly in school.

Sarah points to other examples of students different from herself not working as hard as they should be. For example, she describes what she has observed while tutoring general students:

> I tutor an Algebra II class, since I've already taken it, and I go in and help the teacher and the students. The students in that class are a lot different than the students that I'm normally with. It's a general class. The students just aren't nearly as concerned with getting good grades or advancing quickly, or doing super well in school, like the students I'm usually with.

Given the relative lack of social class diversity at Anderson and the fact that this course is part of the college-prep program,[12] it would be safe to assume that most of these students are not economically disadvantaged. Unlike Sarah's classmate in art (or what she perceives about this classmate), social class is not what makes the algebra students dissimilar to her and "the students I'm usually with" or, in other words, other magnet students. The difference lies in them not being enrolled in SMMP. It also would be safe to assume that there are some variations in the achievement patterns and attitudes in a class of twenty-five students. Sarah, however, makes no distinctions among the students. She cognitively lumps together low achievement, lack of effort and the status of general student. Furthermore, regardless of what individual differences Sarah may have with other magnet students, she emphasizes their similarities while highlighting how dissimilar general students are from them. She constructs a dichotomy that separates herself and other magnet students from everyone else.

Sarah uses these distinctions to explain why she and her SMMP peers are headed toward success and why these students are not. From her perspective, they could be successful in school (and therefore later in life) if they wanted to be. They would just need to work harder and make better choices. She believes that they are choosing not to be successful. This explanation allows her to rationalize why others are not as high achieving as she and other magnet students. This explanation also justifies her schooling and life advantages. Although her advantages make success easier to achieve, she is working harder and making better decisions to get what she wants out of life than others. She deserves to be advancing along the path to success.

UNCOMFORTABLE DIFFERENCES

On the weekends Sarah tries to spend as much time as possible with her magnet friends, playing video games, going to the movies, eating at their favorite pizza place downtown, and just hanging out at one of their houses. As long as they are "hanging out [with each other] then we're having a blast." Consumed with schoolwork, Sarah does not get to spend nearly as much time with her friends as she would like, but when she manages to find the time there is nothing she enjoys more than camping out with her friends.

Last fall, Sarah and six friends finally found the time to get together for a camp out. As typical, they began the evening "gorging on junk food" and playing games that they love making up. For the rest of the night, Sarah recalls,

> We just hung out and talked about everything. We are all very comfortable with each other and talked about everything—science, politics, nerdy things, etc. We are all just really close and don't hold back. Everyone feels comfortable being super geeky and interested in something silly even if everyone else has never heard of it. Overall, we are all very close and it's just great to be that comfortable around people.

Sarah does not always feel as comfortable being around peers as she did during this camp out. In fact, she rarely feels comfortable enough to let her guard down and be as geeky and silly as she wants to be. This time spent with her closest friends gave her a rare chance to do just that.

Sarah feels most comfortable around other magnet students who share her academic interests and ambitious attitudes. As she explains, "I like the people I hang out with because they have similar interests and have to deal with all the academic pressures of the magnet program, too." When like-minded people surround her, especially other magnet students, she feels entirely at ease to reveal her true self. No façade. No worries. No pressures to act differently or be anyone other than who she truly is. Her "inner nerdy self" thrives. But common academic interests and attitudes toward education are not the only similarities between Sarah and her closest friends. As she explains, "Almost all of them are in the same social class as me."

Sarah just recently became aware of this commonality among her friends as she began noticing social class divisions in her school and community. Paying more attention to these divisions she developed a better understanding of her social class identity, which she identifies as "upper middle class" and "privileged." Until she entered Anderson, she never considered herself privileged. Sarah remembers, "I didn't realize that I was part of a higher socioeconomic class because when I was at my private school [Taylor], we were one of the families on the lower end of the income spectrum." She also had limited opportunity to become aware of her class privilege given that no one in her life talks about the advantages that she and those around her enjoy. She explains, "I don't often talk about privilege with my family or peers because it's considered in bad taste to discuss advantages that certain people have over others." In high school she could no longer ignore her advantages. Her status as "not as well off as everybody else" changed when she entered Anderson where, she reports, "I'm definitely toward the higher end of the income spectrum." In describing Anderson's student body, she claims, "There's a large population on free or reduced lunch. And the school covers a variety of different areas of the county. So there's a lot of diversity." Although the percentage of economically disadvantaged students is relatively small,[13] Anderson is much more diverse when it comes to social class than Taylor and the other spaces she ordinarily occupies where "everyone is pretty much well off." Her advantages over others became too apparent to ignore.

Sarah also became increasingly aware of her preconceived notions about economically disadvantaged people. She reports that she cannot help judging "someone walking down the street with their pants sagging and a hood up and loud music playing. I would assume that they were of a lower social class." To Sarah, this person presents him/herself very differently than a privileged person who has "good posture and makes eye contact." Although she became more aware that she makes quick judgments of others based on their appearance and actions, she finds making them unavoidable. She regards her opinions of others as natural because, as she concludes, "Everybody does it." Sarah regularly forms these swift opinions of others including privileged peers who she considers having different interests, attitudes and values from her. Sarah, to some extent, recognizes that these snap judgments often make it difficult for her to recognize any similarities that she may actually have with them.

For instance, she recently attended a birthday party of a childhood friend, Alice. She does not really hang out with Alice any longer because they "don't have much in common." Alice is a general student at Anderson so Sarah believes that the only tie that binds them is that they live in the same neighborhood. When she arrived at the party, she felt "incredibly uncomfortable [because] who I usually hang out with weren't there." Because Alice is a "popular kid," most of the young people at the party were members of this social group. Coming in direct contact with them, Sarah found herself in an unfamiliar situation. She was no longer observing them from a safe distance across the school cafeteria. Surrounded by "popular kids" she felt alone in the crowd. She recalls, "The popular kids were all drinking and just acting, you know, teenagery, and not in a positive way. I didn't think that it was reasonable or normal. They were doing ridiculous types of dancing to rap music and sort of being raucous." Sarah found it difficult to recognize any similarities that she may have with this group. She goes on to say, "There's a bit of, 'Hmm, I really don't know what you're talking about and why you're acting that way,' when I'm around these [popular] kids." Sarah also finds it difficult to relate to other groups at Anderson who similarly engage in "dangerous, stupid stuff." She provides another example by saying, "A lot of kids in my art class like to do drugs and it's just unusual because I hadn't had that pressure to do drugs or smoke marijuana until this year." When faced with an unfamiliar situation like being offered drugs or being at a rowdy party, Sarah freezes up and does not know how to act. She begins to doubt that which she normally never questions, but she somehow always manages "to keep true to myself." She finds a way to stick to her "values and principles in these situations."

Sarah frequently points to just how different all other groups at Anderson are from her own social group. From her perspective, these other groups do not have the same values and principles. They are not as motivated to do well in school. They are not academically achieving at the same level. They are too "teenagery." They are unreasonable and their actions are abnormal. She finds too many differences between her and these other peers to find any commonalities. Even with the "all-purpose nerds" who share similar interests in and outside the schooling context, she finds it difficult to relate to them because "they don't have to deal with the same [academic pressures] as we do [in the magnet program]." She would much rather stay surrounded by her highly motivated, high achieving, affluent classmates in the magnet program—those whom she has determined to be similar to herself.

Part of what makes it difficult for Sarah to get past first impressions of others outside her social group is that she rarely interacts with peers outside SMMP. As noted previously, SMMP students are fairly isolated from the rest of Anderson and, therefore, she has limited opportunity to really get to know general students. This is not the first time that Sarah has been isolated at school; in fact, she has spent most of her educational career separated from her peers on a regular basis. Because she was enrolled in a program for students with disabilities at Taylor, she was often pulled out of her classes for individualized instruction. She spent a significant amount of her elementary and middle school years around the few other students in the program or one on one with her teachers. This regularly isolated her from the larger student body. Although these accommodations during high school do not separate her from peers as frequently or to the extent they did earlier, they do somewhat set her apart because she is the only student in the magnet program with a documented learning disability. Her accommodations, however, do not create a divide between Sarah and other magnet students. She has established close relationships with her SMMP peers because she finds them more alike than different.

In contrast, divisions exist between Sarah and everyone else at Anderson. Although the separation of SMMP students certainly creates and maintains divisions, her perceptions of general students play a greater role in isolating her. Although Anderson students, as a whole, academically achieve at one of the highest levels in the city,[14] Sarah perceives most general students as low achievers. Although most general students are not economically disadvantaged, she considers them to be. Whatever similarities she may actually share with general students, she perceives that they are too different from her to find those similarities or to relate to them. Despite having multiple opportunities to interact with others who she perceives as different from herself, she avoids them and remains far removed from those differences. She moves through Anderson similarly as she rides with her father past run-down sections of the city and the people that live there on the way home. She never stops and attempts to understand differences around her. Instead, she observes them from a comfortable distance.

NOTES

1. We are not providing the sources of these quotations in order to avoid identifying the city. They come from a popular magazine that provides rankings of U.S. cities on a number of economic factors.
2. The average class size is fourteen students, and the teacher-to-student ratio is one to seven.
3. The existing literature on summer learning documents the ways in which these kinds of opportunities create even larger opportunity and achievement gaps between advantaged and disadvantaged students. See, for example, Alexander, Entwisle, & Olson, 2007.
4. It is important to note that Sarah reported that her maternal grandfather has a Ph.D., as stated later in this chapter. She did not indicate what specific career he had but provided other information giving every indication that her mom grew up in a middle-class family. It is reasonable to conclude, therefore, that she labeled her mom's side of the family "lower class" in relation to her dad's side, which is considerably wealthier.
5. Lareau, 2011.
6. Adequate Yearly Progress (AYP) is the measurement used to determine how a school is performing academically according to results on standardized tests. Each subgroup of a school (e.g., special education, English language learners, low income, race/ethnicity) must perform at a particular level on the tests. Therefore the test scores from one group of students do not determine the school's effectiveness or, in other words, whether a school meets AYP. The school is held accountable for the achievement of all individual subgroups.
7. On average, every SMMP graduate is offered five scholarships from some of the top universities in the United States. Although most of the students who attend the program do not need financial assistance to attend college, they are focused on getting scholarships to demonstrate their achievement. It is more about the recognition that comes with being offered a merit scholarship from a top university or, in most case, multiple offers.
8. More specifically, 7 percent Asian Americans, 9 percent Latino/Latinas, 17 percent of African Americans, and 2 percent unidentified nonwhite.
9. As at other schools across the nation, the only indicator used to determine the number of economically disadvantaged students is the number of students qualified for free or reduced lunch.
10. Like most affluent students with learning disabilities, Sarah has received the educational services she needs to be academically successful. In a longitundinal study of services and supports for students with disabilities, Levine, Marder, and Wagner (2004) found that cost, among other issues, are reported as the greatest barriers to service acquisition. They argue that the fact that cost is cited as a main barrier highlights the important relationship between household income

and service acquisition. More specifically, poverty poses obstacles to accessing related services for youth with disabilities and their families. Affluent peers and their families face fewer barriers to service access related to transportation, location, and language. They also do not need to go beyond the school to receive services nearly as often as do low-income students. Therefore affluent students with disabilities receive the services they need most often. Sarah's educational experiences are consistent with these findings.

11. For example, see Wolanin & Steele, 2004.
12. Research studies have consistently documented that college-prep programs enroll a relatively low number of students from traditionally underrepresented groups and from poor families. These programs typically enroll mostly middle- to upper-class and white students. For a review of this body of research, see Howell & Smith, 2011. Moreover, a lack of economic and racial diversity is especially seen in AP courses. For the latest and most comprehensive report on the demographics of AP courses in the United States, see College Board, 2012.
13. Especially compared with the other public high schools in the city. Anderson has the smallest percentage of students receiving free and reduced lunch among the city's five public high schools.
14. This is based on the percentage of students achieving at proficient and distinguished levels on state-mandated yearly tests. Math is the only subject in which Anderson falls below the district average. Anderson performs well on other indicators of student academic achievement, such as graduation rates, attendance, and number of graduating students going to college. In almost all ways, Anderson students, on the whole, achieve at above-average level academically.

7 Leo

Uncertain Future, Certain Success

with Annie Chen

No plans, no goals, just a clean slate.

For most of his eighteen years of life, Leo has rarely followed the crowd. Whereas most nine-year-old boys in his neighborhood and at his school spent hours outside kicking a soccer ball around or planted in front of the television with a video game controller, Leo spent as much time as possible closely watching his saltwater fish and maintaining their habitat. Just before turning nine, he had set his mind to creating a saltwater habitat for multiple species of fish. Determined to make this happen, he dedicated every waking moment to learning how to create the best environment for fish that he did not even own yet. He quickly became obsessed with the project. After Leo had read countless books and articles and watched hours of educational programming on how to maintain a saltwater tank, his grandfather came to appreciate his commitment and bought him a fifty-gallon saltwater fish tank. It took up half of Leo's bedroom and he absolutely loved it. His enthusiasm did not subside in the least after he got what he had been wanting for months. He monitored the water temperature closely, made sure the proper amount of salt was dissolved in the water, kept track of the pH level, and cleaned the aquarium and its contents on a regular basis. Given that maintaining a saltwater habitat is extremely time-consuming and complicated for anyone, never mind for a nine-year-old, adults in his life marveled at how hard he worked to make sure that his fish would thrive. By the time his next birthday came around, he knew more about how to maintain a saltwater aquarium than even the owners of the local fish store.

As he grew older, Leo gradually lost interest in the saltwater habitat he had created and maintained, but he kept his passion for fish and other marine life. Growing up on the northwestern coast, it was "only natural for me to be exploring the ocean." With the same intensity and enthusiasm he had put into creating an artificial saltwater habitat, he jumped into scuba diving at the age of fourteen. Soon after discovering his passion, he took scuba-diving lessons, and his "always supportive parents" bought him the equipment necessary to pursue his deep-sea excursions. Leo soon took on his first job and began working at a local dive shop to learn more about his new interest. By sixteen, he had undergone the training necessary to be a certified rescue diver. Wanting to spend more time with his parents and especially his father, who did not live with him, he convinced them to become certified as well so that they could take diving vacations. Because his parents are divorced, they took turns taking Leo on diving adventures. Although all three of them were never able to dive together, these trips became the most meaningful memories he has of time spent with his parents. In fact, Leo found it quite nice to have such quality one-on-one time with each of his parents, sharing his passion with them as they explored new parts of the underwater world.

In becoming an expert diver, Leo also discovered surfing. Although he never developed the same passion for surfing as he did for saltwater fish and scuba diving, he followed a similar path in becoming a proficient surfer—he learned what he needed to learn primarily on his own. Before long, surfing became second nature to him. For five years now, surfing has been one of his favorite activities. It is something that he does "to clear the mind" when he needs a break from school, family problems or just life in general. The beach and ocean serve as an escape from the world as he rides the waves in solitude. Until recently, surfing was "pretty much the only thing I did that really cleared my mind of everything else." But now playing the guitar is his escape—and his newest obsession.

A couple years ago, Leo picked up a guitar and wanted to learn how to play because he thought it would impress girls. Although not generally a shy person, he often finds himself tongue-tied around girls, having no idea how to initiate contact or what to say when he does interact with them. For Leo, playing the guitar seemed like the perfect conversation starter. What he learned from watching television and observing in real life was that "girls love the guy that can play the guitar," and there just happened to be a guitar lying around his house that had not been used for several years. He explains, "I actually picked up the guitar to try and make myself a little more interesting to girls, I guess. It seemed like a good way to impress girls. Not the noblest reason, but it seemed like a solid plan. So I basically claimed my sister's old guitar that she left when she moved out and taught myself a few chords." His plan worked. In no time, he met his first girlfriend while playing the guitar. Although he had done what he had set out to do, it did not turn out exactly as he had planned.

Playing the guitar became much more than "a pickup line" for Leo; it has become a large part of his identity. Most aspects of his life now revolve around music, learning new material, gaining new knowledge and skills, refining and improving upon what he already knows, and surrounding himself with others who equally share his passion. Leo rarely goes anywhere without his guitar in hand and spends most of his time practicing and "jamming with friends." As he explains, "It was during this time period that I realized how much I love music. The reason I knew this is 'cause I would bail on [my girlfriend] to go play music with my friends. That was when I thought to myself, 'ah crap, total opposite effect.'" Leo's love of music trumped any feelings he had for his girlfriend, which "needless to say, caused the relationship not to last." Not long after picking up the guitar for the first time, his motivation for playing completely changed. In fact, he is at a point where he is "sacrificing relationships with girls and most everything else to play music with friends." All he wants to do is play music, and when he is not playing, "I'm thinking about playing. I'm totally obsessed."

Like the other activities that have captured his attention, learning to play the guitar required a lot of work and commitment. He claims that learning to play "never really came natural" to him. Although he grew up watching his father and older sister play the guitar, "I really didn't have much interest in [playing] and was not really drawn to it." But when his interest was unexpectedly piqued, he practiced for hours and hours every week, which allowed him to learn how to play in a fairly short period of time. During periods where self-doubts about his skills surface, he will "go on a practice binge for like four hours straight and then I'll become exhausted and take the next three days off." Even on these days off, he still thinks about what he could do differently and comes up with plans for improving his skills.

Although he puts a lot of effort and hard work into his ever-changing interests, Leo has had help along the way. At just the right time, he seems to be "fortunate enough to meet people who support me and give me the guidance I need"—family members, the owners of a fish store, and the master scuba dive instructor, to name just a few. In the course of pursuing his current interest, Leo met a jazz musician who came to his school on a weekly basis to work with students who were interested in music. Leo took advantage of the opportunity to learn everything he could about becoming a professional musician. Around that time, he also met "this guy who went to my school and we didn't really know each other before, but I found out he had been playing since he was five and he was really good." He immediately introduced Leo to others who played music and soon after, "they invited me to jam with them, and we all became pretty close." Although Leo had little else in common with his new friends, their shared interest in music was "more than enough" to establish close and meaningful relationships with them. They began spending as much time with each other as possible and "jamming anywhere we could." He fondly remembers one such jam session: "It was winter, and really cold, our fingers were super stiff, and our drummer's fingers were all blistered and bleeding cause he kept hitting his hands on the drum rims. It really should have been a miserable experience, but it was a lot of fun." Moments like this serve as inspiration for Leo to continue his commitment "to be the best musician I can be."

No one has inspired him or been supportive of his past and current passions more than his family. His family provided him with the emotional and financial support necessary to explore his interests—no matter how obscure or unrealistic they might have considered those activities. When he was obsessed with saltwater habitats, his grandfather bought him a tank.

When his attention wandered to scuba diving, his parents bought his equipment and paid for the best training available. Since the day Leo's interest in music sparked, his parents provided him with instruments and practice space. After years of not playing, his father picked up the guitar to make sure that Leo did not have to practice alone when his friends were busy. Over the years, his family found multiple opportunities to support him as he diligently worked toward his goals. Without their support, Leo realizes that he might have never been able to pursue his various interests.

His strong work ethic, extraordinary intellectual curiosity, unwavering commitment to achieve what he sets his mind to, and solid support system make it seem as if he could overcome whatever obstacles he might encounter in achieving what he wants out of life. The problem for Leo, however, is that "I have no idea what I want to do in my life." He currently has no immediate or long-term plans for his future. Although he is increasingly gravitating toward "something in music, whether it's producing or playing," his future remains uncertain. Whereas his interests have varied over the years, he has had little to no interest in formal education. Leo almost dropped out of high school in his junior year and barely managed to graduate. He is now out of school and has no intention of going to college.

PAINFUL EDUCATION

In ninth grade, I had a teacher that I really couldn't stand. It wasn't just me; other kids didn't like her either. I would wake up in the morning and just dread getting up. I hated going to this class, it was always the first one of the day. We had to read To Kill a Mocking Bird *for class, which I think now is a really good book, but at the time, I couldn't stand it. We would read the pages assigned to us, around fifteen or twenty every other day, and the next day come in and discuss them. The thing is, this teacher would then make us listen to an audio book of the pages we just read, then draw a scene from the book. This was for a ninth grade English class! For the whole book, we repeated this pattern, and this may be an exaggeration brought on by how much I disliked the class, but I could swear it took us a good three months to get through that book. It was the biggest waste of time ever.*

I really like reading, and I like good books, but to be stuck listening to some pre-recorded woman from an audiotape re-read what we read was just awful. And the drawing for me was the worst part. I would always just draw some stick figures and would get the same grade as the kids who put so much effort into theirs. I understand art is subjective, but I shouldn't have gotten full points for those crappy stick figures. After a while I just stopped trying. I almost failed that class, and it was literally because I just found it completely boring. No

discussion. No variety. No feedback from our teacher. Doing the same
mindless thing over and over for months.

Leo considers going to school like trudging to the doctor's office to receive a
shot in the arm. He knows the shot is going to be good for him but he is not
going to like it at all. There was not one part of his high school experience
that he enjoyed because "it was just a mindless routine of doing what was
being asked of you day after day." But he knew, at the very least, that he
needed to graduate for his own good. At times it was even difficult for him to
keep in mind that "this is something I needed to do because without [a high
school diploma] I can't do too much with my life." He often needed people
in his support system to remind him from time to time that he should "just
had to go ahead and take the shot and get the pain over with." What made
his schooling seem like such a painful experience was his strongly held
belief that schools place tremendous pressure on students to give up significant parts of themselves in order to be academically successful. Although
he had attended different kinds of schools in various contexts—a large public school, a small independent school, and a public alternative educational
program—Leo adamantly believes that the educational system as a whole
functions to "shoot out generic students like a conveyor belt and strip you
of all your individuality." In an attempt to avoid being "a product of this
factory," he settled for mediocrity at every school he attended.[1]

Leo lives with his mother in a farming area that sits right outside a
very wealthy and touristy coastal town. Hidden behind a thicket of trees
and surrounded by well-maintained gardens, their large home sits on five
acres of oceanfront property. Although the beach in front of their home is
officially public property, it remains undisturbed by outsiders. A massive
building, originally an indoor space for boat building and now what his
family calls "the warehouse," sits next to the main house. Several years
ago, Leo built a skate park in it to continue skateboarding with his friends
in the winter. Then his parents bought him an old boat and he returned the
space to its original purpose. Other structures sit next to and behind the
main house, including a barn, three play houses, a guesthouse, and a massive tree house. His mother's estate provides ample room for Leo to explore
his various interests and "to forget that a world exists off the property."

Anyone living on such a lavish estate could easily forget about what lies
just beyond its boundaries. Their home seems far removed from the realities of their immediate world. Although not far from a wealthy community,
their home is located in a rural area with one of the highest unemployment
and poverty rates in the state.[2] Instead of following in his older sister's
footsteps by going to a school in the wealthy town nearby, Leo began his
educational career at an elementary school close to home and stayed there
until he reached the fourth grade. Like most schools situated in predominantly poor communities, his school did not have nearly the same resources
or overall quality of education as the one in the wealthier community.[3]

This reality was always a concern to Leo's parents, but they allowed him to decide which school to attend. Because he wanted to be close to home and attend school with his neighborhood friends, the choice was pretty simple for him. His parents, however, continued to worry about the poor quality of education he was receiving, especially in comparison with the top-notch education offered at his sister's school. They were also concerned about his meager performance in school, which they concluded was because he was not being challenged enough. After "much discussion and pleading," his parents finally convinced him, just before he was to start middle school, to transfer to the school his sister attended. His parents thought that this change would make him more academically successful, and Leo was willing to give it a try.

Although he was now attending a "higher quality" school, Leo's academic performance went from bad to worse. By the end of his time in middle school, he was on the brink of failing. As with his experiences at his other school, he was "completely bored" in most of his classes and "didn't see a purpose in really trying that hard or doing what I was being told to do." But unlike the case at his previous school, he was now in an unfamiliar environment and without his neighborhood friends; he felt incredibly alone. He did establish positive relationships with some teachers "that really challenged me." Because he respected these teachers, he performed significantly better in their classes than in his other ones. In most of his classes, however, he found what his teachers were trying to teach him and his peers to be "the biggest waste of time." As he further explains, "[My teachers] were teaching us how to basically jump through the hoops that are coming, that we are going to have to deal with later on down the road. It had nothing with what was going on with us now." Halfway through his high school career, Leo was doing so poorly in school that his family needed to find an alternative plan for his education. His father played with the idea of sending him to a private boarding school, but Leo resisted that idea to the point where it seemed like an unlikely option for improving his academic performance. After much deliberation, his parents decided, with Leo's approval, that it would be in his best interest to return to his original school and enroll in Explore, the school's alternative educational program.[4]

Explore is designed to prevent or discourage students from leaving school before they graduate by using alternative approaches to teaching and learning than the ones most commonly found in traditional education. The program focuses on experiential learning that aims to give students more options for exploring their own interests than they would have in the usual school system. Explore students attend classes only a few days a week; the other days are spent completing "various real-world experiences." Because Leo lives on the part of the West Coast well known for manufacturing traditional wooden boats, one of his first "real-world experiences" was working with a local boat builder to learn the craft; he even built a replica of a boat originally used in the area. In the program, he also had opportunities to take "some really cool electives" that offered an alternative to the traditional classes he had found so uninspiring at his other school. With the freedom to explore varied interests in diverse contexts beyond school walls, the program seemed like the perfect fit for Leo. Being situated in a familiar context, which included familiar faces, also seemed ideal.

Because most of other Explore students had also attended Leo's local elementary school, he was acquainted with most of his peers; they were once his classmates and neighborhood friends. Almost everyone except Leo had attended only the local schools. They did not have the same opportunity to leave their small community to attend a better school elsewhere—even if it was just twenty minutes away. Unlike most households in their community, Leo's family had the necessary social, cultural, and financial resources to send him to a school outside their home district.[5] At this other school, he never made lasting friendships because, in part, "I never was too focused on the social aspect [of school]." When he reentered the local school system, part of him welcomed the chance to rekindle old friendships, but it never happened. At Explore, he never found a "network that I could feel comfortable in." He felt too distant and too different from his classmates to establish meaningful relationships with them. Shortly after enrolling in the program, he started going home during lunch period instead of eating in the cafeteria with other students because he always felt "really uncomfortable walking into the lunchroom." It did not take him long to develop a "pretty cynical viewpoint on [Explore] and everyone that went there, so I just didn't think it was worth my time to try and connect with the people that were there." He once again felt incredibly alone within an educational context.

Although Explore offers students multiple opportunities to individualize their learning, they still need to take traditional courses to fulfill graduation requirements. For Leo, the engaging aspects of the program were overshadowed by these requirements because it made the program "basically the same [as traditional schools] with the same mindless, useless requirements." Because of this, he wanted nothing to do with what he considered to be "the mass-produced education" offered at Explore. According to Leo, his school "suffered from the same problem" as other schools in the United States, because his education "wasn't really about the individual student" but instead about "mass producing students in this one way to churn out as many contributing worker bees as possible." As he further explains,

> I do feel like there is a lot wrong with the system. They educate for one type of kid and those are usually the kids that get straight A's and do really well, but aren't necessarily the smartest kids. They are the ones that can do these assignments and typically come from good homes, with the means to support them, and they typically don't have learning disabilities or any other problems. You have to be perfect to be successful. The system doesn't really give you the room to bring your own self into what you're doing.

Leo is partly aware of the contradiction that exists between his own performance in school and his understandings of the "broken [educational] system." According to his own perspective, he should be excelling academically, given his supportive family and demonstrated abilities and eagerness to learn, but he sorts out this contradiction by emphasizing that it was the system that made him unsuccessful. He insists, "I probably could have done fairly good in school and been the kind of student who brings home honor awards and receives top grades, but it just wasn't for me. I wasn't willing to be just another cookie-cutter student."

Leo also contends that he did not receive much pressure from his parents to do better in school. As he explains, "They pretty much allowed me to make my own choices in school. Every once in a while, they would try to get me to focus on school so I could do better, but that never worked, so they took a hands-off approach." On rare occasions when they tried placing pressure on him, Leo threatened to drop out, get his GED, and join the military. Tapping into their deepest fear for his future, they immediately went back to their hands-off approach. Although they wanted him to be successful, his parents thought it was more important for him to make his own decisions and face the consequences of those decisions. Leo believes that his parents would have taken another approach if they were economically disadvantaged because "the consequences would've been more serious." As he further explains,

> If I was from a different social class, maybe my parents would have been pressuring me instead of saying, 'Do what you want in order to be happy.' Instead, maybe they would be pressuring me to go to college so that I could live above the poverty line, then maybe I would have worked harder in school, gotten better grades, and received a Fulbright scholarship to some school.

Because they were much more privileged circumstances, his parents accepted Leo's rejection of the idea of school and felt no real need to coerce him into thinking otherwise. Without much interference, they allowed him "to coast through school."

After attending Explore for just one year, the confluence of his lack of interest and motivation, his skepticism of the education system, and the absence of parental pressure caused him to seriously consider dropping out of school at the end of his junior year. Ultimately he decided, "I would just keep going though I really wanted to drop out and just get my GED." By his senior year, he was "completely exhausted with school" and stopped doing schoolwork altogether. Three weeks before graduation, his teachers informed his parents that he would most likely not graduate, but they were still giving him a chance to finish his missing work. Not successful in urging Leo to complete the work, his parents called on anyone who they thought could motivate him. His two older sisters ended up coming to the rescue. Because both of them lived elsewhere, they were not fully aware of the extent of Leo's academic problems. Individually, they called him in disbelief. "How could you get yourself in this kind of mess," one sister questioned at the start of their conversation. Both of them similarly made the point that "I was too intelligent and had too much to offer to just throw it all away." He did not have an option—he had to do whatever it took "so I could get my diploma." His sisters' tough love snapped him out of his apathetic daze and within three weeks he had completed the assignments he had missed throughout the year. With no time to spare, he made the deadline and fulfilled all the requirements to graduate.

A DEFIANT SPIRIT

Before Leo turned five years old, his family often referred to him as "the complete destroyer." He threw whatever he could get his hands on, yelled as often as possible, and stayed always in motion. His days were spent "trying to destroy anything in my path." Because he was unwilling to sit still for more than thirty seconds, "it was a full-time job for my parents and sisters to keep me occupied and happy." As often as possible, his family took him outside "to release some of my built-up energy by running around, even if it meant running around in circles. I needed to be always moving and on the go." Because of his destructive and rambunctious behaviors, his parents avoided taking him to public places unless absolutely necessary. They especially avoided sit-down restaurants because "I would yell, throw food, and run around." When they went out to eat as a family, they picked up food from a drive-through and ate it in their car to keep Leo in a private, contained environment.

During vacations, however, they found it nearly unbearable to eat fast food the entire time. Finding no way around it, they took Leo out to sit-down restaurants. On one such occasion, they went to an upscale restaurant while vacationing in Hawaii. Without knowing much about what kind of food the restaurant served before arriving, the family was disappointed by the prevalence of pork dishes on the menu. Because they observe Jewish dietary laws, Leo's sisters do not eat pork. Although his parents do not observe kosher laws as strictly, they typically avoid pork products, especially when they eat with the family. At first glance, his parents and sisters "started griping about the menu, trying to find something that wasn't wrapped in bacon, made of ham, or served with a side of pork chops." After studying the menu for quite some time and making special requests, his sisters and parents finally managed to order dishes without pork.

Leo was last to order food. Before telling the server what he wanted to eat, he looked over at his sisters with a devilish grin and then shouted to the server, "I want pig."

"Pig?" she asked, "What kind?"

"I don't care what kind. Anything with pig in it. Give me pig," he demanded and then leaned back in his chair triumphantly. He glanced over at his sisters to see their reaction. After determining that he had success-fully "grossed my sisters out," he felt utter glee and satisfaction.

Leo was too young to remember this restaurant incident; it is just one of the stories that his family has told him about his "hell raising, loud, and stubborn years before I was in school." His parents were certain that he would eventually channel his rambunctious behavior into an aggressive sport and become a successful athlete—probably a linebacker. Even before he was too young to play on a Little League team, they bought him a foot-ball uniform because "I was such a bruiser that they were sure I would grow up and play in some violent sport like football." Although his parents found his difficult behaviors challenging, they gave him the freedom to express his individuality. His parents and everyone else in his world held the expectation that he would use his individual qualities to reach the level of success that other men in his family had achieved in their lives. They nurtured those traits despite the amount of effort it took, for instance, just to have a family meal at a restaurant.

As the only son of an accomplished lawyer, the grandson of a prestigious doctor, and the great-grandson of a successful business owner, Leo comes from a line of highly motivated and ambitious men. His great-grandfather built his own button factory, primarily with the intention of being finan-cially able to put his children and their children through college so they could have more opportunities and financial security than he ever had. His grandfather reaped the rewards of this successful business and was the first in the family to attend college. He eventually went to medical school and became a nationally recognized physician. By the time Leo's father was born, his family had amassed a considerable fortune. Not willing to just glide through an entitled life, Leo's father wanted to achieve the same level of success as his father had but on his own terms. Although he felt pressure to follow in his father's footsteps and become a physician, he chose a com-pletely different career path and became a lawyer specializing in medical malpractice, a career that put him constantly at odds with physicians. Leo is not fully certain that his father "became a lawyer so he could be noth-ing like his dad, but it's obvious that this was part of the reason. I mean, he couldn't have decided on anything more of a polar opposite than what he did." His father accomplished what he set out to do by achieving (and arguably surpassing) his father's level of success. Although the men in Leo's family have achieved great professional success and "worked hard and get the job done," they all made significant personal sacrifices that came at a great cost to their families.

When Leo was in kindergarten, his family moved from Alaska to Wash-ington mainly for the sake of his father's career but also to be closer to their extended family. Shortly after moving to Washington, his father's "work life became incredibly crazy and he was constantly working, even his spare time was spent working." He spent considerably more time away from home than when they lived in Alaska. Although Leo was only six years old at the time, he remembers one instance where his father "was gone for two and a half months working on a big case." When his father's absences became more frequent and lengthy, his mother began suspecting that he was not coming home for reasons other than work obligations. Her suppositions were confirmed when she discovered that he was having an affair with a colleague. Not long after finding out about his affair, she filed for divorce.

Leo distinctly remembers the day when his parents sat him down to inform him about their divorce after he arrived home from school. His mother explained that his father was "going through a confusing time period and he was going to be away," which went right over his head. He was too young to fully grasp what she was telling him, but he nodded as if he understood. Despite not being aware of everything, he understood that his father was leaving. Initially he assumed that this "was going to be a temporary situation and everything would go back to normal and that my dad would be back living with us and we would once again be a family." For reasons still unknown to him, his father disappeared completely from their lives immediately after the divorce. No phone calls. No visits. As time went on, Leo came to the painful realization that "my dad wasn't coming back and everything was different."

Leo says, "Honestly, I don't remember a lot about that time period cause it's just one big blur and I don't generally think about it, mainly because I have a good relationship with both my parents now, and my stepmom, so it really doesn't seem to do any good to dwell on it too much." Although he does not remember much or want to dwell on what happened, his parents' divorce immensely impacted his life and behavior. His hell-raising, loud, and stubborn demeanor suddenly changed. As he explains, "I got very secluded, and submissive, and obeyed the rules. I became well mannered and no longer was 'the destroyer.' It was like overnight, I became a completely different human being." He does not know why he changed so suddenly and dramatically; it was just one of the ways in which he responded to the divorce.

His sisters had their own individual ways of responding to the divorce. Because the oldest one was about to leave home and attend college on the other side of the country, she mostly distanced herself from the family turmoil. His other sister, however, "became a complete wreck," and her life changed entirely after the divorce. To vent her anger and frustration, she resorted to reckless behaviors and became increasingly unstable and violent, eventually turning to drugs and developing an eating disorder. Not too long after the divorce, she was in and out of rehab. Everyone's attention soon became directed toward keeping her alive. With his parents' focus on his sister's life-threatening behaviors, Leo became a "wallflower" and began "to slide under the radar." He wanted "to make sure that my actions and behaviors did not affect anyone negatively." While he watched his sister put a tremendous strain on the family, he tried doing his part to bring some stability and balance by "doing what I was told and not causing any trouble and not having [my parents] need to worry about me." He thought, "They had enough to worry about with my sister and I didn't want to cause them any more stress." While they focused on his sister's troubles, they appreciated his cooperative behavior.

During this time, Leo became increasingly independent, while his parents left him "alone to do my own thing" and "to make my own rules." Because he attracted no attention from his parents with his amiable demeanor, they barely noticed his poor performance in school. Even though they had previously "put a lot of emphasis and importance on getting a good education and put a lot of pressure on my sisters in their schoolwork," they maintained a hands-off approach when it came to Leo and "didn't apply the same pressure" as they did with his sisters. Even during his elementary school years, he was essentially left to make his own decisions about his schooling. His parents did not give him grief or try to intervene as he nearly failed out of school. Able to do as he pleased, "I did only the bare minimum required [in school] and sometimes didn't even do that." Leo is uncertain whether his poor performance in school was a direct consequence of his parents' divorce. As he explains, "I really was never good at school and since my parents divorced when I was really young, it's hard to know whether that was a product of the divorce." He acknowledges, however, "It probably didn't help how I did in school; that's for certain." Whatever impact the divorce actually had on his performance in school, his parents were too occupied with his sister and their own life changes to even notice it.

For several years after his parents' divorce, Leo experienced typical adjustment difficulties; he felt confused by what was happening to his family, fantasized about reconciliation, and experienced difficulties in expressing his feelings.[6] Even though his parents have been divorced for over ten years, he continues to find what happened during those years puzzling and painful. He also continues to yearn for those rare moments when "everyone is together. It doesn't matter what we're doing. All that matters is that we're all together." His fantasies about his parents getting back together are long gone. Although a part of him still wants "all of us to be one family, not two different families," he reluctantly accepts, "The reality is that it's never going to be one family again, and we're not going to be all together that much." It took Leo several years to find ways of dealing with and making sense of his parents' divorce. He eventually decided, "The best way is not to think about it much and just move on." He prefers not "to relive the past" or "revisit painful memories."

Currently Leo and his father "have a good relationship for the most part." When his father finally came back into the picture after being absent for nearly three years immediately after the divorce, Leo quickly forgave him; he was just ecstatic to have him back in his life. They began spending more time together and eventually reconciled hurts of the past. With the two of them spending more time together, he had the opportunity to build a relationship with his stepmother and "even grew fond of her." A couple years after their reunion, though, he discovered some difficult news about his stepmother; she was the woman with whom his father was having the affair that led to his parents' divorce. That realization initially created a rift between Leo and his stepmother, but "I eventually got over it and just accepted that I like her, and we could have a good relationship." Again, his way of coping was "to not dwell on the past."

Living with his mother after the divorce, Leo feels closer to her than to his father. She has been a constant presence and source of support in his life. He reports, "She understands me and is always there for me no matter what." Although they do not always agree, he claims that his mother is "probably one of the most open-minded people I know. I can tell her anything and she will have an open mind to it." Over the years he has adopted many of his mother's understandings and values, especially ones related to their wealth. Her working-class background left its mark on her and powerfully influences her views on their advantaged circumstances. Above all, she taught Leo the valuable lesson that "money doesn't buy happiness." He elaborates,

> My mom and I always talked about what it is to be happy, and is it worth it to work for the monetary gain if all you do is spend all your time making money and have no time for family and friends. She has emphasized the point of how important it is in life to be happy and you don't always find that happiness by making a lot of money.

Leo shares her belief that "actually being wealthy can make you always feel unsatisfied in life. My mom has a saying, which is really awesome, she'll say, 'your needs grow with your income.' The more money you have, the more your needs keep you from being happy 'cause you're always trying to fulfill something that can't be." He holds onto this lesson dearly as he attempts to figure out the next stage of his life.

Although closer to his mother, Leo enjoys a close relationship with both parents and feels that they have been "my main support system, both emotionally and financially." He further explains, "Economically, they totally support me and provide me with opportunities, but they've also been incredibly emotionally supportive. They've always told me that I can do whatever I want to do and that I don't necessarily have to follow what everyone else does just because it brings money." Even though they hold their own visions for his future, they recognize that he still possesses the deviant spirit he had as a young child. They accept that Leo will not follow in the footsteps of others in his family but instead will continue to blaze his own trail in life. He greatly appreciates that "they don't have a cookie-cutter plan for me and they want me to be happy despite anybody else's expectations. They just want me to follow my dreams." He may be uncertain about his future at the moment, but he knows with absolute certainty that his parents will support him regardless of what direction he eventually takes "in the pursuit of my own happiness."

RIDING THE WAVE

When Leo jumps on his surfboard and paddles into the ocean, he does not think about where he will end up or how he is going to get there; he waits for the perfect wave, sets up, jumps to his feet, and glides toward the shore. Whether he makes it there all the way the first time or falls off the board and has to try again, he knows for certain that he will make it to the shore eventually. With no worries and no plans for executing the task at hand, he is just there to ride the wave. He approaches the rest of his life in a similar manner; he just goes "with the flow and I'll see where things take me."

To most of the people in Leo's life, he seems lost to the point where it is nearly impossible to imagine that he will become motivated enough to achieve the same level of success of others in his family or, for that matter, become self-sufficient enough not to rely solely on his family's wealth for the rest of his life. No one in his immediate world questions whether he is capable of reaching success and autonomy, but they doubt his willingness. Their misgivings, however, fade into the background. He hears their concerns but pays little attention to them. As he explains, "People think that I should be actively pursuing a plan and doing things differently. They think I should be going off to college or joining the workforce. They try to offer advice, but it's really not needed and I don't really listen to what they're saying." Although he acknowledges that he has no plans and has not been successful so far in life, he is completely certain that when the opportunity arises to follow his dreams, whatever they may be, he will achieve what he wants out of life.

At the moment, Leo reports, "I'm taking the summer off. My only definite plans right now are to go hang out with friends, play music, go surfing, relax, and get the twelve years of nightmare [that I experienced in school] out of my head." His parents are not "pressuring me to get a job so I can choose whether I work or not. Either way, I'm able to be supported completely financially." Although he has no real need for a job, he has toyed with the idea of going back to work at the dive shop for a few hours each week to continue pursuing his enjoyment of scuba diving. He ultimately decided, "It's better right now not having a responsibility that ties me down while going through this transition." He wants to avoid a similar tedious routine of life that he endured throughout his schooling.

With the same advantages in life, the friends with whom Leo plays music are also fortunate enough to spend their time focusing on music and their other interests without needing to work. Because his friends will go off to college in just a few months and have more concrete future plans, their decision to spend the summer in the same way serves as a form of affirmation for Leo's own immediate plans. It makes his decision to take a break seem more acceptable to himself with his friends, "who know what they're doing," taking the summer off also. He does not necessarily need "to be doing the same as my friends to feel like I'm making the right decision, but it helps now." More important than anything else, spending time with friends will make this summer less lonely and help him figure out his next move in life.

Given his poor performance in high school and his lack of interest in pursuing typical paths after high school, his options for what lies next are limited. With no significant training or experience, his only option for employment would be getting an unskilled job, but he has no interest in doing that kind of work. Without the necessary credentials to gain admission to a four-year college, his only option would be attending a two-year institution; but going back to school is completely out of the question for the time being. Because no viable path seems the right one to take, Leo has decided to hold off on his journey toward the future and "just live in the moment and see what happens." He is certain that "when it's the right time for me to move ahead, it'll all come together."

For the most part, his parents accept that he is taking a break to figure things out. As he explains, "They have always taught me to follow what I want to do to make myself happy regardless of anything else, so they're pretty supportive of me taking the time needed to figure out what will make me happy." Until recently, it never actually occurred to his parents that he might never attend college. They held to a deep-seated assumption that going to college after school would simply be his next step in life. For most of his life, Leo shared their taken-for-granted assumption of college as the obvious next step after high school. Because most members of his immediate and extended family graduated from college, he formed the natural assumption that he would go too.[7] Even though "it was pretty clear to me and everyone else that I didn't like school," attending college was never "up for grabs or really doubted" until he graduated from high school. He does not have many detailed plans about his future but he knows at least one thing for sure—he is not going back to school. When this reality began sinking in, his parents tried to convince him to change his mind. At that point, as he had done in the past when he felt pressure from them, he responded by threatening to join the military. Once again, this threat "made them back off and stop bothering me about it."

While Leo spends time figuring out his future, he casually entertains the notion of working toward a career in music, an idea that emerged when he developed a relationship with the jazz musician he met in high school. At that time, he gathered all the information he could about what it would take to be a professional musician and found it an attractive option for his future. He realizes that it would not be an easy route to take because "only a very few actually make it in that line of work and [are] successful in turning what you do in your free time into an actual career." In thinking about pursuing this career, Leo is not too worried about beating the incredible odds to achieve success but instead is more concerned about eventually losing his "intense interest and passion for music." He goes back and forth on whether his interest in music will last long enough to be worth the time and energy it would take to pursue this option. Given that his interests are always changing, he acknowledges that he may have a completely different focus at some point in the future. He does not know, and nor does anyone else for that matter, how long his current interests will last or what will grab his attention next.

When he sets this concern aside and imagines an eventual career in music, he confesses, with some embarrassment, that his ultimate dream would be to become a rock star. He knows that "this sounds a little crazy, since everybody at some point dreams of being on stage with millions of fans screaming their name." Leo claims, however, that he potentially wants to follow this dream for reasons different from the most common ones. The perks of being a rock star, namely money and fame, are of absolutely no interest to him. As he explains,

> Money and fame don't motivate me. I'm going to be set financially either way so that isn't what I'm after, and I like keeping to myself and just being around my friends and not crowds of people. I have this whole attitude that's inspired me to ignore the glory or money. I'm really after more than that.

What he finds appealing instead is "being able to play music all the time and going on tour and living the nomadic life." Being a rock star "fits perfectly" with what he considers to be the ideal lifestyle. It would give him a chance "not to be tied down and be able to jump around freely while doing what I love."

Reaching musical stardom is the closest thing to a future plan that Leo has at the moment. Although he thinks this would be the perfect solution to do what he loves while avoiding "the dreaded nine-to-five desk job," he realizes that becoming a rock star "may be a long shot" and "it may not turn out as perfect as it seems like it would be." He explains,

> I love the idea that I would get to travel around, meet people, experience new places, and of course play music, but it might not be fulfilling. I might find out I just want to settle down, or we might not be good enough, but I won't fall into the trap of monotony where I have to get a job to pay for whatever. It seems like the perfect life, but there are just a lot of uncertainties.

He understands that inevitable obstacles would stand in his way of becoming a rock star; however, none would be greater than "discovering that I didn't enjoy it as much as I thought I would." More than anything else, he is concerned about the possibility of disliking the rock star lifestyle.

Whatever Leo eventually decides to pursue in life, he wants "to try to live and be happy." He believes,

> I'll be happy doing something where I'm not jumping through hoops. I want to build a life for myself where, of course I'm going to have to jump through hoops, but it's not going to be like it was in school where you have to fill out the timesheets and meet project deadlines. I just think that, for me at least, it's not the way I want to live.

To be genuinely happy, he claims, "It doesn't matter what my income is or what I'm doing with my life. I just need to be enjoying myself. It really comes down to finding and doing something I enjoy." Although he believes that "to really be happy, I need to be able to stand on my own two feet without having to rely on other people to constantly bail me out of trouble or help me pay for things, and to basically be able to support myself," he is completely opposed to doing "some kind of work that I don't enjoy just because I need to support myself." As he further explains, "I think really my biggest fear would be that I end up in that cycle of just getting up, going to a job I hate, getting home, and going to bed. That would be my worst fear."

He is still in the process of figuring out "what would make me happy, but also allow me to support myself," and believes that his advantaged life circumstances "will allow me to pursue my passions and dreams and find happiness easier than a lot of other people who aren't as fortunate as I am." As he further explains,

> I guess I'm pretty confident that I will end up somewhere that I am happy, and if I am not happy I will probably quit that job, move somewhere new, or do something different. If I end up somewhere I'm not expecting to be, it'll be because I want to. I don't have the same worries as many other people that would force me to stay in a job or do something that I really didn't want to do.

He believes that his family's wealth affords him the freedom to search for a career that he truly loves, and he does not "need to think about how much money I'll be making if I love what I'm doing because I'll be completely supported no matter what." For Leo, this is "just the reality of my life. The truth is, I have these advantages that others don't have and they are mine to use or not use as I will." Although he believes that it is "unfair" that others do not have the same advantages he enjoys in life, he concludes, "It's just the way things are, so it's no use feeling bad about [my advantages]." In the end, he has "no guilt about being able to do what I love and knowing that everything is going to work out." His certainty that everything will work out is a driving force behind keeping his future so uncertain at the moment.

With no parental, financial, or other pressures looming over him and unable to "tap into myself to move forward," he lacks motivation to make plans for his future. Leo believes that he is not that different from other privileged young people when it comes to being unmotivated. Although his affluent friends, for instance, have their lives figured out more than he does, "they aren't too pressed about much. Like me, they don't have real pressures to deal with that would make them more motivated." He insists, "Pretty much the only reason they have things sorted out more [than I do] is they're doing what everyone else does and I'm just not into doing that. I don't want to follow the masses and do what everyone is doing." On the surface, his friends seem more motivated because they have concrete future plans, but on a deeper level, Leo claims, "They're just like me and not really that motivated." He further explains, "People with privilege are less likely to be motivated because it's not required and they don't have anything on the line. It's not a 'do-or-die' situation like it is for those less fortunate, so they have to find their motivation elsewhere." From what he has experienced and observed in his immediate world, this lack of motivation is the fate of individuals born into privilege because "they never have to worry about supporting themselves or a family; they will always have a backup plan to fall back on." With a backup plan and no "real" pressures in life, he has yet to find a source of motivation "elsewhere" that requires him to begin planning his future.

With all the humility Leo can muster, he claims that he has extraordinary abilities to learn, and most often even master, whatever grabs his attention more quickly than most people. From past experiences, he also realizes that he has the drive and determination to achieve whatever goals he sets. This awareness of his strengths gives him confidence to believe that "there is really nothing to stop me, as long as I am motivated." He believes that he does not need a college degree or a job lined up through family connections to become successful. In his eyes, passion and a little self-motivation are all he needs to accomplish whatever he wants out of life. For now, he does not need a set plan for his future to be certain about his future success.

NOTES

1. Leo demonstrated an active resistance to school. For more discussion on the various ways in which affluent students contest the various forces imposed upon them in the schooling context, see Howard, 2008.
2. This rural community is not that different from other ones throughout the United States. Using the latest information provided by the U.S. Census Bureau, the Housing Assistance Council (2012) reports that the percentage of people living in poverty is higher in rural communities than any exurban or urban communities in the United States. Nearly one in six families in rural communities live in poverty.

3. For research on unequal funding and resources in schooling and a discussion on how this affects the overall quality of education, see, for example, Biddle & Berliner, 2002; Darling-Hammond & Post, 2000; Education Trust, 2001; Elliott, 1998; Ferguson, 1991; Harter, 1999; Kozol, 1991.
4. Students are generally referred to alternative programs if they are at risk of educational failure, as indicated by various risk factors including poor grades, truancy, and disruptive behavior (Quinn & Poirier, 2007). Barr and Parrett (2001) estimate that the number of alternative programs in the United States is about 20,000. Approximately 39 percent of public schools districts administer at least one alternative program for "at risk" youth. Districts with high minority enrollments and high poverty concentrations are more likely to have such programs (Kleiner, Porch, & Farris, 2002).
5. More specifically, Leo's family not only had to pay an annual tuition fee for him to attend a school outside their home district and provide transportation to and from school every day but they also needed to know how to access information about the available options for his education.
6. For one of the most cited studies on the effects of parental divorce on children before the age of six, see Wallerstein & Kelly, 1975. More recent publications consistently report similar conclusions of this earlier study.
7. For more discussion about how social class plays a role in these assumptions, see Mullen, 2010.

8 Olive

Creating Her Own Space

with Annie Chen

I guess I just feel like there is not that much freedom in my life.

The Westwood High School auditorium is overflowing with spectators who have come to watch the annual spring recital of the Underground Dance Company (UDC), a program that offers a wide-range of dance classes for all ages. The theme for this year's performance is "Hotel UDC," in which each class performs a routine that depicts employees or visitors at a hip-hop inspired hotel. The crowd collectively sighs with delight as the class of four-year-olds jumps and flips out the doors of a prop elevator and, one by one, burst out some freestyle moves. When the curtain drops, the entire auditorium erupts in shouts and applause.

When the curtain opens again, twenty mannequin-like adolescents, all dressed in black and purple with gold accents, stand frozen and the auditorium falls silent. The heavy thump of the music begins, rattling the hearts of everyone in the audience. After five beats, the stage lights flash on and the dancers come alive. Pounding, stomping, and clapping, they execute their routine with military precision. Although there are differences in gender, skin color, and body size and shape within the group, the dancers appear more similar than different on stage, making it difficult to distinguish one from another. Toward the end of the performance, they all line up from shortest to tallest, while the front dancer does a solo move and then falls away, leaving the girl behind her to take a turn. The final performer in line is tall and athletic, with black hair, pale skin, and bright blue eyes. She lunges at the crowd as if she were going to start a fight, drops on one knee, and ends with a tough glare and head nod. This is sixteen-year-old Olive.

Rap music pulses throughout the auditorium; the heads and feet of the audience bounce in time to the rhythm. Olive appears three times during the recital, dancing with the competitive cheer squad, her dance class, and the competitive dance team. To everyone watching the recital, she seems very much in her element each time she takes the stage. Her movements are those of a confident, skilled dancer. The intensity and attitude of hip-hop dancing seem to naturally pop from her limbs. On stage, she flawlessly takes on the persona of a fearless fighter. This character, however, is a far cry from her usual self.

When Olive leaves this hip-hop world, she becomes a courteous, polite, gentle young woman. She exudes the manners she first learned in the etiquette classes that her parents forced her to take before she started school and have reinforced repeatedly in her life since then. With an attentive posture and perfect eye contact, she usually remains a quiet presence around others. She rarely speaks unless spoken to or without reason, choosing instead to observe and listen attentively to the interactions of others. Even with family members and close friends, she finds whatever means possible to direct conversations in such a way that others are doing the talking and she is the one listening.

Because most people mistake her quiet presence for shyness, "everybody was kinda shocked that I liked [hip-hop dancing] so much and really got so into it." She discovered hip-hop when she and her family went to see one of her younger cousins dance in a UDC performance three years earlier. From the moment the first dancers took the stage that evening, she became fully engrossed by the performances. She explains, "I had never really heard hip-hop music before and never saw this kind of dancing." All of what she was witnessing—the music, performers, dance moves, and choreography—captured her interest. She claims, "I knew from that moment, it was going to be something that I was going to love and really want to do." Although ballet has been a facet of Olive's life for as long as she can remember, this form of dance seemed to offer "something that I'd been looking for, but I didn't know that I actually was looking for something like this before being exposed to it." After years of ballet training, she had lost nearly all interest in dance. "I was bored with taking the same dance classes and doing the same thing. I wanted to drop out a few times before [discovering hip-hop dancing], but my parents wouldn't let me," she explains.

With her passion for dance reignited, she convinced her parents to allow her to take lessons at UDC. In an effort to make sure that none of their children felt excluded, her parents also put Olive's three siblings in these classes. In the beginning, they took hip-hop dance lessons with her, but all three quit after one or two sessions. "My sister that is closest to me thinks it's inappropriate," Olive says with a smile, "She doesn't like the hip shaking. She's more into ballet. And my brother and other sister just weren't that into it from the start." Accustomed to doing activities with at least one of her siblings, it was a new experience for Olive to do something completely on her own. The athleticism and skills she had developed from years of ballet training allowed her to excel in this new form of dance rather quickly. Within two years, she became a member of two competitive dance teams and began representing UDC in competitions across the United States.

Olive's passion for this hip-hop style of dance is supported but not fully understood by most people in her life and especially her parents. Cherishing the fact that hip-hop dancing is *her thing* and not something she is made to do, she is "totally fine that people don't get why I love it so much." Her hip-hop dancing has become *the thing* that makes her different from the rest of her family. As such, she defends with every fiber of her being, whenever necessary, her choice to stay involved in this form of dance. Olive says, "Sometimes my parents threaten to take away dance if I don't have good grades or I say I don't want to do something they want me to do. I usually do what they say because I want to keep dancing." She wears modified recital costumes to meet her father's approval, even though she would prefer to wear what everyone else is wearing. She continues with her advanced study of the Japanese language, even though she has little interest in continuing to learn it. She continues with ballet training, even though she has found this form of dance "boring for several years now."

In the world of hip-hop dance, she finds an escape from her normal life, which is consumed by her parents' rules, standards, and expectations. Mainly consisting of school, Japanese language classes, ballet training, family, and church, her busy schedule leaves little time to express her individuality or to pursue her own passions and dreams. Through hip-hop dancing, she has managed to carve out her own space. Moving to the heavy beat of music is the only time that "I completely let go of anybody else's expectations and all the pressures [in my life]." Expressing a tough attitude through dance allows Olive to reveal something inside of her that largely remains hidden. Although her life does not reflect the content of the music she dances to, the lyrics and beat, in many ways, relate to her desire to break away from her current circumstances and appeal to her rebellious spirit. The words speak to her, and the movements give her a voice. While dancing, she feels focused, liberated, and full of energy.

Despite her quiet, unassuming presence, Olive exhibits this same focused confidence about what she wants to accomplish in life. She talks about college and success in her eventual career as if these were foregone conclusions. Yet she has no specific immediate plans for her future. She has not been given adequate space in her life to figure out the exact details of her future plans. She is very aware of what her parents want her to do, but "I'm pretty sure I'm not going to do everything they want [me to do]." Even though she may not know exactly what the future holds, Olive is absolutely certain that she will achieve what she wants out of life on her own terms.

A RESTRICTIVE LIFE

Olive rarely hangs out with anyone other than her family members. The only time she somewhat socializes with nonfamily members is during school hours and the time she spends in enrichment classes outside the schooling context. Even during these times, she mostly keeps to herself, typically avoiding the kinds of interactions necessary to establish meaningful relationships with others. Once in a great while she goes over to a friend's house in the neighborhood without any family members. Moments of going anywhere alone are so rare that "I could list them all in about a minute." Most often, Olive does not "even ask [my parents] for permission to go alone any place [because] I know they're not going to let me."

After recently rekindling relationships with a couple of childhood friends in the neighborhood, she is invited to a birthday party at her friend Jeanna's house, just three blocks from where she lives. Because Jeanna is one of her only friends, Olive really wants to go to her birthday party and finally builds up the courage to ask her mother for permission. Before making a decision, her mother needs to call Jeanna's mother to make sure there will be adult supervision at all times. When she calls, her mother discovers that this is a co-ed party. Although "she's not happy about boys being at the party also," her mother "knows [Jeanna's] mom pretty well and knows she would keep a close eye on everything." After some deliberation, her mother reluctantly gives Olive permission to go to the party.

Olive feels a little anxious about attending the party but does not allow that feeling to overshadow her excitement. Filled with these mixed emotions, she leaves her house without her phone, which goes against her parents' request that she keep her phone with her at all times. After a couple of hours at the party, she finally realizes that she left her phone behind, but "I didn't worry about it since I wasn't far [from home]." The party is everything that she hoped it would be. She is having "a blast" hanging out with Jeanna and making new friends. Although she is usually very quiet in social situations, she feels very comfortable after unexpectedly finding a lot in common with many people at the party, especially shared interests in rap music and hip-hop dancing. Olive pushes past her tendency to remain silent around others and is livelier than usual.

Around midnight, Jeanna asks her mother if she, Olive, and two boys could walk over to the park across the street from their home. The two boys have been flirting with Olive and Jeanna most of the evening and "we wanted some time not surrounded by tons of people." Because there is still plenty of light in the Alaskan summer evening sky and "her mom knew [the boys] since we were all little kids," Jeanna's mother gives them permission, much to their surprise. The four of them walk awkwardly around the neighborhood, brushing shoulders once in a while and discussing teachers, homework, and their dreams of the future. No hands are held. No kissing. When they make it back to Jeanna's house an hour later, one of the boys offers to give Olive a ride home. He is also giving rides to three other people, so it seems safe enough. When they arrive at her house, Olive immediately hops out, thanking him for the ride and apologizing for making him stop an extra time. He smiles at her, sheepishly tells her he was happy to do it, and waits while she fumbles with the combination to her garage door.

When she finally manages to get inside her home, it is close to two in the morning and she finds her parents waiting on the couch with her cell phone in front of them on the coffee table. They are clearly upset, but despite their anger, they realize that "it hadn't really occurred to them to give me a curfew 'cause I never went to a party before." Given that they had not given

Olive a specific time to be home, they express their disappointment in her "poor decision" to arrive home late but "didn't push that point any more." They take this opportunity to communicate very clearly their expectations about how late she should stay out in the future. They are, however, less forgiving about her being in a car with "an unknown boy 'cause they had told me over and over not to ride with anybody without their permission." Although Olive does not fully understand "what they were so worried about," she accepts, with no question, that "they were probably right about the situation and they had good reasons to be worried."

Olive rarely challenges her parents' decisions, expectations, and rules. Most often, she dutifully does what they tell her to do, but that does not prevent her from getting in trouble for making unintentional mistakes due to a mistaken understanding of their instructions. On the night of the birthday party, she simply forgot to bring her cell phone with her. It also never occurred to her what time to come home, because her parents never gave her a curfew, or that she did anything wrong by accepting a ride home. That evening, she made a series of honest mistakes. She almost never deliberately challenges her parents' authority even when she does not fully agree with them. Whatever disagreements she may have with her parents' rules, she has buried them so deep inside her that she is barely aware of them. In those rare moments when her differences of opinion begin to surface, she quickly pushes them down, accepting the notion that her parents know best and are always right. Without a doubt she believes that her parents are leading her in the right direction in life. She fully accepts that they make their decisions and establish their rules and expectations out of unconditional love and unwavering support.

Olive describes her parents as overprotective and talks about their parenting style in ways similar to what has been commonly referred to as *helicopter parenting*, where parents hover over their children and become too involved in their lives.[1] She claims, "My parents know where I am all the time. They're always there looking out for me and don't want anything bad to happen." Her mother, in particular, not only keeps track of her every move but is also often nearby. When her mother is not physically present, she is just a phone call or text message away. In fact, staying in contact with her parents is "pretty much the only reason I have [a cell phone]." She is allowed to text others, but her parents closely monitor her phone usage. They have access to and check her email often to make sure that language and subject matter are appropriate. They also monitor her online activity and do not allow her to participate in any social networking sites, such as Facebook.

Olive is allowed to communicate only with other girls when she texts, emails, and talks on the phone with someone other than her parents. In the past, her parents had said that she would be allowed to communicate more freely with boys and possibly even start dating when she turned sixteen. But when the time came, her parents had changed their minds and explained to her their belief that she was not mature enough to have more interactions with boys or to start dating. Although she is "sorta allowed to have a boyfriend," she can never be alone with a boy. Soon after turning sixteen, "I did sorta have a boyfriend, but we could only see each other at school and it just seemed kind of pointless. My parents won't let me be alone with a boy or let me go see boys outside school, so it's easier to just be friends." Olive has decided to "wait until I'm in college before I start dating and have another boyfriend. It'll just be easier if I wait until then."

Although she has more freedom in her interactions with girls, her friends must gain her parents' approval. She says, "My parents won't let me just hang out with anybody. They want me to be around people with the same values and who won't get me in trouble. They want to be positive that I'm not around anybody who's a bad influence, who'll drag me down." She further explains, "My parents have to know all my friends before they actually become my friend, and [they] have to know their parents also." Her parents have been successful in making sure that "everybody I hang out with is just like me and their families are just like mine." She points out, "Me and my friends don't get into trouble, [we're] really focused on our schoolwork and want to go to college later on; we're all really focused on our goals and the right things." There are some minor differences among her friends and their families, but "we all pretty much have the same values, Christian, go to the same church, vote for the same people since everybody's a Republican, nobody's divorced, live next to each other, and almost the same economically."

Olive rarely leaves the familiarity and comfort of being surrounded by people who are "pretty much alike in about every way," but when she does "I'm pretty much always with someone in my family or someone [my parents] know really well." When her parents are unavailable to drive her to and from school and activities, one of her aunts always accompanies her. Because she is the eldest of all her cousins and most members of her large extended family live within a mile of her home, she spends a considerable amount of her free time at their houses babysitting. Although she regularly babysits outside her home, her parents do not allow Olive and her siblings to be at home without adult supervision. When they go out of town or just out for the evening, one of their grandparents or aunts stays at their house. These moments, however, are rare because her parents "usually don't go anywhere without us" and she typically "can't go anywhere without them."

Olive's parents also maintain complete control over her schooling and activities by selecting her classes at school, lessons outside formal education, and extracurricular activities. As in choosing her friends, she gets "some say in the matter," but her parents ultimately make the decisions. As she explains,

> When I want to do something, me and my parents sit down and we talk, like when I wanted to take hip-hop lessons they listened to me.

They wanted me to stay in ballet, so they said that I could take those lessons if I stayed in ballet. I get some say, but it's mostly their decision about what classes I should take and what I should be involved in.

As with other aspects of Olive's life, she is allowed little freedom to make choices about her education or how she spends her time outside school.

Although Olive wishes that her parents would give her "more freedom" and "allow me to make more decisions," she says, "I think that I'm lucky they care about me so much. They're making sure I stay out of trouble and am going to be successful." For the most part, she understands their over-protective parenting style as demonstrating how much they care for her. She also believes that if they were not as protective, then "I wouldn't be where I'm at today and probably wouldn't be where I'm at in school." Given that she excels academically, has never suffered any traumatic or life-altering negative experiences and that she also avoids drugs and alcohol, she concludes that her parents must be doing what they need to be doing. She sees that her peers, with similarly protective and involved parents, are the ones in her honors classes who are headed toward a successful future. Conversely, her peers without overprotective parents "aren't doing that good in school, don't really pay close attention in school, aren't really making the best choices, and get in trouble constantly." Without as much direction from their parents, Olive believes, "These kids aren't as lucky as me and my friends [who have similar parents], since they probably won't achieve that much and end up not really being as successful [as we will be]." She may not fully enjoy her parents' level of control over her life, but she sees it as necessary for protecting her from harm and failure.

At the same time, however, she partially recognizes that her parents' overprotection has had some negative effects on her life, outcomes typical of helicopter parenting.[2] With limited opportunities to socialize and interact with peers, she has not developed close, intimate relationships with others outside her family. She explains, "I don't have a lot of friends and even the ones I have, I don't hang out with that much besides at school. I have to get good grades or my parents will take away dance, so I don't have much time for just hanging out with friends." Outside school hours, she spends a fair amount of time in her dance class with peers who share her passion for hip-hop. Even though she shares this significant common interest with them, "I'm not really friends with anybody at [UDC]. I mean, we don't live near each other and my parents don't know their parents so we're just friends in class, but that's it." Without significant peer relationships, she often feels incredibly lonely and isolated despite being constantly surrounded by family members and peers.

Olive also experiences some dissatisfaction with her life,[3] frustrated with limited opportunities for expressing her individuality and pursuing her own passions. At the moment, her only true interest is hip-hop dancing, but she questions whether "there is something else out there that I would love even more." With her restricted life, she has not had the kinds of experiences necessary to even begin answering this question. She compares her life to that of living in a confined space surrounded by four towering walls. Although she remains clueless to what lies beyond these walls, she holds a deep curiosity about the world outside her own. Whenever the opportunity arises, she pushes against these walls even though it often seems useless to do so. Once in a while, the walls seem to expand outward just slightly, providing a bit more of her own space in life and moving her closer to discovering the unknown.

ELITE LESSONS

Olive's parents have known each other their whole lives (or at least since elementary school). Both grew up just minutes away from where they live today. Although their families lived relatively close to one another, they grew up in dramatically different worlds, separated by the stark class differences that existed between their families. Her father grew up in a working-class family and her mother in an extraordinarily wealthy one. Olive is unaware of what specifically made their worlds so different but has been told that her mother "had more opportunities to experience things and didn't have to worry about things that much and dad had to work at a really young age and had a pretty tough time as a kid." Whatever home-life differences existed between her parents did not keep them from forming a quick bond when they first met at school. They became "pretty close friends" and shared the same social circle at school. The started dating in high school and then got married after graduating college.

From the very beginning, her parents assumed traditional gender roles in their marriage. Her father started his career in an entry-level position at the oil company where he now holds a senior management position. Although her mother also had the necessary credentials to begin a professional career, she has never worked outside the home. It was decided before they married that "my dad is the breadwinner and my mom stays at home to take care of us and house stuff." Although her mother has never directly complained to her children about not working outside the home, Olive feels that "my mom is a little embarrassed that she is the only [woman] in the family who doesn't work [outside the home] and [instead is] a stay-at-home mom." Her aunts have all built successful careers while being the primary parent for their children.[4] Olive reports, "Some things [my aunts] say to my mom, it's almost like they're telling her, 'I take care of my kids and have a job, why can't you? Why aren't you doing more with your life?'" By not working outside the home, her mother feels that members of her family, and especially her siblings, look down on her.

Even with some shame associated with choosing a different path in life than the other women in her family, her mother has taught Olive and her siblings throughout their lives to adopt traditional gender roles and behaviors. Whereas her parents are overprotective with Olive and her two sisters, they give her younger brother more autonomy. Olive claims, "It's like [my brother] has different parents than me and my sisters. He goes over to his friend's house without even asking and roams around the neighborhood as he pleases. [My parents] don't give him the same restrictions. He has way more freedom." She does not fully understand why her parents give her brother more freedom but believes it has something to do with them "not [being] as worried about him and his safety as they worry with us." Whatever their reasons may be for allowing her brother more autonomy, "[my parents] have different opinions about what's best for the girls versus the boy."

Along with placing different expectations on their children, her parents reinforce traditional gender roles and behaviors through gender-stereotypical activities. Olive explains,

> My brother always did typical boy kinds of things like playing hockey and football . . . [My parents] put me and my sisters in more girly kinds of things like ballet. [My sisters and I] could play sports too, but they put me in tennis, [which is] not as rough and physical as hockey.

Supplemented by their parents' lessons about gender-appropriate roles and behaviors, these activities have been incredibly important instructional spaces for Olive and her siblings in learning that males should be assertive and competitive whereas females should be more passive and supportive. As early as she can remember, Olive's parents have taught her to conform to prescriptive gender norms, mainly through their modeling of these norms and the activities they chose for her.

In addition to these lessons of gender, her mother was determined to teach her children the ways of knowing and doing that she learned growing up in wealth. Although Olive's family has been firmly situated in the upper middle class for almost her entire life, their financial circumstances pale in comparison to those of the extended family on her mother's side. Because their immediate family is "not quite as [financially] comfortable as my aunts and uncles and my grandparents," her mother wanted to make sure that Olive had the same opportunities and experiences as everyone else on her side of the family. She believed that the best way to bridge the gap was through educational experiences both within and outside the schooling context. Soon after she began walking, Olive started ballet training. Then she took etiquette classes to develop proper communication skills, social behaviors, and table manners. She also had lessons outside her formal education in art history and appreciation, opera, tennis, swimming, and piano, to name just a few. She visited museums and attended operas and other kinds of performances. Her family also traveled on a regular basis, giving her additional opportunities to experience new cultures. Since birth, Olive has participated in a seemingly endless succession of experiences to provide her with the knowledge and experiences that her mother associated with wealth.

When the time came for Olive to enter school, her parents had their eyes set on a prestigious magnet program, Academy of World Languages (AWL), at an elementary school outside their local district. They wanted her to attend not only for its reputation for being one of the best elementary educational programs in the city but also "because they wanted me to be bilingual." For her mother, knowing a second language was yet another quality she associated with wealth. Because AWL uses a lottery selection process, Olive's parents used connections for her to gain admission. In this dual-language program, students are taught literacy skills and content in English and one of five languages: Japanese, Spanish, German, Chinese, or Russian. Upon acceptance, students are offered a spot in one of the language tracks. Although Olive's parents preferred one of the other languages, she was assigned to the Japanese track. She reports, "Even with Japanese, they were still happy that I got into the program because they knew it was my best option and I would gain a skill that most people don't have." From kindergarten through middle school, she spent half of her school days taught in English and the other half in Japanese.

Most AWL students continue the program through high school, but Olive's parents believed "the high school program didn't really have a very good reputation and wasn't really rigorous enough." They worried that "I wouldn't be as prepared for college if I stayed in the program in high school." After nine years in the program, Olive started looking for something different in her education. Although she enjoyed her educational experiences at AWL and preferred staying in the program among familiar faces, "part of me was ready for a normal school, so I didn't really mind going to another school." But the decision of what school she would attend was not hers to make. When it was time for her to enter high school, her parents decided that she would transfer to Westwood High School, the public school closest to their home and the same school they had attended. With the school's reputation for educational excellence and its record of success in helping students gain admission to competitive colleges, they felt that this was the best option. They also "liked the fact that my uncle[5] teaches [at Westwood] and he could look out for me and make sure everything's okay." Leaving the only school she knew and her friends behind, Olive was incredibly sad about the move, but she ultimately understood why her parents made this decision.

However, she found two other decisions that her parents made in conjunction with her transfer less acceptable. Westwood offers five different academic programs outside the core curriculum: Fine Arts, Highly Gifted, International Baccalaureate, School through the Arts, and World Languages (which does not include a Japanese track). Olive explains, "These programs are like different little schools within the big one. [Westwood is] a really big school, so these break it down a lot so you get more individual attention from your teachers, and what you learn is more geared toward your interests." After discovering these programs, she wanted to enroll in the School through the Arts program so that she could focus on dance. Her parents, however, quickly nixed that option. She explains, "My parents said that it wouldn't look right on my college applications. They said that it would hurt me getting into a good college so they said no to that right away." She "begged and pleaded" with them, to no avail. They had already decided that she was going to enroll in the honors program and had not even given these "special programs" a second look.[6]

They also wanted her to continue her study of Japanese and made arrangements for her to take language classes at the local university. With approval from Westwood administrators, her parents decided, as Olive explains, "that I take classes at [Westwood] only in the mornings and then had to leave school every day after lunch." She was incredibly upset to have such a disruption in her class schedule. But she was given no other option; "I had to take Japanese, no choice about that." Unlike her response to her parents' decision to enroll her in the honors program, she resisted this one. "I told [my parents] at first that I wasn't going and if they made me then I wasn't going to try and I would fail out," she says. They responded harshly to her threat: "I was on restriction for a long time and they said that if I didn't take Japanese and do as well as I could do then I couldn't stay at [UDC]." Her parents were successful in quickly and effectively squashing Olive's unusual display of resistance.

At the beginning, Olive found Westwood to be a strangely different world. She explains, "It was so different than what I was used to, a lot more crowded and noisier." The size of the student body is not only larger than that of her elementary school but also more diverse. In many ways, Westwood reflects the integrated diversity of its surroundings. Class and race lines are seemingly blurred in this medium-sized city in Alaska. There are certainly wealthier and whiter neighborhoods within the city; Olive lives in one of them. But for the most part, class and racial divisions are not as clearly established as they are in other cities across the U.S. For instance, although several homes are valued at well above a million dollars in Olive's neighborhood, her family lives only a block away from several families living in extreme poverty. Like the other pockets in the city where the majority of affluent residents live, the realities of the economically disadvantaged surround her family and affluent neighbors. Situated within this integrated city and affected by the ways in which schools in Alaska are funded,[7] Westwood is a setting where "kids from really poor backgrounds who don't even have places to live are going to the same school with kids whose parents are multimillionaires . . . [and] most [of the student body] are minorities." Of the nearly sixteen hundred students, 47 percent are economically disadvantaged and 56 percent are students of color.[8]

This diversity, however, is virtually nonexistent in Olive's honors classes.[9] Student demographics take a noticeable turn in the honors program, where the vast majority of students are white and affluent. For most of the school day, students very much like Olive surround her; she is almost entirely separated from other Westwood students, seeing them briefly in hallways as she makes her way to classes, and in the cafeteria during lunchtime as she sits and socializes with other honors students. Even when she encounters students different from herself, she avoids associating with them. In fact, she barely even acknowledges their existence, keeping their circumstances and realities that are different from her own far removed from her daily life. Within this diverse context, she remains isolated from racial and class differences.

She was also isolated from others different from herself at her previous school. Although the school that housed the Japanese language magnet program was not as racially diverse as Westwood, the student body was fairly diverse when it came to social class. However, almost all students enrolled in that magnet program came from affluent families. Olive and her classmates spent most of their school days separated from nonmagnet students, encountering them only during lunchtime and recess. Because their classes were held in a separate wing of the school building, "it seemed like we were going to a different school than everybody else [outside the magnet program]." Although she was given opportunities, albeit limited ones, to interact with nonmagnet students, she stayed mostly in the social and academic enclave of her magnet program. As an honors student, she continues to attend what seems like "a different school" than that which most other Westwood students attend.

Olive remains isolated even within the honors program. Because she leaves school right after lunchtime almost every day, and engages in activities that take up most of her time outside school hours, "I feel like it really disrupts everything for me and doesn't really give me much time to just hang out, since I feel like I'm always going somewhere." With her busy schedule and her parents' restrictions on when and with whom she may socialize, Olive has not established meaningful relationships with anyone at school. Not having close relationships with her peers makes Westwood yet another lonely place in her life.

During lunchtime, she often pays little attention to what others at her table are discussing. As she is lost in her thoughts, she notices members of the track team sitting at a nearby table. She wistfully admires their visibly close bond with each other. As she watches them laugh and joke around, she imagines what it would be like to be a part of their group and to have such close friends who supported her. Because she has never experienced the sense of community and belonging among peers demonstrated within this group, she can barely envision what this would mean. Even as she daydreams about having such meaningful relationships at Westwood, she is quickly brought back to reality as she leaves the cafeteria to meet her mother, who is waiting outside the school's entrance to take her elsewhere.

TROUBLING UNKNOWN

Now that Olive and her three siblings are all teenagers or about to be, her mother has decided that it is time for their bedrooms to reflect their individual personalities. She sits down with her children to help them decide an overall theme and dominant colors for their bedrooms. In the end, Olive's two sisters decide on "a classic yet modern" theme, which according to Olive means, "their rooms have really light colors and look really girly." Her brother, who could not care less about what his room looks like, lets his mother pick vintage sports posters and paint the room light blue and his bedroom furniture navy blue. "It looks very boyish, so he liked it," she explains. When it comes time for Olive's room to be redecorated, "I wanted something completely different from them." Excited about the opportunity to create another space in her life that reflects her individuality, she wants her bedroom to look like UDC's dance studio with its royal purple walls marked with silver and black graffiti.

At first, her mother flatly refuses because she feels like "having the walls painted a dark color would make the room seem like a depressing little hole." In response to her mother's attempts to have her consider other options, Olive says with a shrug, "If I can't decorate it like I want, like you said I could, then I don't want anything to do with it." Both refuse to back down from their position on the matter for nearly a week. Finally, her mother budges a little and asks her to choose whatever colors she wants and that she will find a compromise. Olive also wants to find common ground with her mother. She explains, "I figured that my mom was right that it wouldn't be good to go with the dark colors, so I picked neon green and electric teal and wanted silver and purple graffiti." Olive shows her mother the exact colors on the Internet, and her mother reluctantly agrees to try and find something similar.

Their mutual willingness to find common ground, though, does not last very long after "my mom brings these samples from the paint store home to show me and they're completely different from what I showed her." Her mother's attempt to find something similar is "a complete fail." After other unsuccessful attempts at convincing Olive to choose alternative colors, "I was so over it by then."

"You only want me to have the same room as my sisters," Olive yells, "Why even pretend like you're giving me a choice?"

Her mother calmly replies, "That's not true. I want your room to reflect your personality, but I'm not having a room in this house look so different from everything else."

"You don't understand anything about me and what I want. You're just not listening to me," Olive responds in a lower voice. Her mother walks away without saying a word. The fight ends, as well as their plans to redecorate her room.

Several months later, her father takes Olive and her siblings on a camping trip the weekend before her birthday. While they are away, her mother decides to end the standoff with Olive and redecorate her bedroom. Despite wanting to make the room correspond with other rooms in their house, she ultimately decides to try her best to do what Olive really wants. Knowing that she will never quite understand her daughter's tastes, she enlists the help of her younger sister-in-law, asking her to buy the paint and choose whatever colors she thinks Olive would want. When her helper returns with the neon green and electric teal that Olive had requested in the beginning, her mother is taken aback but agrees to it. They spend the weekend furiously giving the room a makeover.

When Olive returns from the weekend and discovers her new room, she is ecstatic. It is exactly what she initially imagined: The walls and furniture painted with her color choices, purple comforter with black graffiti-like designs, and several blank canvases hanging on the wall ready for the graffiti that Olive will create with the three cans of sliver, teal, and purple spray paint sitting on the dresser. At that moment, Olive and her mother forget their earlier disagreements. She reports, "My mom liked how it turned out and I was happy that she actually did what I wanted and it reflected who I was and not something else." For Olive, this is a small yet important victory in her quest to express her individuality and set herself apart from the rest of her family.

Throughout her life, she has found similar opportunities to distinguish herself from her immediate family and those around her through minor acts of rebellion. By most standards, however, it would be difficult to consider her rebellious. She rarely disobeys her parents or other authority figures in her life. She meets her parents' expectations for her performance in school and activities outside the schooling context. While following the rules of her restricted life, however, she finds ways to carve out spaces and locate moments when she can disrupt and challenge her present circumstances.

In fourth grade, for instance, she found such an opportunity during her teacher's lesson on diverse holiday celebrations. Just before winter break, the teacher asked Olive and her classmates if any of them celebrated Hanukkah. Without hesitation, Olive raised her hand proudly. When the teacher asked some follow-up questions, she remained silent. "Thankfully, she didn't make me answer and just dropped it and went on with what she was teaching. I guess she thought I was too shy to speak in front of the class," Olive explains. That afternoon, her mom received an email from the teacher asking if she could send in a menorah and anything else Olive would like to bring to share with the class about their Hanukkah celebrations. Not sure what to think, her mother waited until dinner to bring up the email, asking Olive what her teacher meant, given that their family was not Jewish.

"I raised my hand when she asked if anybody celebrates Hanukkah," Olive clarified.

"Why would you raise her hand knowing that we're not Jewish?" she asked with a confused look.

Shrugging it off, Olive casually responded, "It seems more fun. And Aunt Lucy is Jewish, so I thought I could be too."

"You can't be Jewish. You're Christian," she responded firmly.

A look of deep disappointment came over Olive's face. "It never occurred to me before she said I couldn't be Jewish that I couldn't be what I wanted to be. This was really the first time that realization hit me. I was really upset when my mom told me this," she recalls. Sensing her disappointment, her mother ended the discussion with what she considered a compromise. "We'll go over to Aunt Lucy's house during their celebration and learn what they do," she informed Olive, who found this alternative "just okay." Her family ended up not going over to her aunt's house to join them in their celebration of Hanukkah that year. But shortly after this dinner conversation, Olive was pleasantly surprised when her Aunt Lucy gave her a menorah, candles, and a dreidel for Christmas. Since then, her family has gone to their house each year for one night of Hanukkah. With great satisfaction, Olive reports, "Every time we go over there I'm really happy. We wouldn't be celebrating with them if I hadn't raised my hand in that class [during fourth grade]. I'm proud that I made something like this happen."

Olive continues to be interested in converting to Judaism but will decide what to do after she leaves home. She no longer accepts what her mother said when she was nine years old. As she explains, "I know that I can [become Jewish] if that's what I decide, but just not now. So I know that I *can* do it, just *can't* while living at home. I'll have to wait 'til later." As she has gotten older, she has become increasingly convinced that Judaism makes more sense to her and reflects her own thinking and beliefs more than Christianity. She has no idea if she will ever muster the courage to oppose her parents' expectations and go through with the conversion, even when she no longer lives at home. For now she simply takes satisfaction in knowing that this is at least an option for her. Until she has more freedom to make her own decisions in life, Olive plans to keep this idea of possible conversion to herself.

Olive's urge to be different from her parents has grown stronger since she began taking hip-hop dance lessons. The freedom that she experiences in this form of dance provides her a sense of autonomy and a medium for expressing her individuality. She wants this freedom to spill over into the other spheres of her life. An increasingly dominant part of her wants to break away from all the restrictions shaping her everyday life, but she knows that most aspects of her life will not be liberated until she leaves home. As the time for her to leave home for college quickly approaches, she finds all the unknowns that she will inevitably encounter away from home both exhilarating and frightening. As she explains,

A big part of me can't wait 'til I go off to college and get to live on my own and see things that I don't even know exist. But another big part of me finds this all seems really scary; I'm going to be in a completely different place and nowhere near anybody I know. I don't even know if I'm ready for all this sudden change, but I try not to think about that too much and focus just on the positives.

She tries not to think too deeply about what lies immediately ahead of her because the troubling unknowns overshadow her excitement about discovering a world outside her own.

Even though she is still figuring out which college she wants to attend and what she wants to study, "I'll probably major in dance or something like that and go to college in New York, but I haven't completely decided everything yet." After graduating from college, she believes, "I'll probably become a dancer. But I want to teach dancing, not be a performer. I love to perform, but it's really hard to make any money as a performer. Dance teachers get paid by the hour, so that makes more sense. I can make more money that way." Olive claims, however, "Making money isn't my main goal, but I want to have enough to be comfortable in life. My main goal is to do something that makes me happy, that I'm really into and want to do." To a lesser extent, she also wants "to do something that helps others, to give back and help people that haven't had the same opportunities, those less fortunate." She realizes that "it's probably going to be really difficult" having a career that would allow her to live comfortably, do what she enjoys, and "to give back." In the end, "I'll be happy if I can eventually support myself by doing something that I love doing."

This does not necessarily mean that she will abandon her current intentions "to give back." As she explains, "If I can't help the less fortunate in my [eventual] job, then I'll do it when I'm not working." Throughout her life, her mother has taught her yet another lesson about what it means to be wealthy by reinforcing the idea that a responsibility to help those who are "less fortunate" comes with their wealth. Olive did not really learn this lesson until she had an experience in sixth grade that made her aware not only of the disadvantages of others but also of her own advantaging circumstances. She recalls,

> There was this girl who sat near us at lunch. She always had a hot lunch. One day, she stopped having lunch and after a couple of days I asked her why. She said that her mom didn't get paid for another week, so she couldn't have lunch until then. I told my mom about it, and after that my mom made sure she had lunch money. I remember that was the first time I realized that some people don't have food and that those people go to my school. They aren't just, like the homeless people downtown; they're right next to me.

After that experience, Olive started paying attention to the social and economic differences around her. "I know those differences were around me before, but it was like I never saw them until I finally noticed them. And then [those differences] were everywhere," she remembers.

With her mother's previous lesson about the responsibility that comes with wealth making more sense after this experience, "I wanted to find ways that I could help out other kids that didn't have money for lunch." Soon after, she began holding a bake sale in her neighborhood to benefit a local charity that provides free school breakfast and lunch to economically disadvantaged students. She baked and called her friends and relatives to donate goods to sell for the fundraising event. "We didn't make a lot of money, but that didn't matter because it felt good helping others that aren't as lucky as I am." Every year after that, Olive organized a bake sale to raise money for this cause; the sale has become one of the largest annual events in her neighborhood. She plans to continue doing this kind of charitable work throughout her life. Although she has not developed meaningful relationships with "those less fortunate" at school and in her community and may never have these relationships in her life, she wants to help them nonetheless.

Because her parents repeatedly emphasized the value of helping disadvantaged people, they are pleased that she has adopted this value and that her future plans include a commitment to charitable acts. They are, however, less satisfied with her plans to pursue her interest in dance at a college that may well take her far from home. Olive claims,

> They're more unhappy about the fact that I'll be moving so far away; they'd prefer that I go to a school on the West Coast or somewhere closer. And they never understood why I love dance. They would be happier if I focused on ballet or more classical dance, but they know that I don't want to do that since I love modern dance. So they aren't happy, but they're leaving it up to me.

Although her parents want her to attend a good college, Olive believes that they do not care, to a certain extent, what she ends up studying when she gets there. Earning a college degree and building a successful career are not their main hopes and dreams for her future. Above everything else, they want her to find a good husband who will provide her and her future children with the privileged lifestyle to which she is accustomed. In other words, they want her to follow in her mother's footsteps.

Even though Olive wants something completely different, she somewhat fears that she will end up reliving her mother's life, returning eventually to the restricted world that she wants to escape. With a limited view of what lies ahead, too many troubling unknowns exist for her to be completely certain that this is not her fate. She desperately hopes to escape this fate, but if she does not, "It'll be because that's what I wanted and what made me happy." She knows with absolute certainty that she will achieve the happiness and freedom she wants out of life. Most often, fears of reliving her mother's life quickly fade. At least at the moment, her urge to break away from her current circumstances, so she can create her own version of her future self, seems too strong to be overpowered by anything or anyone, including her parents.

NOTES

1. The phrase "helicopter parenting" has been used mostly in popular media but increasingly also in scholarly works to describe a phenomenon of a growing number of parents in the United States who are obsessed with their children's success and safety, vigilantly hovering over them, sheltering them from mistakes, disappointment, and risks, insulating them from the world around them (e.g., Gibbs, 2009). Researchers have found that affluent parents adopt this parenting approach more than low-income parents. For more discussion on the relationship between social class and the helicopter parenting approach, see Nelson, 2010.
2. Disagreement exists in popular and scholarly works on the consequences of helicopter parenting. Some authors and researchers argue that in today's culture and economic downturn, helicopter parenting ensures productive adolescent development. Aucoin (2009) argues, "Some researchers have begun to argue that late adolescence and young adulthood are such minefields today—emotional, social, sexual, logistical, psychological—that there are valid reasons for parents to remain deeply involved in their children's lives even after the kids are, technically speaking, adults." Although several have heralded the benefits of this parenting approach, most scholars and authors argue that it leads to negative outcomes in children, including higher levels of depression and anxiety. Several studies also suggest that children of helicopter parents are more likely to feel less competent and less able to manage life and its stressors (e.g., Schiffrin et al., 2013). Although the debate over the consequences of helicopter parenting is fairly new and ongoing, most argue that these and other negative outcomes outweigh any potential positive effects.
3. For several years, Olive has received treatment for depression and anxiety. She did not want to discuss her depression and anxiety during the interviews. For ethical reasons, we did not ask her additional questions about a subject that she did not want to discuss further. She only felt comfortable enough to disclose that she has received and continues to receive mental health treatment.
4. Even though her aunts are gainfully employed outside the home, it is important to emphasize that they still take on the role of primary parent. Therefore they continue to assume, at least in part, prescriptive gender roles.
5. Given that she previously described the careers of her mother's siblings and their spouses as high paying and high status, it is important to note here that she is referring to an uncle on her father's side of the family.
6. The honors program is outside the Highly Gifted special program.
7. The funding for the majority of public schools in the United States comes from three levels: local, state, and federal, in that order. On average, the federal government adds less than 10 percent to local education budgets. Funding from the federal and state governments typically makes up less than half of the funding. Most funds are provided through local taxes, which explains why there are large differences in funding between wealthy and impoverished communities (Anyon, 2005; Education Trust, 2001; Kozol, 1991). However, Alaska is one of the very few states where the majority of funding

for public schools comes from the state, in order to avoid the extreme funding inequalities that would occur if the state used the traditional model for school funding. Several remote, sparsely populated school districts in Alaska incur significant costs, owing to their isolation and extreme climate, which are dissimilar to other districts. These districts are also located in the state's poorest communities. It would be impossible for these school districts to fund their public schools with the low amount of revenue generated from local taxes. The state, therefore, provides appropriate funds to all school districts to maintain equitable funding for all.

8. More specifically, the student body is made up of 15 percent Asian American, 13 percent Latino/Latina, 11 percent bi/multiracial, 10 percent American Indian/Alaska Native, and 7 percent African American.

9. This lack of diversity in honors classes is not unique to Westwood. Numerous research studies have found that even when students attend heterogeneous schools, the results of tracking show that students of different social classes do not have the same opportunities for learning (e.g., Anyon, 1997; Apple, 2001; Oakes, 1985). More specifically, low-income students are overrepresented in low-status courses and underrepresented in high-status ones (e.g., Brantlinger, 2003).

9 Jacob
Dancing through Life

with Kelsey Cromie

Dancing is my escape. It takes me to a place where I can go and be myself without having to be criticized or told what to do.

From the moment seventeen-year-old Jacob enters the stage, he carries with him an air of confidence, grace, and strength. When his dance performance begins, the energy immediately changes throughout the auditorium as his body eloquently communicates what he wants to share tonight in his two-minute solo. Through his contemporary style of dance, he tells the audience a story about his built up frustration and anger toward the "closed" world of dance he is forced to reckon with. Although the common belief is that this world is accepting of nonnormative gender expression, he warns others that this is a "dangerous misconception." As he explains, "When it comes to dance performance, males *must* perform in a manly manner and females must be feminine." He believes that the restrictive gender roles in the larger society dictate the norms within the dance world, leaving no room for an effeminate male persona. Male dancers must "act how society tells you that you should; act like a man."

Jacob's performance mostly conveys the conflict he experiences in challenging traditional gender roles. His emotions produced by this conflict are brought out by his big swipes of arms, kicks, fists, arches, and jumps. His toe slides to the floor show a moment of hesitation and giving in, but they quickly give way to his continued struggle. He lashes out and lets his anger explode. The end of his dance contrasts with the more contained movements at the beginning as he swirls around the stage with clenched fists, dropping to the floor and breathing heavily on the ground. The sequence of his movements communicates his inner struggle and the anger building up inside. He never resolves this inner turmoil in the performance because his struggle will continue throughout his life. When Jacob is no longer dancing, the stage goes dark, the music stops, and a controversial statement from Nigel Lithgow, executive producer of the television show *So You Think You Can Dance*, appears on a large screen in back of the stage: "You are the reason fathers don't want their sons to dance."

Jacob's performance was part of the International Schools Activities Conference (ISAC) annual cultural event, which showcases student performances from international schools located in six different Southeast Asian countries.[1] Beforehand, students compete to be one of the two students selected from their schools to perform at the event. Although Jacob has only been dancing for a little over two years, he won a spot. He began dancing shortly after his family moved from the United States to Malaysia, when his father became the chief operating officer of one of Asia's largest companies. Unlike his previous schools, his school in Malaysia, the Southeast Asia International School (SAIS), offers an extensive dance program. He initially joined the program to find his artistic home in this new, unfamiliar context, but then "it didn't take long for me to figure out that dance is just my passion." As he further explains, "When I perform, it's this kind of otherworldly feeling that it's so much joy. Even if I'm bleeding or if like I'm tired beyond belief, I'm just so thankful that I actually get a chance to be able to do what I love." Although he loved dancing, he was not very good at the beginning, especially in comparison to most of his peers, who had been dancing since early childhood. Soon, Jacob began to take additional classes outside school and spent summers training in New York. Because of these experiences and his natural talent, he quickly became the most talented dancer at SAIS.

A couple months before the ISAC cultural event, students in the dance program were instructed to choreograph a performance that expresses a word summarizing how society viewed them. Without much hesitation, Jacob chose the word *effeminate* to express not only his understanding of how others see him but also his frustration about the restrictive gender boundaries within his immediate world. Although mostly accepted as an openly gay male at his school, he feels that he must act "manly" to be fully accepted by others. Because he resists conforming to male gender norms, he often finds himself "in these tiring situations where I can't be my true self and feel all this pressure to become this certain way." He rarely caves in to this pressure but never really expresses how he feels about it. Through dance, he decided to break his silence. In the event program, Jacob included a brief artist statement about his performance: "I am the male, *feminine* you might say. I want to dance the girl's part but I am not allowed. I'm tired of being guarded and want to be accepted for who I am without compromise." Prioritizing the performance over his academics, he spent weeks choreographing and then rehearsing a two-minute performance that would powerfully and effectively convey this statement. In the end, his hard work paid off. Echoing the feedback that he received from several others, his dance teacher told him, "There wasn't one person there who wasn't moved [by your performance]."

Although Jacob uses this performance to express something that he cannot quite communicate verbally, he often has "no filter when I talk, well I think before I talk, but I just say what's on my mind most of the time." He claims that his experiences growing up in different parts of the United States and now living abroad, to some extent, have made him confident enough to be so open and honest around others. "Moving so much I've been the new kid at school I don't know how many times. At first, it was hard adjusting to new places, but then I just got to a point where I said, 'fuck it, I'm just going to be myself,'" he explains. But more important than these experiences, Jacob's confidence has emerged from the fact that he is different from most others around him. He claims, "I'm an odd child. Since I'm different from other kids, I either had to be comfortable with that or go hide in a corner. I decided to be comfortable with who I am."

Although being gay certainly makes him feel different, he claims that other aspects of his identity equally set him apart from most people in his immediate world. Until he moved to Malaysia, he attended schools and lived in wealthy suburban communities where he was one of the few students of color and the few non-Christians. His mother is originally from Venezuela and his father from Iran. Because of his mixed race heritage, as Jacob explains, "I'm technically biracial but I don't really consider myself that way." Culturally influenced more by his mother's side of the family and "'cause that's what I look like," he identifies as Latino. When it comes to religion, however, "I had no choice in that. My mom is Catholic, but I had to be Muslim because that's what my dad is." Although his parents hold different religious beliefs, they both emphasize the importance of "religious values and staying true to religion, like not doing anything that would be bad in the eyes of God." Quite opposite from his parents, Jacob does not "really follow any faith right now 'cause I'm trying to see what I believe in." Even though he is figuring out his religious beliefs, culturally he identifies as a Muslim.

Currently situated in much more diverse contexts than when he lived in the U.S., he remains different from others around him. As he points out, "Me being [Latino and Muslim] I'm not just sort of your everyday white boy, you know, like your typical WASP American." He is quite happy that he has managed to carve out his own separate identity in the contexts he currently occupies. Although he is distinguishable in almost any context as a gay Muslim Latino, these characteristics alone are not what set him apart from others. Jacob puts a great deal of effort and energy into making sure that he is different. He is not, however, trying to be different only for the sake of being different but instead primarily to be himself.

SHATTERED IDEAS OF FAMILY

Over spring break, Jacob travels to London on a school-sponsored trip. Without much adult supervision, he spends the week "going around the city and doing typical touristy stuff and living it up with my friends." He enjoys the week just hanging out and relaxing with his friends, having freedom from his normal responsibilities and, more importantly, being independent from any parental supervision. While in London, his parents, two older brothers, and uncle spend the week vacationing at his family's beach house on the Florida Coast. This is where Jacob's family goes whenever possible. Their beach house is "sort of my family's retreat from normal life."

Toward the end of the week, one of his brothers gathers the family to tell them that Jacob is gay. Just a few weeks before, Jacob came out to his brother looking for support. As he explains,

> I told him because I needed him to help and his support. I was in a relationship with a guy who was a complete dick. I was being bullied mercilessly at school by this group of assholes, getting beat up and called names and harassed. I came to him and thought he would be there for me.

But Jacob held a mistaken view of how his brother would respond to his plea for help. Instead of supporting him through this difficult time, his brother began treating him very much like those who were tormenting him at school. Even though his brother had a negative reaction, he did worry about Jacob's safety and decided "to out me to the rest of family because he told me that 'I wanted to protect you.'" His brother's news hit the rest of the family "like a ton of bricks, because they never suspected [that I'm gay]."

A couple days later, Jacob's father and two brothers pick him up at an airport about a two-hour drive from their home. Shortly after picking him up, his father begins repeating over and over, "We know about you." At first Jacob has no idea what he is referring to, but then he glances over at his brother and everything starts piecing together. He recalls, "I had that moment of realization, 'Oh shit, my brother told my parents.'" Not knowing how to respond, Jacob remains silent. His father continues, "We know about you." Intermittently, he asks, "Do you think you're making a good decision?" Without giving Jacob a chance to respond, he asserts, "This is a family decision."

When they arrive home, his parents call a family meeting to discuss what they repeatedly refer to as, "the situation" because, as Jacob explains, "they couldn't even say the word *gay*." At the gathering, his parents and two brothers initially take turns blaming themselves for "making" him gay. His mother claims she babied him too much as child because he is the youngest. His father wishes that he made Jacob play "manly sports," the kinds of sports that his straight brothers played all their lives. His brothers fear that their playful wrestling when they were younger was too homoerotic. They soon stop taking responsibility and place the blame entirely on Jacob for making "the wrong decision about my life." By the end, his parents develop a plan for helping him make better decisions or, in other words, a plan to change his sexual orientation. They pull him out of all activities and closely supervise his actions "to make sure I wasn't acting gay."

For the next two weeks, "it was unbearable. [My parents and I] were constantly arguing. They were controlling my every move." To avoid the "complete and utter hell" at home, he stays late at school, arriving home hours after the school day ended. When he finally comes home, he goes directly to his room where he stays until he leaves for school the next day. After several weeks of this routine, his mother informs him, "You're not talking to the family anymore so we're going to therapy." Initially, Jacob is relieved to hear this because he thinks, "great, therapy is going to help us talk through things that we needed to and going to improve the situation and sort out problems." His mother further informs him that she has scheduled their first session and that the entire family will be there, including his oldest brother who attends college in another state.

As Jacob enters the therapist's office, he notices a crucifix hanging on the wall and a Bible on a side table. He thinks, "It's like weird to be this obvious about your religious beliefs in this kind of setting." Jacob is confused further when the therapist begins by leading them in prayer. "Is this how people normally begin therapy sessions?"

After the prayer, the therapist asks Jacob, "Do you know why we're here today?"

"Because I'm gay," he anxiously replies because he uses **the word** that the rest of his family has avoided saying out loud for several weeks.

In a raised voice, the therapist responds, "Yes, of course that is the root of the problem. But we're also here because you're disappointing your entire family. Do you know how much you're hurting them?"

Not knowing how to respond, Jacob sits quietly and remains so for the rest of the session. He recalls, "It was like I didn't know how to react. It was too confusing to make sense of what was going on. And it wasn't like anyone was giving me a chance to talk. They were just yelling at me." For the next hour, Jacob listens to his family members share how his "decision" hurts and disappoints them. After what seems like an eternity for him, the session ends as it began—with prayer.

Only Jacob and his parents attend the subsequent therapy sessions. And like the first one, he rarely gets an opportunity to speak. With each session, his confusion about what is happening increasingly turns to frustration and anger. Eventually he reaches a point where "I had it. I said to myself, 'enough is enough, I can't go through this shit anymore.'" Incensed, Jacob decides to do some background research on the therapist and discovers that he heads an ex-gay organization and does not have the proper credentials or license for mental health practice.[2] It takes a few days for this information to sink in fully, but when it does, Jacob decides he will do whatever it takes to end therapy. He says, "I just couldn't believe it. My parents were making me go through ex-gay therapy without telling me that this was what all this was about. I wasn't about to play their game." He waits until their next session to unleash his fury. He interrupts the therapist during beginning prayer, discloses what he has discovered, and then lets out what has been pent up for weeks. For several minutes, he and the therapist engage in a shouting match. His parents are mostly bystanders, too shocked at what is occurring to speak. But they eventually intervene when the therapist looks like he is about to strike Jacob. His parents end the session and take him home.

Shortly after this, Jacob falls back into his old routine of staying late at school to avoid interacting with his family. He mostly keeps busy preparing for the end-of-year drama showcase of student-produced one-act plays. With three friends he rehearses a play that he has written about "typical high school life." At the showcase, his other classmates, parents, and even his drama teacher find out what the play is actually about. Jacob plays a sexually confused student, struggling with homophobic bullying at school and an abusive home life. In front of his parents and a few hundred other people, he plays the main character in a play about his own life. For Jacob, the play is the "ultimate payback for putting me in ex-gay therapy." He knows that he has done what would hurt his parents the most—publicly embarrass them. He stays the night at a friend's house so he can avoid seeing them later that night. His mother tries to reach him by phone, but he does not answer.

When Jacob returns home the next day, he finds that his belongings are scattered across his bedroom and immediately notices that some of his clothes, jewelry, pictures, and books are missing. He goes downstairs to ask his mother what happened. She informs him that she threw away anything that "looked gay," insisting, "I'm your mother and I know what's best for you." Jacob storms to his room and begins packing clothes and other essentials. "I just didn't feel safe at home. I felt like I was going to do something that I was going to regret, so I needed to get out of there," he explains. Coping with recurring suicidal thoughts for the past few months,[3] he worries that he is going to hurt himself if he does not leave. After packing a couple duffle bags, he walks out the front door unnoticed. He finds a place for the night and then leaves his mother a voicemail to let her know that he is not coming home for a few days.

He attends school but stays in the counseling office to avoid running into his brother and others who would tell his parents that they saw him. After three days of staying at different friends' houses, he finally talks to his mother on the phone. She tells him that she needs him home "to avoid embarrassing the family." His father's work friends are coming over to dinner and she does not want them to suspect that anything is wrong. Jacob agrees to return home and "put up a good appearance for everybody's sake." When he arrives home, his mother "unleashes on me. She is yelling at me, telling me that I'm grounded and I won't be allowed to go anywhere." He ignores most of what she is saying while making his way to his room. Just before he is out of earshot, she informs him, "By the way, your dad accepted the position in Malaysia. We're moving there." Jacob closes the door to his room and tries to keep his composure as he gets ready for the dinner party.

Jacob describes the aftermath of his family's discovery that he is gay as "hell year." During that period of his life, Jacob reports, "I had no time to do any schoolwork and I wasn't home most of the time, so my GPA went from a 3.9 to a 2.7. I was seriously depressed and couldn't get out of [my depression]. My whole world turned upside down." Although this period was incredibly difficult, he stresses,

> I'm kind of happy I went through that hell year because it made me who I am today. It made me optimistic and I've kind of looked at everyone in the way that you can't judge them for who they are. My parents come from very religious backgrounds, so I don't look at them for what they put my through, because that's all they know and been exposed to. I accept that they're probably not going to change and that's who they are and I don't want them to change me for who I am so I probably shouldn't try to change them.

When he emerged from the emotional turmoil of hell year, Jacob had formed different understandings about his family. As he explains, "The idea that family is always here for you was shattered. I no longer could rely on them, which, up to that point, I always took for granted that they would be there no matter what—that's what family is supposed to be about, I thought." He previously thought of his family as "loving and caring, being supportive, giving me unconditional love." He now understands that this was not "a complete picture of what [my family members] are really like."

Jacob claims that his parents' goals and dreams of him changed after they learned that he is gay. As he explains, "My dad wanted me to be a doctor and then, after he found out and all that, he goes 'okay, just be something manly,' and I was like, 'no, fuck you, I'm going to be a dancer.'" He says that his parents "kind of just gave up in general on what they had imagined for my life." According to Jacob, their only concern became about him "staying in a high social class, like they want me to do something later on that will give me money." Although he wants to eventually make enough money to live independently from his parents and be comfortable, he claims, "I don't really care too much about being well off; I'd just rather do something that makes me happy and that I love." Although his parents abandoned their hopes and dreams for his life, they still "kind of clash heads" on what lies ahead for him.

Soon after moving to Malaysia, Jacob's home life became more tolerable. His parents' way of dealing with "the situation" was "just to ignore it and hope I would change." Not talking about him being gay, they rarely argued. About a year ago his mother began surfacing the subject of his sexuality in their conversations, giving some indication that she had become slightly more tolerant. Jacob claims that she is in "that awkward stage of beginning to accept my gayness . . . where she asks stupid questions." When he recently went to the doctor for an annual physical, for instance, "She asked me, 'Are you going to get horny when the [male doctor] sticks his finger up your butt?' It was way over the top." Although her questions about his sexuality often embarrass him, he answers them as openly and honestly as possible. For Jacob, her questions give some indication that she is beginning to accept him for who he is.

ESCAPING FROM HOME

A photo of Jacob's family appears in the main city newspaper just before their first Christmas living in Malaysia. In their upscale hotel penthouse, his family is gathered around a Christmas tree, hanging light-colored ribbons and ornaments. In the background, his father stands on a stepladder placing a gold star atop the tree. Everyone is smiling and laughing. The description below the photo capturing this moment simply reads, "bonding time." The article begins by describing how they are acclimating to their new surroundings while maintaining their cultural heritage and family traditions during the holidays. It then quotes family members explaining what Christmas means to them. His parents and second oldest brother, who lived in Malaysia for their first year, emphasize the importance of family. Being the youngest, Jacob is the last to be quoted: "For me, it's about spending time with people you care about and cherishing the time spent together." The article ends with his father recounting the family's time spent at a soup kitchen giving out meals to the poor and homeless and donating to various charities.

As they appear normally to the outside world, the article depicts a picture-perfect family. Jacob, however, is successful once again in providing a small light into reality. In his quote, he intentionally refers to "people you care about" instead of "family" to disrupt the notion that "we're just a happy family who love spending time with each other." As he further explains, "It wouldn't be honest to say that I like spending time and being around them, since I don't, even [at the holidays]." To most readers, his choice of words is too subtle to even notice that he did not refer to his family directly. Jacob knows that he cannot disrupt his family's public appearance too much. He is completely content with his action going unnoticed because "I was honest with myself and that's what mattered."

Although Jacob does not want to spend time with his parents and brothers, he still needs family-like relationships in his life, ones that are built "on unconditional love, support, helping you maintain a balance, [and] being there for you." Driven by this need, he formed a "chosen family"[4] during hell year with four friends who were experiencing similar troubles at home. They quickly became the integral foundation for support, survival, success, and love in Jacob's life. As he explains, "I don't really know how to explain our level of closeness. It's . . . , I don't know, it's like they're just people I want to have in my life. Because I don't want my family that much, they kind of balance out my life." He refers to these four friends as his *epiphinistas* "because when we were eating at this diner one day, I had an epiphany that I love them more than I love Lady Gaga, which is a big deal!" From that moment on, Jacob claims, "They are my real family." Because his epiphinistas all live in the U.S., Jacob rarely sees them in person. They manage to maintain a close relationship "through Skype, text, email, whatever it takes to keep in touch."

Although Jacob's relationship with his parents improved after moving to Malaysia, he continues to avoid being around them whenever possible, even to the point that he moved out of their penthouse to an adjacent apartment two years ago. But they have complete access to his apartment and make him share what they call "quality family time" each evening, which mostly consists of "us eating dinner either at home or we go out and talk about what happened that day." He goes on to say, "Thankfully it doesn't last that long. My dad is usually too tired and wants to go to bed." After dinner, he heads back to his apartment and, most often, does not see his parents until the next evening. Even with this limited interaction with his parents, "I don't want to be [at home] and find some way not to be there." Most nights he waits until he knows his parents are asleep and then goes out with his friends to nightclubs.

He arrives to school on most mornings hung over from the night before. At seventeen, he is under the legal drinking age but reports, "if you're a westerner they don't care; as long as you have money and you can afford the drinks, they don't really care how old you are." Given how often he frequents nightclubs, Jacob's weekly allowance "doesn't even come close to covering how much it costs to go out." To make up the difference, he sneaks into his parents' bedroom to take another $200 to $500 from their safe on a weekly basis. He explains, "I have a money situation because my parents don't tend to give me a lot. Thankfully I know the password to their safe, so it's easy for me to go out and go shopping and all that." He does not feel guilty for stealing money from his parents because "I need [the money] to escape the bullshit [at home]. I need to go out and paint the town lights purple and be someplace where I can be myself."

Nightclubs allow Jacob to escape the realities of home, but no place compares to his school. He feels safest and most comfortable being himself while at SAIS because, as he explains, "It's an open campus, and if you're gay people just accept you here. I'm loud, outgoing, and more who I am." What makes SAIS so accepting is that an individual's differences "are like no big deal here. Everybody's different, so it's kind of hard saying you need to be this one way when there isn't really just one way to be here." The community at SAIS is very diverse in most respects, especially in comparison to Jacob's previous schools. It is an international school at which twenty-six different nationalities are represented and twenty-one different languages are spoken[5] in Jacob's class alone. Overall, students come from sixty-two countries, with approximately 23 percent of the little over six hundred students from the United States. The SAIS community is made up of multiple nationalities, cultures, and religions and is also somewhat diverse when it comes to sexual orientation.

SAIS takes pride in the fact that their students come from places all over the world and diverse backgrounds, but as at most other elite private schools, there is little diversity when it comes to social class.[6] With the highest tuition of any school in the city and limited financial aid available to offset costs,[7] almost all SAIS students come from wealthy families. Because it is regarded as the most prestigious school, students' families are some of the most politically and socially powerful as well as wealthiest in the city of over 7 million people. This extraordinary amount of wealth and power makes SAIS not nearly as inclusive or diverse as school officials and others in the community claim and possibly want it to be. As an elite private school primarily for wealthy expat students, SAIS is, by its nature, an incredibly exclusive community.[8] The school's exclusive character is immediately evident to the outside world. A security team stands guard at the entrance to the school around the clock, screening everyone before admitting them and searching every car that enters campus for explosive devices. Everyone inside, including students and teachers, wears an identification badge to show that she or he belongs there. The tight security procedures are just some of the visible indications of how exclusive this community is. SAIS's exclusive character is partly what makes this a comfortable environment for Jacob. He has spent most of his life in affluent communities, isolated from the rest of the world. He, therefore, finds the wealthy community of SAIS, separated from its surroundings, comfortably familiar.

At the same time, Jacob has found the unfamiliar aspects of SAIS even more important in feeling safe there. Far more diverse than his previous schools, SAIS has provided him with opportunities to become more "accepting toward all different cultures, ethnicities, nationalities, races, and people in general." Becoming more accepting allowed him to form meaningful relationships with his peers that he would not have otherwise formed as he broadened "who I considered my friends, and that's been amazing. I found people who accept me for who I am because I accept them." In many ways, his acceptance of others has been important in accepting himself more. "I always felt alone and that gets tiring after a while. I now have an amazing friend group—not just friends who don't live near me—and that's, in a weird way, been really, really helpful. I'm not as depressed because I have accepted that this is who I am and they helped with that," he explains. Through his meaningful relationships with peers, he finds support and acceptance that he does not get at home.

ADVANTAGED CIRCUMSTANCES

Water gushes down the hill flooding the trails. Jacob and his classmates are slipping and sliding, barely able to make it down. When they finally reach the bottom, they discover that the shallow river they waded across earlier is raging and much deeper. "It was a little stream when we were going up. I mean, we barely got our feet wet," Jacob recalls. They have no other choice; they must cross the river to make it back to their campsite. After some deliberation, the tour guide comes up with a plan. He ties one end of a rope to a tree and then crosses the river to secure the other end to a second tree so that the students and teachers can use the rope to pull themselves across the river. Jacob volunteers to be one of the first to cross the treacherous water. "I could feel my heart racing. I was nervous as hell but I just wanted to get it over with." When he reaches the other side, he looks down and discovers that a few leeches have attached themselves to his feet and legs. Flailing his arms and legs in all directions, he starts "freaking out and didn't want those things on me, but I didn't know how to keep them off." The tour guide is too busy assisting the others to help Jacob. He finally calms down enough to pick them off and throw them as far away as possible.

It takes nearly three hours for the rest of his classmates and teachers to make it safely to the other side. By the time they reach the campsite, the rain has stopped but "everybody's wet and [we] have no way of getting dry. It was just a yucky night; all of us are cold and miserable." Gathering around a fire to get warm, a teacher asks the students what they learned today from their experiences. One of them quips, "Don't try to start up a hill in rainy season." Another adds, "And when it starts raining, then make sure not to spend another two hours on top of a mountain." Students take turns complaining about their adventure today. The teacher finally interrupts them to emphasize the important life lessons they should have learned about teamwork and community. The students listen half-heartedly at first to her impromptu lesson but soon go back to moaning about what Jacob considers to have been "their near-death incident" earlier that day.

Every year at SAIS, groups of around twenty students and two teachers go on a Global Action Program (GAP) trip to a neighboring country to live and work together for a week of service outreach, cultural immersion, and outdoor adventure. It is a week of hands-on opportunities intended "to deepen students' understanding of the region and grow through service opportunities, all the while discovering more about themselves and their individual strengths."[9] Two months after enrolling at SAIS, Jacob attended his first GAP trip in Vietnam, where they had the "near-death incident." Although he has been on two GAP trips since then, he found this first one most valuable because "I was new at [SAIS] and I got really close with people. I also was pushed out of my comfort zone almost the whole time. I never did anything like that before." During the Vietnam trip, he recalls, "I started to realize that I was taking a lot for granted, that I was a lot luckier than a lot of other people in the world." All three of his GAP trips have given Jacob meaningful opportunities to challenge his taken-for-granted assumptions of self, others, and the world around him.

Back home in Malaysia, he sporadically volunteers at "an Afghan refugee center, down the street from where I live, for little kids without homes and kids that don't have the chance to be educated." At the center, he teaches children English and occasionally gets the opportunity to give them a dance lesson. He regrets that "I don't make it there nearly as often as I would like to with rehearsals, schoolwork, and all the college stuff," because "I realize I've been privileged; I've gone through some rough times too, but in different ways than they have. I want to be able to be a helping hand to other people that are going through rough times in their lives." Although SAIS does not require Jacob to perform additional community service on top of the GAP trips, his parents, guided by their religion beliefs, have always emphasized the importance of service. "It's both a Muslim and Catholic thing. Since we're privileged, we have an obligation and sort of a responsibility to give back to people who aren't as fortunate," he claims.

Above religious obligation or anything else, Jacob is primarily driven to engage in service to alleviate his feelings of guilt associated with his privilege. He says, "I just feel guilty that I have so much and that there are people everywhere who aren't as lucky as I am." Volunteering at the local refugee center allows him "to feel good about what I'm doing and good about myself overall." Provided with opportunities to reflect on his advantages in life, he feels more at ease with being privileged. He explains, "I think this [volunteer work] has made me think about all the opportunities and experiences I've had, and in weird ways makes me feel better about [my privilege] because I cherish it more." Appreciating such advantages is "not always easy to keep in your mind because it's just your life. It's your world and you really don't think of things that are common in your world." His volunteer work, in particular, gives him a context for making his advantages seem a little less ordinary.

He believes that appreciating his advantages, even part of the time, sets him apart from most of his privileged peers. As he explains,

> Because I appreciate what I have, my advantages are more about loving to experience things, like I love going out and feeling different emotions and seeing different kinds of people and I like more of the societal aspect. Most people who have similar circumstances as me go and spend $10,000 on Gucci and get whatever they want, but it's not something that I do so much. Their ideas of their privileges are different than mine and maybe even somewhat similar. I do like to spend money, but having experiences are more important.

Upon further reflection, Jacob sees more commonalities between himself and his privileged peers than he likes to admit. Although he believes that he mostly appreciates what he has, he blames his "love of fashion" for always wanting more. At least two or three times a week, he goes clothes shopping. He confesses to being "somewhat materialistic cause I'm a shopaholic." But he quickly argues, partly in jest, that it is only natural for him to be materialistic because "I'm a gay man, so I like to wear nice clothes." For the most part, he maintains, "In reality I'm not really that materialistic other than buying clothes. When it comes to like 'oh I have the newest iPhone' or 'oh I have the PS3, let's go home and play it,' not really for me, not so much, unless it's clothes." Ultimately, he finds a way to distinguish himself from other privileged people and rationalize his materialistic side enough to feel good about his privilege.

Glimmers of his awareness and appreciation of his life and schooling advantages are often overshadowed by what he takes for granted. Most often, as he explains,

> I take money for granted a lot. I don't appreciate enough where I live and where I go to school and all the opportunities that I actually get. When I think back, I'm like I don't really know how many other people in the world really get a chance to do something like this. I haven't thought about it that much.

When it occurs to him that he is taking his advantaged circumstances for granted, feelings of guilt once again emerge. He says,

> Whenever I used to go shopping I would always take my mom's credit card and not think twice about it, like I'd pay for myself and pay for other people. I started taking some things for granted. That's kind of one of the last things on my mind, because we are well off. It's really not fair compared to the financial situation of so many people in the world at this time. When it comes to my attention, I feel pretty guilty about it all, and then I try not to take it for granted anymore.

Since he is unwilling to kick his shopping habit, his feelings of guilt are instead alleviated by his efforts to appreciate what he has and not taking it for granted.

Before moving to Malaysia, he rarely thought about his advantages or even the topic of social class differences. He claims,

> Social class doesn't matter as much in the U.S. as it does [in Malaysia]. Well I mean in different times, your social class mattered more 'cause if we're in the twentieth century or nineteenth century, it'd have a lot to do with who you are and what you can amount to in your life. Nowadays it's changed, but it's still similar in some ways. If you are less privileged back in the U.S., you're probably going to work more than someone who is more privileged. The kind of the worldview of life is almost altered slightly from the situations you're in. If you're less privileged you just have a different way of looking at life.

Believing that social class has almost entirely faded as a force in American life, Jacob rarely thought about his advantages when he lived in the U.S. Although he partially realized class differences exist in the country, he rarely witnessed those disparities firsthand. "I didn't really have to think about it because it wasn't really a big deal," he adds.

When he moved to Malaysia, class differences became more apparent in his daily life. He explains,

> Stark class differences are really common here in Malaysia, so it's kind of like we're living in the 1920s back in the U.S. That sort of brought it to my eyes how there are people doing things for me and there are people that call me sir and I'm only like seventeen so that's weird for me. A really big thing here in Malaysia is if they call you boss, that means that you have sort of like a higher social class than they do, that they need to respect you, even if they're in their eighties and you're twelve. That is what really set the whole standard for me and how I kind of got to understand social class.

No longer able to ignore class differences in the contexts he occupies currently, he is uncomfortably reminded of his high-status class position. In efforts to become more comfortable with his privileged status, he attempts to bridge the divides between himself and others by acknowledging and interacting with individuals different from himself whom he sees on a daily basis. He says,

> When I go home, I actually love talking to maids. I actually sat down and played cards with them. There's a lot of people you see every day around you that are almost like servants to you. I hate using that word, but they really do cater to you and take care of you.

But he claims that the rigid class hierarchy in Malaysia prevents him from establishing the kinds of relationships he wants with those working for his family. To his disappointment, "I genuinely feel like the people that work at my hotel and for my parents would not be as nice to me if they didn't know whose son I was. I'm sure they would treat me different than they do."

Class barriers stand in the way of his ability to form relationships with others from a different social class. But it is still important for him to make efforts to form these relationships so as to maintain a positive self-image, even though he knows he will not be successful in the end. By making these efforts, he believes, "I'm not looking down on people. I don't like looking down on people 'cause I feel like you're not respecting them if you are, and it makes me feel yucky about myself. Showing people respect I feel like I'm respecting myself also." He also wants to be perceived by self and others as a sharing person. As he explains,

> I've been lucky enough in my life to have what I need and even more than I actually need. Realizing how lucky I am makes me want to share my privileges and opportunities. I really don't think it's fair that they have to

suffer while I'm taking the easy way out. I just need to feel like I'm sharing what I have with people who don't have the same privileges.

Jacob has difficulty identifying specifically how he shares his privileges with others besides through his sporadic volunteer work. Regardless of how much and often he actually shares, he understands himself as someone who is sharing, especially with those from a lower social class.

With facile liberal, egalitarian sentiments, Jacob expresses the unfairness of his advantages in life. He observes,

> A lot of people go through a lot of crap in their life, like unnecessary crap. They shouldn't have to go through that. When I think about it, I've had somewhat of an easier life, like I've had a difficult time with my parents and all that. It's almost like there are equal opportunities, but the opportunities are really only there if you have the privileges to get it.

He concludes, "This is just how life is. It isn't fair to everyone always." He accepts unfairness as natural and unavoidable.[10] Jacob firmly believes that individuals can overcome unfair obstacles to achieve whatever they want in life. As he explains, "It's really saddening that people have to go through this crap in life, but they don't have to stay where they're at. They can work for a better life. How they better their lives is really what creates the outcome of it all." Again, he asserts, "Your social class doesn't really affect how happy you are or what you want to do with your life, it just affects how you live at the moment and not where you can head in life. That's up to the individual." He attributes social class differences, therefore, more to individual efforts and choices than unfair societal circumstances.[11]

NEW YORK OR BUST

Jacob barges into his guidance counselor's office nearly at the midway point of his senior year. For several months, he has had frequent conversations with her about what schools are a good fit for him and the overall college admissions process. The previous night, while lying in bed for hours thinking about his post-SAIS plans, it occurred to him that he knew very little about how to get financial aid or scholarships. As soon as he arrives to school, he goes directly to her office. Accustomed to Jacob's unscheduled visits, she stops what she is doing and looks up at him. Without giving her a chance to greet him, he impatiently asks, "I need to apply for financial aid for college. How do I do that?"

"What are you talking about?" she asks.

"I know nothing about how you get financial aid and scholarships to pay for college," he explains.

She replies sarcastically, "You live in a penthouse and you've only flown business and first class your entire life. You're not going to qualify for financial aid." She goes on to inform him that his grades are not good enough to receive merit scholarships. Sensing that there is more behind his question, she asks him what he really wants to know. After some hesitation, he admits, "I don't know how I can pay for college without my parents' help." Aware of his strained family relationships, she talks with him about how to afford the costs of attending college, giving him information that she rarely offers to SAIS students. At the end of their conversation, she confirmed what Jacob already knew at some level; he needs his parents' financial support for at least four more years.

Jacob's request for information about financial aid reveals just how much he looks forward to the day when he can declare independence from his parents. After hell year, he decided, "I'm going to stop talking to [my parents] after college. I'm cutting them out of my life completely then." Looking for a drastic change in his life, he only wants to "stay in contact with my epiphinistas 'cause I consider them my real family. Everyone else, who knows? But definitely not my parents." As the time for him to leave home for college quickly approaches, he grows increasingly impatient to break free from them, but he knows now is not the time because needs their financial support during college to achieve his goals in life. Part of what makes it a bit more bearable to have them in his life for four more years is the fact that "I'll be going to school back in the U.S. and they'll be over here. I'll probably only have to see them once or, at the most, two times a year." For now, as he further explains, "I'm stuck with them. I just have to keep focused on what I eventually want."

Jacob has a clear goal for becoming self-sufficient while doing what he loves. His eyes are firmly set on becoming a professional dancer:

> Dance and theater are really what I want to do with my life. I know that it probably won't get me a lot of money and most of the time I probably won't have a job directly related to dancing and theater, but I'm willing to move through all that, like do whatever I need to do to get what I want to do, what I love to do.

Although he is determined to make it as a professional dancer, he realizes the road ahead will not be easy. He believes, "Achieving what I want is gonna be hard! It's gonna be a lot of work, especially for me, since I want to go into performing arts. I want to be dancing and acting and I know that it's going to be rough." What makes the difficult road ahead seem somewhat easier is that he knows "this is what my heart tells me I need to be doing with my life; this is where I feel my essence is."

Jacob also believes that his advantages make it somewhat easier for him to achieve what he wants in life because he has been given "more opportunities to get where I want to go than other people." Spending summers in

New York City, being trained by top professionals, and attending a school with an extensive dance program, to name just some of these opportunities, will place him ahead of most who share his aspirations. As he explains, "I've had the money to go and get classes and go to this expensive school where it just so happens there's a dance team, and I just have had so many opportunities that others don't have." But at the same time, he feels a tremendous sense of pressure because of his advantages. He continues, "I really feel like I have to grab hold of what I have been given in life while I can so that I can establish a future. If not and I just sort of don't take advantage of my advantages, then I guess life will kind of bite me in the ass." He does not want "to realize later on that I could have done so much more with my life, and from my privileges that I had, but never really took action on it."

Jacob sometimes worries that he will not make it as a professional dancer because he sees "so many people who are much more talented than me, and they're working so much harder than me. When it comes to my future, I kind of feel like I really need to start busting my ass or else I'm not gonna go anywhere with it." From time to time, his doubts make him "alter my goals a little bit 'cause I start to hesitate about whether or not I can make it." But his love of dancing allows him to overcome these worries and, as he explains, "I always end up going back to what I want to really do in my life." Jacob is a firm believer that nothing should stand in people's way of achieving what truly makes them happy in life. To keep focused on what he wants to do in his life, "I set strong goals for myself and keep set on them, so then I can work harder to maintain them and go back to [those goals]." Although he has some worries, he is confident that he will work hard enough, stay focused on what he really wants, and be determined enough to overcome any obstacles he may face in pursuing his goals.

Jacob sees his parents as the "only real obstacle I'm facing now 'cause they don't have the same goals as I have for my life. They have another plan for me." His parents believe his plan to become a professional dancer is a "pipe dream" and "to this day they want me to have a backup, which means like don't do that, just do this instead. They don't think that I will succeed in getting where I want to be in life." Their doubts about his future success serve as motivation for him. As he explains, "I'm really gonna need to work and prove to them, and to myself, of course, that I can do what I want to do with my life and be as successful as I know I will be. Them lacking faith in me just motivates me that much more." But he knows that it will take more than their disapproval and his intrinsic drive to keep him working toward his goal. He will need to rely on others, namely his epiphanistas, other friends, and teachers, who "will push me into doing what I love, what I really want to do with my life. They're the ones that will really push me into doing what I want to do and into overcoming the obstacles." He cannot make it entirely on his own; he needs emotional support from others. But he is confident that he will achieve what he wants out of life without any support—emotional or otherwise—from his parents.

To some extent, Jacob knows when he severs ties with his parents that "it's gonna be a little bit of a rough patch." He also partially understands that "since I'm gonna need to support myself somehow I'm really gonna to need to work hard and make sure that I'm pushing myself to my fullest and trying to be the best that I can be so that I can get more job opportunities and sort of be financially stable." But he does not fully grasp how drastically his life circumstances will most likely change[12] when he breaks free from his parents. Moments like when he asked for information about financial aid from his guidance counselor reveal just how unaware he remains about the extent of his family's wealth. Above all, he takes wealth for granted, believing wealth to be a fixed stock that always has been and always will be around—even when he becomes self-sufficient.

Later in life, Jacob wants to maintain the privileged lifestyle to which he is accustomed; but eventually doing what it would take to make enough money to do so is not a priority. He fully realizes that he will most likely not make a lot of money as a professional dancer. As he explains, "I know it's going to be hard surviving on what I'll make as a performer; I probably won't make tons of money." Like most struggling artists, he plans to have "a day job to give me money I need to support me so I can do what really want to be doing." However, he has little understanding of how these changes in his financial circumstances will affect his lifestyle and has little to no inter-est in thinking about this too much. For now, making money is not enough of a priority for him to sort out any financial details in his future plans. "I'm sure of it will all work out in the end," he asserts confidently.

What is a priority, however, is to find happiness. He wants to be like most of the people who surround him in his everyday life. As he explains,

> With my dad and his company we have to go to a lot of functions and all that, so I tend to meet a lot of rich, happy people, or at least they seem happy. I also meet some of the families that live here and a lot of them are so happy with their life and don't have a care in the world and it makes me like really wish that I can get to that point in my life at one point.

Not content or happy with his life, he feels, yet again, different from most others around him. Yet he is hopeful that he will be happy one day. He maintains,

> I have hope that I'll have that kind of life eventually. The factors that play into me enjoying life and being happy would be having someone I love, being happy with the situations I'm in, being happy with my job or where I am, and who my friends are and with my family, and just sort of enjoying the small things in life and not taking what I have for granted. Really living to the fullest each day and enjoying life while you can, and not wasting it and sort of thinking about the future and not

focusing on the past. It's really living in the moment and making the best of everything you have.

At the moment, these factors are mostly absent from his life. The hurts and disappointments of the past continue to cast a massive shadow. Still needing to heal from the past, he finds it difficult to live fully in the present or to focus as much as he wants on what lies ahead.

Although Jacob still needs to sort out most details of his future plans, he knows where he is heading in just a few months when he graduates high school. At the halfway point of his senior year, he has not completed one college application or fully prepared for his upcoming auditions at performing arts schools. Nevertheless, he remains confident that "everything's going to work out" and he will be in New York City next year to begin his journey toward becoming a professional dancer. He is doing everything he can to redirect his attention to what immediately lies ahead of him, for it is the only light that pierces through the shadow of the past.

NOTES

1. The International Schools Activities Conference includes varsity-level competition among schools in Malaysia, Indonesia, Thailand, Taiwan, Singapore, and the Philippines in sports, fine and performing arts, and academic contests.
2. Jacob's therapist practiced what is often referred to as "reparative" therapy. For nearly three decades, the major professional associations of mental health practitioners and researchers in the United States have recognized that homosexuality is not a mental illness. They are highly critical of attempts to change sexual orientation through "reparative" therapy. For example, see American Psychiatric Association (2000). Until recently, this harmful psychiatric treatment was only offered to adults, but now the organizations offering this form of therapy primarily target adolescents. For more information about the harms of this treatment for adolescents, see Price, 2012.
3. Jacob does not provide a lot of details about his suicidal thoughts and we, as the research team, decided not to push him for additional information about this subject for ethical reasons. He briefly discussed his suicidal thoughts in explaining how he has suffered from depression since his freshman year of high school, when his family found out about his sexuality. To date, he has not received mental health services for his depression. We therefore felt that it was unethical to dive deeply into issues with which he had not been helped to deal by receiving treatment.
4. Ryan (2009) found that just over two thirds of LGBT young adults had experienced at least some level of rejecting behavior from their parents or caregivers, and roughly 42 percent had families who were "rejecting" or "extremely rejecting." Rejected by their family of origin, many LGBT youth form family-like relationships with people to whom they are emotionally close and whom they consider "family" even though they are not biologically or legally related.
5. Although English is the language of instruction, the majority of SAIS students are not native English speakers.
6. Although independent schools have become increasingly diverse, the vast majority of students who attend these schools are still children of the wealthy. More specifically, the president of the National Association of Independent

Schools has stated that only families in the top 4 percent economically could readily afford a private school education for their children (Bassett, 2006). See also Gaztambide-Fernández, 2009.

7. Financial aid is made available only to native Malaysians.
8. Gaztambide-Fernández (2009) argues that elite schools like SAIS are by definition exclusive.
9. Quoted from school materials about the program.
10. As other researchers have found, Jacob accepts and even expects his own advantages even though he speaks about how unfair his advantages are. See, for example, Mickelson, 1990; Olson, 1983; Howard, 2010.
11. Jacob's beliefs are consistent with what Brantlinger (1993) found in her in-depth examination of affluent and low-income adolescents' perceptions of their educational experiences. The adolescents in her study cast class differences as the inevitable outcome of personal characteristics. Brantlinger's comments are also consistent with Bourdieu's (1984) observation that affluent people assume that low-income people prefer their disadvantaged lifestyles.
12. Jacob has highly valuable forms of social and cultural capital that he can rely on throughout his life to maintain access to economic capital. For a discussion about the importance of social and cultural capital in maintaining class privilege, see Bourdieu, 1977, 1986.

10 Negotiating Privilege

The eight adolescents showcased in this book are more different than they are alike. However, the common qualities of their self-understandings—*confident, isolated, certain, independent, hardworking, and scripted*—reveal how they are similarly constructing and cultivating privilege. Through these portraits, we see that privilege is not just about what these adolescents have or possess, although that is part of it; their privilege also involves intrinsic aspects. Within the body of literature on privilege, the significance of these aspects is often overshadowed, because the focus remains on privileged people's advantages rather than on how they actively leverage those advantages to maintain and advance their privileged positions and circumstances. Bucking this trend, the portraits in this book turn attention primarily toward the intrinsic aspects of privilege. This is not to deny or diminish the importance of advantages that the adolescents have over others; it is, in fact, to underline the relationship between their advantages and their self-understandings in order to uncover the ways in which they actively construct privilege.

Although the adolescents have extraordinary advantages in life and schooling that reinforce their class positions, their privilege is more than these advantages; it is a crucial part of themselves and their self-understandings, which they continually renew, recreate, defend, and modify.[1] Their capacity to understand themselves and to act on those understandings plays an equally important role in the production of privilege. As such, their privilege is about agency as much as it is about advantages.[2] Even though human agency exists within the contradiction between people as social producers and as social products, self-understandings are neither imposed nor stable. Individuals mediate cultural meanings and have the capacity to transform these understandings in order to interrupt the cultural processes that validate and support privilege. With the agency to form their own self-understandings, privilege, therefore, is not something the adolescents are passively given or possess; instead, it is something they actively construct and cultivate. Moreover, although everyone has the agency to form and develop particular self-understandings, the advantaging circumstances enjoyed by these adolescents undoubtedly grant them a greater capacity than disadvantaged individuals have to form their own self-understandings and also use those understandings in ways that protect their class interests.

The adolescents' stories of self, others, and the world around them reveal that privilege is a lens through which they form their self-understandings. Their perceptions, interpretations, feelings, and actions are shaped, created, re-created, and maintained through this lens of privilege. Although the various educational contexts they occupy on a daily basis—such as home, community, and school—function to instill particular ways of knowing and doing, their self-understandings are ultimately constructed in relation to, and in coordination with, the ideologies and emotions they absorb and that give their lives meaning. In this chapter, we revisit the six common qualities of their self-understandings to reveal the various ideological operations and strategies the adolescents employ in constructing and cultivating privilege. We then explore the role that particular emotions—*worthiness, integrity, and happiness*—play in this process. The chapter ends by considering how their self-understandings, and the ideologies and emotions behind these understandings, give direction to what they imagine for their future lives.

IDEOLOGICAL NEGOTIATIONS

Ideology plays a critical role in maintaining and advancing the dynamics of power and oppression[3] through the "production of principles, ideas, and categories that support unequal class relations."[4] Dominant ideologies of the larger society often work like a "network of templates or blueprints"[5] through which actions, experiences, and understandings of individuals are expressed and constituted. As familiar and respected systems of representations and complexes of narratives,[6] ideologies mediate people's self-understandings in profoundly influential and often unconscious ways.[7] However, the meanings imbedded in these ideologies take on different values and forms as individuals mediate these cultural meanings in constructing their self-understandings. Ideology and self-understandings meet at the boundary between individuals' inner and outer worlds. Their self-understandings are produced in relation to and coordination with the ideologies that they adopt and to which they give meaning.

In this section, we identify manifestations of ideologies in the adolescents' self-understandings. We make use of John Thompson's modes of ideological operations and symbolic construction strategies[8] to illustrate how an interlocking stock of ideas is used to construct and maintain a particular lens through which individuals form their self-understandings. Ellen Brantlinger asserts, "[These ideas] back normative practices to support the elevated status of dominant groups, thus allowing stratified social relations to seem right, natural, and inevitable."[9] These ideological operations and strategies, however, are not simply principles and ideas that the adolescents know and use in negotiating their advantages. The ways in which they use particular ideological moves reveal the medley of forces at play in constructing privilege as a central aspect of their self-understandings.

Isolated: "They're Just Too Different"

Situated in contexts that reflect the diverse social world, the eight adolescents come in contact with others different from themselves on a fairly regular basis in their everyday lives—predominantly at school and within their communities. Even when they are located mostly in an affluent bubble, like Kayla, who lives in a community and attends a school with almost entirely other wealthy individuals, they encounter others who are different from themselves by stepping outside their immediate world on a regular basis, traveling extensively, engaging in community service and other extracurricular activities, and attending social events, to name a few. Most of them hardly ever occupy spaces exclusively with individuals just like themselves. Yet they rarely interact with those differences surrounding them in their daily lives.

Within these various diverse contexts, the adolescents position themselves socially in ways that allow them to avoid and remain far removed from differences. Although all of them claim not to use class, race, or any other form of difference as a basis for establishing friendships or determining how they interact with others, their most meaningful relationships are almost entirely with others more alike than different from themselves, especially when it comes to class. They all have developed and maintained a few close friendships across religious, national, gender, sexual identity, and/or racial lines, but none of them have meaningful relationships with others who are socioeconomically disadvantaged. Granted, their immediate worlds generally have greater diversity in forms other than social class, which makes it more likely and even more possible to establish meaningful relationships across these other forms of difference. However, even Olive and Leo, who attend school with and live near more disadvantaged people than the other adolescents, rarely interact with others outside their own social class for very long or in significant ways. By having no meaningful relationships with economically disadvantaged individuals and only having a few friends who are different in other respects, they remain primarily isolated from the differences existing around them.

Although these adolescents have few meaningful interactions with economically disadvantaged people, those of the lower class are symbolically visible in their stories of self, others, and their immediate world as a group who share virtually no commonalities with them. They use *fragmentation ideological operations* (dispersing others capable of mounting a challenge to the dominant group) to differentiate themselves from people without their advantages. Like most affluent Americans of all ages, they often refrain from expressing certain views and using derogatory language when explaining social differences so as to project a politically correct image; they talk about others from lower social class groups in ways to avoid being seen as prejudiced.[10] Using *euphemisms* (describing actions or social relations to elicit a positive evaluation), the adolescents attribute differences between them and disadvantaged people to personal choices. They position themselves, and others like them, as superior to disadvantaged individuals, as when Meredith claims that disadvantaged individuals do not work hard enough and are not determined enough to change their life circumstances, and Sarah describes "general students" as less motivated, poor decision-makers, lacking certain positive values, and lazy. Such *unification operations* (embracing individuals in a collective identity)—using the ideological strategies *standardization* (promoting shared and acceptable symbolic exchange) and *symbolization of unity* (constructing a collective identity)—allow them to enclose the group with whom they identify while casting others outside their own group as being too different.

For Jacob, his sexual identity also contributes to the formation of an isolated quality of his self-understandings. Enduring homophobia in his daily life, mostly at home but also at times in his school and community, tremendously affects his self-understandings, relationships, and interactions with others. As with Kayla and Marcus, the two other adolescents of color in this study, Jacob claims that being Latino does not play a significant role in setting him apart from others within his immediate world.[11] From his perspective, no single racial group, including white, is advantaged over others within his school and community. When it comes to his sexual identity, however, he experiences marginalization on a daily basis, setting him apart from others within these contexts. Unlike the ways in which he remains separated from others outside his own social class, though, the isolation associated with his sexual identity results from the oppressive conditions he endures rather than his use of ideologies in the service of class domination.

Scripted: "Anyone Can Be Successful"

Although the adolescents identify as privileged, or in the case with Herman "privileged enough," and acknowledge shared interests and attitudes with their affluent peers, they follow a particular cultural script to *displace* (transferring connotations to others) and *rationalize* (defending a set of social relations) their own advantages. While pointing out commonalities with their affluent peers, and especially when employing *standardization* and *symbolization strategies* to differentiate themselves from low-income individuals, they concurrently contrast their own qualities with those of other privileged individuals in their immediate world. Through these contrasts, they minimize the significance of their advantages and *rationalize* those that they more readily acknowledge.

Five of the adolescents (Sarah, Herman, Meredith, Olive, and Kayla) establish this contrast most powerfully by locating themselves within middle-class boundaries. Situated in the neutral and undefined middle allows them not only to set themselves apart from other privileged people but also to avoid taking on the negative characteristics that they associate with being upper class or rich, such as being entitled, ungrateful, and snobbish. Although identifying in the middle, these five partially acknowledge their advantages by locating themselves in the upper part of that middle, but they eschew a high-status identification by minimizing the importance of their advantages in various ways, as when Herman identifies himself as being in the lower end of that upper part, Meredith and Sarah claim that personal characteristics outweigh financial circumstances, and Olive emphasizes the fact that her immediate family's financial circumstances pale in comparison with those of her extended family and others. Similarly, Marcus, Leo, and Jacob,[12] who locate themselves in the upper class, diminish the significance of their advantages by claiming that their eventual success will depend completely on their merits, efforts, and choices. They also deflect attention from their advantages by placing more significance on faith, family, and health, as does Marcus, and happiness, as do Leo and Jacob. All of them use distinctions between themselves and other privileged individuals—such as in their values, work ethic, gratefulness for their advantages, and willingness to "give back"—to establish a sense of being worthy of their advantages.

Using *legitimation ideological operations* (representing domination as just and worthy of support), they also justify and veil their advantages by discrediting others from lower social classes. Although the adolescents do not fully establish a cultural deficit position to explain the disadvantaging circumstances of individuals from lower-class groups—that is, they do not make reference to their intellectual abilities—all but Leo[13] cognitively lump together the lack of success, indifferent attitudes, and poor decision making with a lower social class (and for Sarah and Meredith, laziness is added to the mix).[14] In speaking about their low-income classmates, for example, most of them claim that low-income students do not work as hard and are less motivated to do well in school than themselves and even other affluent students. Once again, they contrast their personal characteristics with those of others but establish more rigid distinctions between themselves and disadvantaged people than they do in differentiating themselves from their privileged peers. In so doing, they establish a stark social class dichotomy that separates them further from lower classes than those above them on the socioeconomic spectrum. In spite of five of them placing themselves in the middle, they, as well as the other three, anchor themselves in the upper part of the class system in establishing distinctions between themselves and the lower classes. For most, this positioning against the inferior traits of low-income individuals allows them not only to construct class superiority, but also to further establish the worthiness of their advantages.

With facile liberal, egalitarian sentiments, the adolescents partially acknowledge that the disadvantaging circumstances of low-income individuals make it more difficult for them to accomplish what they want in life and to achieve success than it is for them and other privileged people. They acknowledge the unfairness of a reality in which others do not have equal advantages in life and schooling. Yet they accept—employing forms of *reification ideological operations* (representing a transitory historical state as natural and permanent), and particularly *naturalization strategies* (portraying social creation as the inevitable outcome of innate characteristics)—the unfairness of others' disadvantages as natural and unavoidable. For the most part, the adolescents accept and even expect their advantages in life and schooling, even though they speak of fairness.[15] In their narratives and stories of self, others, and the world around them, they straddle an ambiguous position on their advantages and the disadvantages of others. Glimmers of their awareness of social class inequities in their immediate and larger worlds are overshadowed by ideologies that divert attention from and *rationalize* their advantages and the disadvantages of others.

The scripted quality of the adolescents' self-understandings is also evident in their plans for the future. Except for Leo, they all have a very clear path laid out before them toward achieving their goals and preserving their class privilege: accumulate the credentials necessary to gain admissions to a selective college or university, maintain high academic performance and gain valuable life and work experiences during college, either continue on to graduate school or enter the workforce, and achieve success in their respective professional career. They are determined to follow this clearly defined pathway to achieving success. Even Leo, who originally lacked interest in pursuing a path similar to that of the other adolescents, had a change of heart after working at minimum-wage job for a couple of months. He is now starting down the same path that the others are taking toward certain success.

Hardworking: "No Shortcuts to Success"

"The new elites are not an entitled group of boys who rely on family wealth and slide through trust-funded lives," Shamus Khan argues, but instead, "they firmly believe in the importance of the hard work required to achieve their [current achievements] and the continued hard work it will take to maintain their advantaged position."[16] Similar to what Khan found in his study of students at the elite St. Paul's School, the adolescents in this study do not want to rely on their family's wealth to achieve their goals. Although they know they will become successful later in life, they do not plan to take shortcuts but instead to work hard enough to deserve their future achievements. As noted previously, they partially acknowledge that their schooling and life advantages make it easier for them to achieve their goals than for others who are disadvantaged. To some extent, most of them also understand that disadvantaged individuals do not have the same chances as they have and must work harder than they do to achieve what they have now and will have later in their lives. However, they firmly uphold the meritocratic belief that anyone can achieve what he or she wants in life and draw on examples in their lives to present as evidence that success is achieved through hard work, such as the upward mobility of Sarah and Meredith's grandfathers, Olive's father, and Marcus and Kayla's parents.

Using *reification ideological operations* and particularly *naturalization strategies*, they portray their current and future success as the natural and essential consequence of their hardworking characteristics. For instance, high achievement in school—demonstrated by high tracks, top grades and ranking, and often awards, to name a few—figures prominently in all of their stories and narratives of self except for Leo, who instead emphasizes his achievements outside school, as in music and scuba diving. They *dissimulate* (deflecting attention away from domination) advantages beneath their own personal characteristics by equating academic achievement or, in the case of Leo, other forms of success with hard work; in so doing, they further establish their worthiness for those advantages. They frame their advantages—such as having the financial, social, and cultural resources for private tutoring and other forms of individualized instruction, summer enrichment programs, out-of-school activities, additional college counseling, and/or preparatory programs for college entrance exams (and in the case of Leo, music equipment, and scuba diving trips and lessons)—as relatively insignificant in their achievements, proclaiming they would be as successful even without those advantages. All of them claim to appreciate these advantaging opportunities but contend that they themselves are ultimately the driving force behind their successes.

To emphasize this point further, employing *narrativization strategies* (embedding justifying actions in stories), most of the adolescents claim that if they did not have their same advantages, they would continue to be academically successful and proceed on the path toward achieving what they want in life. In this hypothetical situation, they believe that they could overcome any challenging obstacles associated with being disadvantaged to gain success, because this hardworking quality is such a central aspect of who they are. The inverse of seeing their hardworking quality as what would lead them to success despite challenging circumstances is the implicit criticism of others who have not overcome those obstacles. Once again they position themselves as superior through *differentiation strategies* (disuniting groups through construction of divisions, distinctions, and characteristics) by establishing clear distinctions between themselves and disadvantaged individuals—who, in their perspective, do not possess their hardworking quality, because if they did they would not be disadvantaged.

Independent: "Making It on My Own"

Largely adopting the individualism of mainstream American culture, independence appears prominently in the adolescents' narratives and stories of their self-understandings. Like most Americans, and especially other advantaged individuals, they think in terms of their individual qualities rather than some characteristics—such as race, class, gender, and so forth—ascribed to them.[17] They take the position that what they have accomplished in life up to this point is a product of their own merits and hard work and that their future success depends on continuing to work hard, develop the necessary skills and knowledge, and acquire additional credentials. Using *naturalizing* and *eternalization ideological strategies* (emphasizing permanent, unchanging nature), they adamantly contend that their personal characteristics (namely their work ethic, good decisions, skills, and knowledge) are what really matter, not anything or anyone else, especially their schooling and life advantages. Taking this stance, they downplay their advantages to emphasize the individual characteristics that they have cultivated. By contending that they are completely responsible for their current and future circumstances in life, they assert their independence from, among other things, their advantages.

Although they maintain that their current and future accomplishments are ultimately up to them, all except Herman reluctantly acknowledge that they must rely on others for support at this point in their lives. In contrast, Herman uses *dissumulation operations* and *narrativization strategies* to claim that he relies on others outside his family more than he actually does so as to deflect attention away from his advantages. Like the others, however, when it comes to his family, he maintains that he is on his own. In fact, like the other three males, he puts a great deal of effort into finding ways to avoid receiving support from his family, such as making connections with potential benefactors and applying for scholarships and grants to support his filmmaking endeavors. Some of the adolescents, particularly Marcus and Herman, even find it difficult to divulge just how much help they receive from their families and/or others. But at the same time, all of them are grateful for the support and guidance that their friends, teachers, and family provide, or, in the case of Jacob, his "epiphinistas." Wanting to avoid being perceived as ungrateful, they recognize and at times highlight just how valuable these sources of support are for maintaining current achievements, pursuing interests and passions, and gaining future success. Simultaneously, they reduce the significance of others' support by claiming that nothing else *really* matters other than their own merits and hard work. Therefore, even though they appreciate the support that they receive from others, they find it largely unnecessary.

Their efforts to separate themselves from their parents, especially by not following their footsteps, figure consistently and prominently in the adolescents' stories. Most of them spend a considerable amount of time and effort seeking ways to set themselves apart from their parents; for example, Marcus pursuing endeavors that will help him gain financial independence, Olive finding any chance to rebel against her restrictive life, Jacob spending late nights at school or nightclubs to avoid his parents, Herman limiting the time that he spends with his parents, Kayla not taking over her family's business, and Leo resisting his parents' expectations and aspirations for his educational attainment. Although they all have their own ways of asserting independence from their parents, they share the common desire to distinguish themselves, express their individuality, and carve out their own spaces in life. For them, being independent from their parents embodies their firmly held belief that it is their own merits and hard work, not their advantages or support systems, creating their current circumstances and leading them toward certain success.

Confident: "Not Afraid to Take Risks"

As descriptors, *confident* and *certain* are often used synonymously to describe a person who possesses self-assurance and/or unquestionable thoughts about something or someone. However, significant distinctions between these two qualities surface from the adolescents' stories of their self-understandings. Their confidence is revealed primarily through their actions and knowledge of skills and abilities, whereas their certainty appears through their feelings and emotions, which are mainly connected to their visions of the future. Moreover, the two qualities reveal conflicting features of their self-understandings, because confidence invites possibilities and allows flexibility, whereas certainty shuts down alternatives and maintains rigidity.[18] This is not to suggest that these two traits of their self-understandings are unrelated. As with the other four qualities, there is a symbiotic relationship between the two; confidence builds their certainty and vice versa. Although closely interrelated, each quality is a distinctive aspect of their self-understandings.

The adolescents have cultivated a level of confidence that allows them to be comfortable and assertive in just about any situation. At school and on stage or sports field, for example, they express their individuality, are assertive through their words and actions, take on challenging tasks or approach difficult situations head-on, and are poised to overcome any obstacles. Of course they feel most at ease in contexts that are most familiar and unthreatening, such as school, social gatherings with peers, and/or home; but even in strange and riskier environments and situations, they continue, for the most part, to assert themselves and to feel comfortable in their own skins. Even Olive and Jacob, who do not feel completely at ease being themselves at home, manage to carve out spaces within their home lives to challenge and disrupt the conditions that make them feel uncomfortable and/or threatened. Their self-confidence allows them to find opportunities to be themselves even in their restrictive or unsupportive home environments. However, the various contexts that most of them occupy on a regular basis encourage them to be assertive and risk takers. All of them except Olive are given tremendous freedom in their daily lives to make their own decisions and to figure out the world around them and their own place in that world. Even though Olive is not given the same amount of freedom at home or even at school as the other seven adolescents, she is given some opportunities in these contexts to assert her individuality and pursue her passions and finds other spaces, like a dance studio and performance stage, to take risks and to figure out what she wants in life.

Although their parents, teachers, peers, and others hold particular expectations, the adolescents are given multiple opportunities to develop their own goals and dreams. Even Kayla's father, who places tremendous pressure on her to follow his footsteps, Olive's parents, who place multiple restrictions on her life, and Leo's parents, who desperately want him to develop specific goals for his future, ultimately allow them to decide what path they will take in life. To a lesser extent, the other five adolescents are also feeling pressure to earn top grades, participate in various activities, attend a particular kind of college, and/or pursue specific goals favored by their parents, teachers, and/or peers, but at the same time, they are supported, encouraged, and given the room to make their own decisions. On the whole, their parents, friends, teachers, and others firmly hold trust and confidence in them that they are making the right decisions, doing what they need to be doing, and heading in the right direction in life or, in the case of Leo, will eventually be on the right path. Others' support, trust, and confidence in them play an incredibly important role in fostering their confidence.

Although the adolescents partially recognize the role that others play in building their confidence, none of them directly acknowledges the influence that their advantages in life and schooling have on making them feel more at ease taking risks and asserting themselves in most contexts. Using *dissimulation* (concealing or denying domination in ways that deflect attention) and *reification ideological modes*, and especially *displacement* (transferring connotations to something or someone else) and *naturalization strategies*, they primarily explain the development of their confidence as the natural result of their actions and personal characteristics. In other words, they mostly believe that being confident is just who they are and a product of their own doing. Their achievements figure prominently in their explanations of the key factors behind their confidence. Because success is equated with their merits, they understand their confidence as an inevitable consequence of what they have accomplished. They also believe that their confidence leads to success, suggesting that being confident is an innate characteristic and not just a by-product of their success.

The adolescents explain away or avoid acknowledging any role that their advantages may play in fostering their confidence, such as the safety net created by their families' wealth, which makes risk taking less risky than it would be for disadvantaged individuals without that security. *Euphemisms* woven into their narratives and stories of their self-understandings give some indication that they realize a safety net exists to catch them if necessary, but Leo is the only one who directly acknowledges this security in his life. However, he quickly claims that this protection from "real failure" is actually more of a disadvantage to him and his affluent peers because it causes them to be less motivated. Like most others, he does not recognize the role of his advantages, and the security that comes with those advantages, in building his confidence. Meredith somewhat acknowledges, indirectly, that her advantages have some influence in making her more confident. Although she does not fully establish a connection between her family's economic resources and her opportunities to travel, she believes that her traveling experiences have been significant in building her self-confidence. But like the other adolescents, she mainly gives herself credit because she believes that she takes advantages of, and even creates, some of the opportunities during her travels that, in turn, foster her confidence. In the end, all of them mainly attribute their confidence to their own doing and innate characteristics.

Certain: "Everything's Going to Work Out"

All the adolescents except Olive and Leo have laid out a clear path for achieving what they want in life. The most immediate step in their plan for certain success is gaining admission to a prestigious college or, in the case of Marcus, gaining valuable work experience during college. Given that most of them who are still in high school maintain a nearly perfect GPA, have earned high scores on college entrance exams, and are participating in a phenomenal array of extracurricular and service activities, they are on the right track to getting into the college of their choice. Marcus is also on the right track by working as an intern, day trader, and website developer while excelling academically. These six firmly believe that they have done, are doing, and will continue to do what is required to achieve their ultimate goals in life. Sarah is certain that she will become a chemical engineer; Marcus and Kayla hold the same certainty about eventually entering the business world; Herman has no doubts about becoming a screenwriter; Jacob is certain that he will become professional dancer; and Meredith knows that she will reach her goal of becoming a physician. With absolute certainty, they know that they are heading toward a successful future.

Olive is less clear about her future plans but is leaning toward a career in teaching dance. Whatever she eventually decides, she knows without question that she will achieve what she truly wants in life, which is less about her eventual career, and more about gaining happiness and autonomy. Like the others in high school with more specific goals, her most immediate plan is to gain admission to a college of her choice, and she is on track to accomplish this goal without much standing in her way other than her parents. Leo is the only one without any set plans for the future; in fact, he has no specific immediate or long-term goals at the moment. Although his future remains uncertain, he believes that when the opportunity arises to follow his dreams, whatever they may be, he will realize those dreams. Like the other seven adolescents, he looks toward the future knowing that he will achieve eventual success.

All of them unquestionably believe that they will maintain their advantaging circumstances in life. Those with specific goals realize that their plans may change and some of what may influence their plans will be out of their control. However, like Olive and Leo, they believe that whatever changes may occur, they will achieve success, maintain their class position in society, and eventually get what they want in life. They are determined not to let anything stand in the way of achieving their ambitious goals or, in the case of Leo, realizing his dreams. To some extent, they recognize that they will not need to overcome too many obstacles in achieving their goals. They are partially aware that their life and schooling advantages make anything possible. At the same time, they feel that their current advantages do not necessarily guarantee their own versions of success. Most of them could easily follow someone else's version. For example, Kayla and Marcus could slide through college and still take over their family-owned businesses; Olive could follow her parents' wishes and rely on her future husband to maintain her advantages; Leo could use his family's connections to begin following a similar path that the other men in his family have taken in their lives; and Jacob could maintain a relationship with his parents after college and rely on their wealth to pursue his passion for dancing. None of them want to take what they consider to be the easy, yet not necessarily uncomplicated, route to success by relying on others, primarily their family, to maintain the privileged lifestyle later in life to which they are now accustomed. Instead, they firmly believe in the importance of carving out their own paths to success. For them, this is the only path that will lead them to what they truly want in life.

Although they want to create and follow their own paths, they know, to some extent, that they must rely on others, and particularly their families, to propel them toward a successful future. Most of them, somewhat reluctantly, acknowledge that they cannot achieve their own versions of success completely on their own; they must rely on others. Although Jacob, Olive, and Leo, for example, are not following their parents' wishes for their future, they avoid pushing the boundaries set by their parents too far in order to continue receiving the support, financial and otherwise, they need to pursue their passions and dreams. Like most of the others, they are maintaining a delicate balance between going after their own plans and following their parents' expectations, believing, to a certain extent, that their parents' continued financial support is conditional. But at the same time, most of the adolescents still take their family's wealth for granted, believing wealth to be a fixed stock that will always be around, even when they become more self-sufficient or even if they do not meet the understood conditions set by their parents.

Inevitably, this fixed security in their lives plays a significant role in developing their certainty about the future.

AFFECTIVE NEGOTIATIONS

Although ideology is a crucial component of the processes involved in creating the lens of privilege that shapes the adolescents' self-understanding, affect is equally important. Affective responses or emotions are structured by people's forms of understanding and, specifically, by their self-understandings.[19] In an extension of this idea, Catherine Lutz argues that although most emotions are predominantly viewed as universal experiences and natural human phenomena, emotions are anything but natural or universal.[20] Although people may experience similar emotions, meanings for those emotions are implicated by one's self-understandings. However, just as self-understandings link the personal and the social,[21] emotions are more than individual responses; instead, they are constituted relationally in sociocultural contexts. Emotions, Lutz contends, "can be viewed as cultural and interpersonal products of naming, justifying, and persuading by people in relationship to each other. Emotional meaning is then a social rather than an individual achievement—an emergent product of social life."[22]

In this section, we identify three affective expressions—*worthiness, integrity,* and *happiness*—implicated by the adolescents' self-understandings and constituted relationally in the various educational contexts they occupy. Although the meanings that form and support their self-understandings involve an amalgam of emotions—from the pity, guilt, and discomfort aroused by awareness of others' disadvantaged circumstances to the emotional toll of enduring the stress and anxiety over the high expectations from parents and other adults in their lives or a troubled home life—these three positive emotions play important roles in affectively negotiating their advantages. Establishing and sustaining a sense of worthiness, integrity, and happiness provide a framing of self, enabling these adolescents to feel more at ease with their privileged status, to reduce negative feelings associated with their advantages, to provide a stabilizing force in their lives, and to give meaning and direction to their actions and plans. These affective responses interface with their ideologies in constructing and maintaining privilege as a central aspect of their self-understandings.

Worthiness

Privileged individuals usually have a sense of entitlement to the advantages they enjoy.[23] They embrace a deeply held belief and feeling that they are deserving of whatever rights and advantages they have in their lives, because these benefits are understood, to some extent, as a natural consequence of their actions, merits, and decisions, and, to a larger extent, as a taken-for-granted reality of their lives. With a sense of entitlement, advantages are not only expected but also firmly protected. In fact, as Karen Rosenblum and Toni-Michelle Travis point out, the sense of entitlement that "one has a right to be respected, acknowledged, protected, and rewarded . . . is so much taken for granted by those of us in non-stigmatized statuses, that they are often shocked and angered when it is denied to them."[24] However, a sense of entitlement is more than expecting and protecting existing advantages but also "a pervasive sense that one deserves more and is entitled to more than others."[25] As such, the sense of entitlement to existing and future advantages powerfully influences self-understandings and guides present and future actions.[26]

The adolescents certainly create and maintain a sense of entitlement to their advantages. For example, this is clearly evident in the ways that they take their families' wealth for granted, believing wealth to be a fixed stock in their lives. However, they firmly believe that their present and future success depends on *who they are* and *what they do* rather than *how wealthy they are*. They primarily frame their success not as deserved but rather earned.[27] Instead of entitlement, the adolescents develop and maintain more of *a sense of worthiness*. Even though they have extraordinary advantages, they want to prove to themselves and others that they have earned and will continue to earn their achievements in life. They downplay the influence of their advantages and redirect the focus toward their efforts, choices, values, and actions as the main explanation for those achievements. Their sense of worthiness plays an important affective role in how they frame, to themselves and others, their present and future success: "it is a product of what they have done and not where they are from."[28]

Although the adolescents partially acknowledge that their wealth provides social, cultural, and economic resources that give them unfair advantages in life, they deny that these advantages carry any real significance in their achievements. They employ a cultural frame that enables them to focus on the ways in which their achievements are an effect of what they do.[29] In so doing, they understand their advantages as having little to do with where they are or where they will end up in life. Through this dismissal, they minimize the unfairness of their advantages so as to establish and maintain a more positive association with those advantages. Believing that they are not relying on their advantages to gain their achievements, they avoid negative feelings such as the guilt, shame, and discomfort often associated with having unearned privilege, especially when those advantages are acknowledged even partially.[30] Their sense of worthiness allows them to accept their unearned advantages without harm to their sense of self; it allows them to feel at ease with being privileged.

Their sense of worthiness, therefore, performs a crucial affective role in how the adolescents come to see themselves in a positive light. Because their advantages are framed as insignificant, the adolescents are not held accountable for their privileging circumstances. They deny their advantages give them a competitive edge over others and therefore avoid being implicated in others' disadvantages. Although they never acknowledge that advantages come at the expense of others,[31] their stories of self, others, and the world around them reveal that they have some notion of the injustices associated with advantages, which explains, in part, why they minimize and distance themselves from their advantages. Holding a firm sense that they have earned—or in the case of Leo, will earn—their place ahead of others because of their merits and hard work, they affectively negotiate their advantages, and the relationship between those advantages and others' disadvantages, to cultivate a positive sense of self.

Integrity

The adolescents' self-understandings provide a framework for how they think about themselves, what they tell others about themselves, and how they live their lives. They develop and maintain a *sense of integrity* to act congruently within that framework. The word *integrity* comes from the Latin adjective *integer*, meaning whole, entire, and honest. As bell hooks argues, "A simple way to understand integrity is to know that it is present when there is a congruency between what we think, say, and do."[32] As an affect, integrity is the inner sense of wholeness and honesty that depends upon the extent to which individuals act according to the values, beliefs, and understandings they claim to hold. The adolescents spend a considerable amount of time and effort to act congruently with their self-understandings in order to keep their sense of integrity intact. As an affective means of maintaining balance between their actions and understandings, their sense of integrity is a stabilizing force in their lives.

All the adolescents would claim that they maintain a solid sense of integrity even though their self-understandings are filled with contradictions and their actions are not always consistent with their stated beliefs and values. For the most part, they are unaware of these contradictions and inconsistencies, but when they do become conscious of them, they quickly sort out the conflicts. This is clearly seen in the ways in which they resolve the contradictions often reflected in their ideas about the significance of disadvantages and advantages in people's lives. On one hand, they believe that unfair circumstances prevent disadvantaged individuals from achieving success and acknowledge that their own advantages make it easier for them to achieve what they want in life. But, on the other hand, they believe that hard work leads everyone to success, and they downplay the significance of their advantages and others' disadvantages. Taking the safest and easiest route, they resolve contradictions by siding with what they consider to be the most widely held belief: that nothing is more important than merit and hard work in order to achieve what one wants in life. They avoid taking a potentially controversial stance that would require further explanation and justification, thus, prolonging or even intensifying the incongruence.

At these moments, they maintain a sense of integrity by taking what they perceive to be the most acceptable position and then convince themselves and others this particular position represents their true beliefs. In so doing, conflict is resolved; congruence reestablished between what they say, think, and do; and their integrity is maintained.

Even Herman, who contradicts himself more than the other adolescents, finds ways of maintaining a sense of integrity. He sees himself, and wants to be perceived by others, as honest. He represents himself in particular ways by following the script that he has constructed for communicating his self-understandings. The script allows him to establish and sustain an image of being honest. This image is not only useful in representing himself to others in a specific way but also in maintaining a particular sense of self. This image is constituted relationally, linking the personal and the social.[33] Contradictions in his narrative often arise when he discusses topics that force him to go off script, such as his class privilege. By claiming that he is lost for words or confused by the questions being posed to him, he quickly dismisses his inconsistent statements without damage to his valued image. He then makes efforts to get back on script as quickly as possible.[34] As with the other adolescents, creating and upholding a particular public and internal image of self—not only as one who is honest but also as possessing other positive attributes such as kindness, compassion, and goodness—is important to Herman for maintaining congruency between his actions (e.g., what he tells others) and his self-understandings (e.g., what he tells himself) and therefore for fostering his sense of integrity.

Happiness

It is not too surprising that happiness is one of the adolescents' main goals in life, given that there is probably no other goal in life than wanting to be happy that "commands such a high degree of consensus."[35] Sara Ahmed argues, "Happiness is consistently described as the object of human desire, as being what we aim for, as being what gives us purpose, meaning and order to human life."[36] The adolescents' goal of being happy gives purpose to what they are doing at the present while directing them down particular paths toward the future. They believe that happiness comes with maintaining their academic success to gain the credentials necessary for continued success, accomplishing what they want out life, and earning enough money to maintain or advance their socioeconomic status.[37] Posed as central to their happiness, these interrelated goals give meaning and direction to their present actions and future plans.

If happiness is understood as an emotion or inner feeling state, the adolescents at the moment are not particularly happy for a number of reasons. For most of them, their unhappy state is primarily attributed to the pressure and anxiety placed upon them by the grueling college admissions process. In addition to the competitive and time-consuming nature of this process, there are a lot of unknowns about their lives after high school, when they will be living away from home for the first time and entering unfamiliar contexts. Although they are excited about the significant changes that are about to take place in their lives, anxiety and stress about the unknowns overshadow any positive aspects of the upcoming transition to college. Other conditions in their lives also contribute to their unhappiness: Olive and Jacob are troubled by the problems they are facing at home; Kayla feels overwhelmed by the tremendous amount of pressure her parents are placing on her; Marcus feels incredibly lonely at his new university and longs to return to his more enjoyable past; and Leo feels uneasy about the life choices confronting him. These and other realities of their everyday lives are preventing them from feeling as happy as they believe they should be.

Although happiness is often understood as a private or interior state, several scholars explain happiness as more than *feeling good* but instead as involving cognition and evaluation. As such, happiness must persist beyond a particular moment[38]; it is a way of evaluating one's life and "overall quality-of-life-as-a-whole favourably"[39] and "mediates between individual and social, private and public, affective and evaluative, mind and body, as well as norms, rules and ideals and ways of being in the world."[40] The adolescents' happiness, therefore, does not stand apart from the world around them but instead is attached to how they make sense of themselves and their place in that world; it is connected to their self-understandings. Framing their advantages as an effect of what they do, for example, illustrates not only how they use ideological operations and strategies to rationalize those advantages but also how they negotiate their self-understandings in particular ways in their pursuit of happiness.

In pursuing happiness, they are intentionally pursuing something that they consider to be good, meaningful, or virtuous because happiness involves "moral distinctions insofar as they rest on ideas of who is worthy as well as capable of being happy 'in the right way.'"[41] Happiness, thus, involves a form of orientation; their lives are being directed in specific ways with the assumption that happiness is "to follow from some life choices and not others."[42] As an affective form of orientation, their pursuit of happiness is crucial for *understanding themselves as good*. Their happiness is directed toward specific versions of goodness; for instance, what Meredith, who plans to become a physician in Central America, understands as good is different from the version crafted by Marcus, who plans to have a career in the finance industry. Although their versions of goodness differ, their life plans are similarly aimed toward achieving what they want in life and maintaining their social class position while at the same time being productive citizens and contributing meaningfully to the world around them in a variety of ways, such as engaging in community service and charitable acts and using their wealth in other ways to benefit others. Their career goals function not only as a means to achieve a level of happiness that is not yet present but also to experience, at least in part, the affective rewards of working toward the promise of greater happiness. In the present, their happiness resides in the certainty that they will realize their goals and therefore that promise.

NAVIGATING SHIFTING SOCIAL AND ECONOMIC LANDSCAPES

The eight adolescents featured in this book are coming of age in unsettled economic times. As economies have become global, the supply of high-paying jobs with health benefits, vacation time, and pensions in the American labor market continues to dwindle, while the number of low-paying, unstable jobs with none of the aforementioned "perks" continues to grow.[43] Competition for the increasingly fewer "good" jobs is fierce, and it is widely argued that access to these jobs is closely tied to high levels of education and, at the very minimum, a college degree. At the same time, and perhaps consequentially, four-year colleges and universities, especially top-ranked institutions, have become more selective, with higher admissions standards; they have also become more expensive while providing less financial assistance. As if these unsettling economic realities generated by a shifting global economy were not enough, these eight young people were entering adolescence at the onset of a severe economic crisis that enveloped most of the globe. Over five years after the eruption of this crisis, the U.S. economy is still struggling to recover, with sustained, relatively high rates of unemployment, continued deleveraging by corporations and households, fiscal tightening, heightened sovereign risks, and slower growth powerfully feeding into one another. [44] Nearly everyone in the U.S. was, and many people continue to be, a casualty of this global economic crisis.

In both popular culture and social sciences, many scholars and writers claim that the shifting social and economic landscapes of what has been termed the *new economy* has brought about "an anxious affluent"[45] and particularly produced the troubled and uneasy identities of the middle class, so drastically different from earlier depictions of a complacent and comfortable middle class that dominated popular and scholarly works in the last century. As Jacob Hacker argues, "The insecurities that were once limited to the working poor have increasingly crept into the lives of middle-class—and even upper-middle-class—Americans."[46] More specifically, several scholars assert, "The stable, middle-class, emotional economy, in which satisfactions, entitlements and a sense of ease balance fear and anxieties is now beginning to topple, as risks threaten to outweigh familiar securities."[47] It is argued that the social and economic instabilities generated by the new economy are having a profound influence on the lives and self-understandings of young people from all social classes and are shaping the ways in which they, especially the affluent, imagine their lives differently than previous generations. As Jane Van Galen maintains, "Those who in previous generations may have assumed that the professional positions were theirs for the taking are now more likely to contract themselves (and in the process, reinvent themselves)."[48]

These eight affluent adolescents do not seem to share the uncertainties and anxieties about their future lives that young people from lower classes or, as several suggest, other young people within their own social class are experiencing in these turbulent times. Without question, they know that they will achieve what they want in life, maintain their privileged positions in society, continue to enjoy a lifestyle similar to that of their families and others in their communities, and become successful in their eventual careers. In many respects, they have good reasons to be so certain about what lies ahead for them. Although the current social and economic landscapes are shifting, young people who come from families in the top 20 percent are likely to remain at the top. Furthermore, those at the top of the economic spectrum are becoming wealthier in recent years, as the gulf between the haves and have-nots has widened. Even during the latest financial crisis, the wealthiest Americans weathered the severest economic downturn in eighty years better than everyone else and emerged from this crisis with an increased net worth. High stock prices, rising home values, and surging corporate profits have raised the recovery-era incomes of the most affluent Americans, while the incomes of almost everyone else are still weighed down by high unemployment and stagnant wages.[49] In the U.S., class inequalities are back to levels not seen since before the Great Depression, with the top 10 percent of earners now making the most on record—half of all income—as the bottom 90 percent continue to see their net worth and earnings decline.[50]

Even though the adolescents only have partial understanding of the myriad ways in which their lives are shaped by their relative power and privileged status, their current advantaging circumstances undoubtedly influence the absolute certainty they hold in imagining their future lives. It is also highly probable that not all affluent adolescents have this same level of certainty, given that there is significant variation among individuals of all social classes, including those at the top of the socioeconomic spectrum. However, how these eight adolescents imagine their future lives offers intriguing glimpses into how they construct meaning to secure and possibly even advance their power, status, and advantages. Of course their advantaging circumstances provide more direct access to such futures than for others without those same advantages.[51] But their self-understandings, constituted in relation to their advantages, play an equally important role in realizing what they imagine for their future lives. Through their self-understandings, they are actively constructing and cultivating their own privilege. This lens provides them with a compass to navigate the shifting landscapes of the new economy in ways leading them to the future lives they imagine at the present.

NOTES

1. Ahearn, 2013.
2. Scholars are increasingly emphasizing the important role of agency in the production of privilege and thus moving away from only considering the role of advantages. See, for example, Howard, 2008; Khan, 2011; Reay, Crozier, & James, 2011.
3. Brantlinger, 2003; Thompson, 1990.
4. Apple, 1992, p. 127.
5. Geertz, 1973, p. 11.
6. Brantlinger, 2003.
7. Althusser, 1971.
8. Thompson, 1990. Specific uses of particular operations and strategies are in italics with a brief definition of each in parenthesis.
9. Brantlinger, 2003, p. 9.
10. In Brantlinger's (1993) in-depth examination of affluent and low-income students' perceptions of their educational experiences, low-income students claimed that affluent students taunted them with "stupid" and "dumb" even though the affluent students in her study never used such labels for economically disadvantaged students. The affluent students in her study, however, communicated that low-income students were less advanced academically than students of their class. See also Brantlinger, 2003; Howard, 2008.
11. Several researchers have found that race plays a significant role in elite contexts, particularly schools (see, for example, Gaztambide-Fernández, 2009).
12. Important to point out that none of the female adolescents identify as upper class even though Meredith and Kayla come from families with wealth and annual incomes equal to those of the three males.
13. Leo, in fact, argues the exact opposite by claiming that privileged individuals are less motivated because they are not in a do-or-die situation.
14. Some did this indirectly through their discussions about the qualities of other affluent students.
15. For example, Mickelson, 1990; Olson, 1983.
16. Khan, 2011, p. 14.
17. Khan, 2011.
18. Pekar, 2013.
19. For example, Rosaldo, 1984.
20. Lutz, 1988.
21. See Apple & Weis, 1983; Wexler, 1992.
22. Lutz, 1988, p. 5.
23. For example, Pease, 2010.
24. Rosenblum & Travis, 2012, p. 203.
25. Campbell et al., 2004, p. 31.
26. Gaztambide-Fernández, Cairns, & Desai, 2013.
27. Khan (2011) finds a similar distinction in his study of students at St. Paul's School. He explains, "Students work to frame their success not as deserved but earned. It is a product of what they have done and not where they are from. This framing . . . works against our very common, age-old suspicion of entitlement and the nagging feeling that the rich succeed just because of who they are. St. Paul's students seek to replace that frame with one that is based on achievement" (p. 48).

28. Khan, 2011, p. 48.
29. Stuber, 2010.
30. For example, Goodman, 2000.
31. Privileged individuals tend to lack the kind of critical analysis of their own privilege that highlights how their advantages are related to the oppression suffered by disadvantaged groups (Gaztambide-Fernández & Howard, 2013; Stuber, 2010).
32. hooks, 2009, p. 192.
33. See Wexler, 1992.
34. This pattern for resolving inconsistencies is similar to how the affluent mothers in Brantlinger's (2003) study resolved dissonance between their liberal identity and conservative viewpoints. Like Herman, the mothers used particular ideological moves to establish and sustain a particular image and to disguise choices in conflict with this image. Using excuses and caveats in their narratives, the mothers rationalized their choices and dismissed any inconsistencies.
35. Frey & Stutzer, 2002, p. vii.
36. Ahmed, 2010, p. 1.
37. The common belief, in the U.S. and other western societies, is that wealth brings happiness. However, several scholars point out that the accumulation of wealth does not lead to the accumulation of happiness. As Richard Layard (2005) argues, "As Western societies have got richer, their people have become no happier" (p. 1). This has led some scholars to argue for the need to "uncouple happiness from the accumulation of wealth" (Ahmed, 2007, p. 122).
38. For example, Ahmed, 2007, 2010; McMahon, 2006.
39. Veenhoven, 1984, p. 22.
40. Ahmed, 2007, p. 124.
41. Ahmed, 2010, p. 12.
42. Ahmed, 2010, p. 54.
43. Lareau, 2011.
44. United Nations, 2013.
45. Harris, 2007.
46. Hacker, 2006.
47. Reay, Crozier, & James, 2011, pp. 2–3. See also Kalleberg, 2009.
48. Van Galen, 2007, pp. 4–5.
49. Lowrey, 2013.
50. Gibson & Perot, 2011.
51. Gaztambide-Fernández, 2009.

11 Transforming Self-Understandings

with Kelsey Cromie

A little over a year and a half has passed since we ended the formal interviews with the eight adolescents. Meredith, Herman, Kayla, Sarah, and Jacob have graduated high school and are now attending college or taking a gap year to travel. Olive is in her final year of high school and Marcus is in his second year of college. Leo still lives at home and is now taking classes at a local community college. Some significant changes have occurred in their lives; most are living away from home for the first time, entering new contexts, and/or embarking on new challenges. But most of them have not altered their goals and plans for the future much; only a few considerable changes have occurred for some of them over this period of time. All of them, though, are exactly where they want to be and where they believe they should be.

For five of them, their plans for the future remain pretty much the same. Moving forward in realizing her dreams of becoming a missionary doctor in Central America, Meredith is majoring in pre-med at her top-choice university and continues to travel regularly and extensively. Marcus continues to stay busy with his entrepreneurial endeavors. After his first year of college, he completed a finance internship set up through family connections. Kayla relinquished soccer and her dream of traveling abroad to focus all her energy and time on gaining admission to an elite college. After stressing over thirteen college applications, she was accepted to a highly selective university in California, where she is majoring in business. Sarah received acceptances with generous scholarships to several prestigious universities. After much deliberation, she chose an engineering program at a university that emphasizes individual learning. Although not accepted to his first-choice university, Jacob is thrilled to be attending college in New York City, where he is pursuing a degree in performing arts with an emphasis on dance.

For the other three, some unexpected changes occurred over the past year. Herman got into his top-choice liberal arts college in New England but deferred his acceptance to take a gap year. His decision to spend a year traveling and "living the life of a filmmaker and screenwriter" instead of going immediately to college was made "sort of at the last minute." Before gaining acceptance to college, he had never seriously considered taking a gap year, but after dealing with the stress of the college process, he felt that he needed a break from academics. He spent the first few months traveling Europe and then started working on a film that he plans to enter into competition next year. At the end of her junior year, Olive surprised everyone by abruptly quitting hip-hop dancing and then focusing more on ballet training. Tired of seeing her parents use her continued involvement in hip-hop dancing to make her do things that she did not want to do, she decided, "I'll just do it when I'm in college [and not living at home]." After spending the summer surfing, playing music, and hanging out with friends, Leo's parents made him get a job. After a couple months of delivering pizzas, he concluded, "This was really a shitty job, not something I wanted to do for very long." Working at this job led to a change of heart about continuing his education. He is now taking classes at a community college and plans to transfer to a four-year institution in a couple of years.

As they continue along their life paths, both major and minor changes in their plans will likely continue to occur, since things rarely go exactly as planned in life. Although certain about their future success, the adolescents expect to modify their plans as they encounter unforeseeable obstacles and opportunities, gain new knowledge and experiences, and discover new interests and passions. Those who have a clear plan realize, to a certain extent, that they will undoubtedly take a few detours and maybe even change direction completely as they balance their expectations with realities. Those with less defined plans anticipate exploring several avenues and revising their future plans multiple times in determining what they want out of life. Viewing unexpected changes more as possibilities rather than limitations, all of them firmly believe that they will be able to incorporate these modifications into their existing and/or future plans to keep them on track toward eventual success.

As noted in Chapter 1, their understandings of self, others, and the world around them will also undoubtedly change, given that the development of self-understandings is an ongoing process. The portraits presented in this book provide a view of these adolescents' self-understandings at a particular moment in their lives. Their self-understandings will continue to be shaped and reshaped by the complex interactions and mediating factors of their everyday realities and lived experiences.[1] As they enter unfamiliar situations and contexts, form new relationships, and gain additional experiences and knowledge, they will encounter new and old cultural meanings and practices that will influence their ways of knowing and doing. These meaning and practices will continue taking on particular values and forms as the adolescents mediate these cultural resources in the ongoing construction of their self-understandings.[2]

UNINTENTIONAL INTERVENTION

At the beginning of this research, we were not expecting to see many changes, if any, in the adolescents' self-understandings over the course of the study.

We began our interviews to clarify more fully how privilege is constructed and cultivated through our participants' self-understandings. Although participatory action research (PAR) emphasizes individual and social change and rests on the idea that "the social world can only be understood by trying to change it,"[3] we engaged in these collaborative, transformational efforts primarily to advance *our own understandings* and not those of the adolescents. Beforehand, we did not fully consider the unavoidable ways in which this project would influence the adolescents' self-understandings. Soon after beginning the interviews, it became clear to us that the adolescents' understandings would be affected by their engagement in a process that gave them opportunities to sort out, discuss, and reflect on their self-understandings and the concepts of privilege and social class, an unfamiliar process to all of them. At the conclusion of the interviews, we asked them to reflect on the overall interviewing process, and their responses confirmed what we had sensed: this process, to varying degrees, had influenced their understandings. As we continued working with them while we analyzed data and constructed the portraits, they gave us additional information on what changes had occurred in their understandings.

While participating in this project, the adolescents found themselves thinking more about social class and their own privilege and paying closer attention to the differences (or lack of differences) between themselves and those around them. Sarah reported, "The questions that you asked [during the interviews] made me rethink things and think more about some other things that I hadn't really even considered before [participating in this study]. It was hard not to keep thinking about what we had talked about during the interviews even when they were over." She further explained that during the interviewing process, "I'd talk with my mom a lot about these sorts of things and sort of paid attention to social class dynamics in school, and what I assume people's social class is and whether they associate with people who appear to be in the same social class." Kayla also noticed and thought about social class differences more than she had before the study. "I think it was right after the first [interview] we did that I kept thinking about all the differences between people and thinking about privilege after that. When we talked about all this more, [these topics] occupied my thoughts even more and I would catch myself trying to notice the things we talked about [during the interviews]," she explained.

Meredith initially did not believe "anything new changed in my thinking [by participating in this study]," but upon further reflection, she realized, "I started noticing more just how much I take for granted and I didn't think that I did take things for granted; it was just an eye-opener." She used an example to explain this further:

> Right now, we're making plans for prom and just seeing how, even though we are splitting everything up, we end up paying a ridiculous amount of money for everything when you add it all together. And just

that we all kind of expected it, like we all knew we were going to go and that our parents were going to pay it. Before we started talking about privilege, I don't think that I would have noticed just how very lightly we're taking all this.

Olive also began paying more attention to her own privileged circumstances. Before participating in the study, "I hadn't thought about privilege that much really, it was just something that existed, like something not to do with me and not tied to a person but [that] just existed." Over the course of the study, she increasingly noticed, "Privilege pertains to a lot of aspects in a person's life. Their privilege is kind of a big factor in someone's life, like as in a part of their past or what they're going to be. I realized all this was more connected to me than I used to think it was." With this increased awareness, "I started see a lot of differences at school. I just think like there are all these reasons why some kids seem so different, instead of just saying that this is probably just who they are. They don't have the same advantages in life, and this makes them seem more different than they actually are. It gives me a different perspective about them."

For Leo, his involvement in this study led him to redefine how he understands social class. He explained,

> I used to just define social class as a tax bracket; it's how much money you make. But after the questions [during the interviews] and thinking about that, I changed how I see social class to something a lot more than just about how much my parents make and not really directly connected to me. My social class impacts everything, a lot more than I originally thought.

Similarly, Marcus developed a broader definition of social class:

> You kept asking me to define social class [throughout the interviews]. I didn't know how to answer it when we first started talking and I still don't know exactly, but for different reasons [than at the beginning of the interviews]. It's just too complicated, something that I can't exactly put words to. But, and I know this is going to sound odd [given what I just said], how I define it has changed; I see it in a broader sense.

Like all the adolescents, Leo and Marcus increasingly considered the social and cultural elements of social class as well as the economic factors. By expanding the definition, they came to understand social class as a salient factor in individuals' lives—including their own.

Herman was surprised at the changes in his thinking that occurred by participating in the study. He noted, "I went into [the study] thinking that I wasn't going to change the way I see things or learn something. I don't know what I was expecting exactly, but I started sensing these changes

in how I thought about socioeconomic issues." In reflecting on his understandings before the study, he recalled, "Honestly, before this whole interviewing, I had not really thought about my social class or the social class
of others and how it affects and shapes a person." He reported that the
interviews gave him an opportunity "to consider a lot more what socioeconomic impact has upon an individual, and how it really affects your life in
multiple aspects and what you do and don't do." Jacob also believed that
the interviews provided him the context for "thinking about how these
conceptual questions, like what does social class and privilege mean, apply
to your own life." Like Herman, Jacob began recognizing "how what level
of privilege you have impacts your decisions and how you act, and you
can't really know how much it impacts everything, just some things." Our
discussions gave all of them opportunities to form deeper understandings
of the various ways in which their advantages shaped their everyday experiences and lives, actions, and understandings.

The adolescents entered this project with little to no prior explicit experiences of interrogating their self-understandings and the concepts of social
class and privilege. Occasionally a teacher, parent, and/or other significant
person in their lives had asked them about their understandings of self,
others, and the world around them, had pointed out their advantages and
the disadvantages of others, and had discussed the social class divisions
around them and within the larger society. All of them had engaged in
community service activities and some of them had gone on service trips to
distant places within and outside the U.S. They reported that these activities and trips had been meaningful learning experiences, helping them to
gain knowledge about the realities of others different from themselves and
their own advantaging circumstances. Finally, they had absorbed cultural
messages through various sources in their lives—such as media, schooling, family, and community—that taught them important lessons about
the concepts of social class and privilege and about who they are, how
they should live and relate to others, what is important in life, and what
the future holds for them. These prior learning experiences had influenced
how they think about others, how they view and feel about themselves, and
what they know about social class and privilege.

Although meaningful, these experiences mainly focused on building
new *knowledge* rather than forming or transforming *understanding*.[4] The
adolescents, for example, know from these experiences that social class
inequalities and other forms of injustices exist in local and extended communities, that privileged individuals have advantages that many others do
not have, that advantages make it easier for individuals to achieve what
they want out of life, that people without advantages encounter obstacles
in life that are incredibly difficult to overcome, and that they are privileged
whereas others from lower social class groups are disadvantaged. In many
ways, knowledge gained from these experiences allows them to maintain
an abstract, impersonal distance from the very inequalities and injustices

that they have learned about; they see these topics as more relevant to the lives of others different from themselves and often outside their immediate context than to their own lives and experiences. These prior learning experiences did not give them opportunities to form understandings, which, as Katy Swalwell points out, "requires empathy and a willingness to implicate oneself in the issue at hand—a much more difficult task."[5] Even in activities purportedly designed to increase one's understanding of their privilege and the oppression of others, such as community service activities and service trips, these adolescents took the relatively easier option of building knowledge of privilege and oppression rather than forming understandings that would establish a connection between these concepts and their lives.[6]

We do not want to overemphasize the influence this study had on the adolescents' understandings of self, others, and the world around them. Nonetheless, the changes that occurred in their self-understandings, no matter how minor, suggest something potentially powerful about the process used in this research project. In this process, we, in our facilitating role as researchers, did not lead them to a particular version of themselves, others, and the world around them or suggest how they should think about their own privilege. We did not attempt to build their knowledge of privilege, oppression, and other relevant concepts but instead focused on what they already knew. This is not to suggest that privileged individuals do not benefit from being offered alternative versions and new forms of knowledge but that it is through sharing what they know that privileged individuals' taken-for-granted, commonsense understandings of themselves and others can be questioned, examined, and possibly even challenged.

INTERROGATING OURSELVES

We began this research to advance our understandings of how privilege is constructed and cultivated through the eight affluent adolescents' self-understandings. As noted in Chapter 1, our project added a friendly amendment to how PAR is commonly understood by defining "our community" as privileged young people instead of just those within the Colby College community. We went into the project, however, with our local community in mind. Consistent with PAR's emphasis on action, we felt an imperative to put our data to use in raising awareness of class privilege within our community. Going into the project, our goals were to provoke an awareness of various issues related to class privilege and to push members of our community to reconsider everyday assumptions that keep class privilege hidden, not talked about, and unexamined. We planned to use data from our project on affluent adolescents' self-understandings to encourage such reconsideration.

Our efforts to further develop a critical awareness of our own self-understandings were also central to this project. During this project, we submitted our own privilege to the same analytic rigor that we took to explore the eight adolescents' self-understandings. This analysis gave us opportunities to examine aspects of our self-understandings "that are ordinarily invisible" because they are "ordinarily lost in silence."[7] It allowed us to more critically interrogate what had become taken for granted and ordinary in our own self-understandings. As we explored the adolescents' self-understandings, we included our own understandings in the mix. We brought these understandings together both in harmony and counterpoint, creating opportunities to explore more deeply how privilege is constructed and cultivated through our own and others' self-understandings. As one student co-researcher explained, "We looked at parts of the adolescents' self-understandings that nobody pays attention to because they're so normal. But paying attention to those aspects led us to turn the mirror on ourselves and pay closer attention to those parts in ourselves that we normally don't think about."[8] Another student co-researcher added, "We ended up studying ourselves as much as we were studying the adolescents."

Turning our scholarly gaze not only toward the adolescents but also inward engaged us in a process that provided valuable learning opportunities. Over the course of the research project, we constructed new ways of thinking about privilege and our own social class identity. Thinking differently, however, did not necessarily mean that we had achieved clarity about privilege and our own social class identities. Several student co-researchers reported at the end of the project that going through this process produced more questions than clarity about their privilege and their social class identity. One of them explained, "I think through doing this research study, my understandings of my own social class and my understandings of social class and privilege in general have become a little distorted. I haven't sorted it all out yet. I have too many questions." She added, "Coming up with all these questions is a good thing, because it's making me question things I never did before. It's making me realize that I need to be [asking] these questions and even newer ones to develop a critical awareness of my privilege."

This questioning became not only an important part of our efforts to work toward a critical consciousness of our privilege[9] but also to wrestle with the troubling concept of class privilege. One student co-researcher reported, "All these questions that naturally came up when we were researching gave us chances to look more deeply within ourselves while at the same time helping us understanding the theory and research that we were reading about privilege and how it works." For most student co-researchers, the project provided the kinds of enriched, active learning experiences to enhance their "textbook learning." As one co-researcher explained,

> Conducting this research study was an effective approach to learning about social class and privilege and ourselves. We got to look at multiple personal instances of privilege and compare and contrast them against one another in a personal way. Watching our participants change their

views, as well as classmates come to conclusions or realizations about privilege, be it their interviewee's or their own, made privilege a discussion and debate, a fluid topic, as opposed to a term discussed in a book. This made us think differently about privilege and our [social class] background.

We saw connections between what we were reading and what we were discovering through this research project. These connections allowed us to explore the potential of different perspectives and theories for illuminating particular practices as a basis for developing critical insights and ideas about how privilege is created and maintained not only in the participants' lives but also our own.[10]

Another important connection that enhanced our understandings was with the participants. A student co-researcher remarked, "What helped me in my understandings about privilege, and especially my own privilege, was the connections we made with the adolescents. In reading their transcripts and interviewing one of them, I was able to see parts of myself through the eyes of others." Another co-researcher similarly explained,

> This research project has been extremely influential for my ways of thinking about my privilege and just the concept itself. Most notably, while interviewing, analyzing, and talking about Kayla, I became more acutely aware of my perceptions of my own privilege. Growing up in a similar community as Kayla, I recognized a lot of the same things she expressed in our interviews. In this way, the research project truly did serve as an exercise in reflecting on my own privilege and the ways privilege is tied to my identity, whether I would like to admit it or not.

For most of us, "the adolescents were additional sources that we could learn from; their interviews served as another text that [let us] learn more about ourselves and about privilege," as a co-researcher explained.

For Howard, this project enriched his understanding of the power of joining with others to engage in research. In particular, he learned to participate *with* young people in the research process and to further appreciate what young people can accomplish in changing the world around them when given the opportunity. Through this project, Howard discovered pedagogical possibilities for creating a supportive learning environment for affluent college students to question their assumptions and understandings about themselves and others. More specifically, he further developed particular pedagogical principles and practices for leading affluent students to uncomfortable places in learning about class privilege: balance the emotional and cognitive components of the teaching and learning process; support students individually and collectively; build and maintain respectful relationships with students; attend to social relations between students; emphasize student-centered learning through reflection and experience; and value awareness, personal growth, and change as learning outcomes.[11] As with his co-researchers, Howard formed new understandings about his own privilege and how privilege works through self-understandings and developed new skills to work with others more effectively for social change.

WHERE DO WE GO FROM HERE?

The research project reported in this book ended up providing all of us-the twenty-four researchers and eight adolescents—with valuable learning experiences for becoming more aware of our self-understandings and the relationship between those understandings and our advantages. Engaging in a process that allowed us to sort out, discuss, and reflect on our self-understandings and the concepts of privilege and social class affected the ways in which we think about ourselves, others and the world around us. Most of us emerged from this research with a greater capacity to question our assumptions about ourselves and others, more willingness to acknowledge the significant role that our advantages play in our lives, a deeper understanding of our privilege and the concepts of privilege and social class, and an increased interest in learning more. For the researchers, we ended our research with a broader understanding of the possibilities for changing the world around us and seeing ourselves as agents of change. For all of us, our understandings, to varying degrees, were transformed through our participation in this project.

Where do we go from here in our learning? What other opportunities will we have to advance our understandings? How can we continue what we started in this research project? Since our immediate and larger worlds are structured in ways that conceal how privilege works and thus keeps our advantages invisible and unnamed, it is likely most of us will not have many opportunities like those we had in this project to sort out, discuss, and reflect on our self-understandings and to advance our understandings of privilege and social class. As an invisible presence, our privilege will rarely come up in our everyday lives, even though privilege plays a deeply important role in how we understand ourselves and others and what we do in the world in which we live.

Most of us, though, will be offered valuable opportunities—as within classrooms, workplaces, our families and communities, religious institutions, and community service activities—to advance our *knowledge* rather than our *understandings* of the concepts of privilege and social class and possibly even our own privilege and social class identity. Like other privileged individuals, for example, we will probably focus on knowledge of the injustices associated with privilege rather than understanding how these injustices are created and maintained and how we are implicated, because it will be easier for us to deplore injustice "than to take responsibility for the privilege some of us receive as a result of it."[12] It will take intentional efforts on our part to seek out opportunities to learn more, further develop our understandings, and continue the efforts that began in this project.

Over the past ten years or so, scholars have increasingly offered conceptual, pedagogical, and research frameworks for creating such opportunities for privileged individuals. Inspired by Paulo Freire's work on the pedagogy of the oppressed[13] and Peggy McIntosh's "knapsack of privilege,"[14] we have seen the emergence of a pedagogy for the privileged[15] and a pedagogy for the oppressor.[16] Even though much of this work occurs in educational institutions, these approaches are also taken into government and community-based forums to make privileged individuals more aware of their advantages.[17] In related efforts, scholars are proposing intersectional strategies for dismantling privilege,[18] undoing privilege,[19] and deconstructing privilege.[20] A few scholars are also outlining approaches of a social justice pedagogy specifically designed for developing the critical consciousness of privileged students[21] and for engaging privileged individuals at all ages in social justice efforts.[22] These scholars join others in proposing ways for privileged people to become allies with oppressed individuals and groups.[23] In a similar vein, others are offering strategies for engaging in critical dialogue with those who are oppressed.[24] Although each of these works offers different approaches and frameworks, there is a fair amount of agreement that transforming the understandings and actions of privileged individuals is essential for challenging privilege.

In addition to processes aimed at transforming privileged individuals, several scholars emphasize the need for engaging in processes that challenge the institutionalization of privilege within societal systems. As Bob Pease points out, "changing people in privileged groups will not itself abolish privilege any more than empowering the oppressed will eliminate oppression."[25] Transforming the understandings of privileged individuals to increase their critical consciousness will not be in itself enough to address the processes involved in the production and maintenance of privilege. Since privilege is generated and reinforced at the personal, cultural, and structural levels, "privilege is rooted in societies and organizations as much as it's rooted in people's personalities and how they perceive and react to one another."[26]

In fact, the effects of macroeconomic policies and the social class divisions of the larger society often overshadow efforts by individuals to interrupt privilege.[27] These larger realities lead some scholars to doubt whether efforts to change individuals actually bring about any changes other than to individuals. Andrea Smith maintains that even these personal changes are ephemeral and often do not lead "to any political projects to dismantle the structures of domination that enabled their privilege."[28] Given this, she concludes, "The undoing of privilege occurs not by individuals confessing their privileges or trying to think themselves into a new subject position but through the creation of collective structures that dismantle the systems that enable these privileges."[29] Like others,[30] she believes that "individual transformation must occur concurrently with social and political transformation."[31] The question of how to engage privileged individuals in such a process then arises.

This book reflects our efforts in carrying out a project that interconnects personal and social transformation. From the outset, we wanted to push local and larger audiences/readers to reconsider everyday assumptions that keep class privilege hidden, not talked about, and unexamined. We wrote this book to encourage such reconsideration. We also put our data to use by engaging the Colby community in dialogue about class privilege, locating problems within our community that the data brought to light, and developing action plans for addressing those problems. We broadcasted these action plans in multiple ways—public forums, the campus newspaper, campus-wide electronic postings, flyers posted around campus, "table tents" in the dining halls, and meetings with senior administrators, faculty, and staff. When what we discovered through our research was widely disseminated, it sparked conversations across campus, challenged common understandings of social class, increased awareness of topics rarely considered within our community, and established a collective of individuals committed to changing practices and policies that advantaged some at the expense of others.

Through this project, we joined others who are engaging privileged individuals in collaborative, participatory, embodied, and arts-based research projects that emphasize both increased awareness and action. Some underlying tenets inform the majority of these projects, including our own: a collective commitment to explore an issue or problem; a desire to engage in self- and collective reflection; a joint decision to engage in action; and the building of alliances in the planning, implementation, and dissemination of research.[32] These aims are achieved through a living dialectical process that changes researchers, participants, and the contexts in which they act.[33] These efforts are providing conceptual, pedagogical, and research frameworks not only for advancing our individual and collective understandings of how privilege works but also for enabling individuals to contest, reframe, and challenge privilege. While these efforts are opening up new opportunities for individual and social transformation, we must continue to move toward a future yet to be imagined. Transformational work never ends.

NOTES

1. Howard, 2008.
2. For example, Tappan, 2005, 2006.
3. Brydon-Miller, Greenwood, & Maguire, 2003, p. 15.
4. This point is informed by the work of Leonardo (2009), who distinguishes between racial understanding and racial knowledge. He makes the point that white people have a fair amount of knowledge about race but largely lack racial understanding. Swalwell (2013) argues that this distinction is relevant to other forms of privilege, including class privilege.

5. Swalwell, 2013, p. 25.
6. For more discussion on why affluent adolescents are likely to focus on knowledge rather than understanding, see, for example, Howard, 2008; Rothenberg, 2002.
7. Greene, 1988, p. 19.
8. This and other quotes from student co-researchers are a part of a teacher research project that Howard conducted to explore what they learned about the concepts of social class and privilege and about their own social class identity through this PAR project. To gather data for this project, he administered pre- and post-course questionnaires, asked students to write self-evaluations, and kept a teacher journal. For the pre-course questionnaire, student co-researchers were asked to describe their social class identity and prior experiences doing research and learning about the concepts of social class and privilege' they were also asked questions about their expectations and concerns going into the project. The post-course questionnaire included questions about their learning experiences during the various stages of the PAR project. At the end, student co-researchers wrote self-evaluations of their overall performance and contributions. They were also asked to reflect on the influence this project had on their understandings of social class and privilege. While working with students on the project, Howard engaged in his own reflection through journal writing. He recorded thoughts, observations, and evaluations of the group's collaborative efforts.
9. Freire (1970) argues that questioning is essential for working toward critical consciousness. As individuals do this, they should learn to question society, see through versions of "truths" that teach people to accept unfairness and injustice, and become empowered to define, envision, and work toward social justice. This process requires individuals to become aware not only of the realities that shape their lives and the lives of others but also of their own abilities to transform those realities.
10. Kemmis & McTaggart, 2005
11. Adams, 2007.
12. Rothenberg, 2002, p. 1.
13. Freire, 1970.
14. McIntosh, 1988.
15. Ann Curry-Stevens (2007) identifies six steps to a pedagogy for the privileged: gaining awareness of oppression, understanding the structural dynamics that hold oppression in place, locating oneself as oppressed, locating oneself as privileged, understanding the benefits associated with privilege, and understanding oneself as being implicated in the oppression of others and acknowledging oneself as an oppressor.
16. For example, Breault, 2003; Kimmel, 2010.
17. Pease, 2010.
18. Hobgood, 2009.
19. Pease, 2010.
20. Case, 2013.
21. For example, Seider, 2009; Swalwell, 2013.
22. For example, Goodman, 2000, 2011.
23. For example, Bishop, 2002; Case, 2013; Edwards, 2006.
24. For example, van Gorder, 2007.
25. Pease, 2010, p. 170.
26. Johnson, 2001, p. 35.
27. Howard (2008) argues that we can only imagine and work toward interrupting privilege given the policies and divisions of the larger society that generate and reinforce privilege.

28. Smith, 2013, p. 263.
29. Ibid.
30. For example, Golash-Boza, 2013.
31. Smith, 2013, p. 263.
32. MyIntyre, 2008.
33. McTaggart, 1997.

References

Adams, M. (2007). Pedagogical frameworks for social justice education. In M. Adams, L. Bell & P. Griffin (Eds.), *Teaching for diversity and social justice* (2nd ed., pp. 15–33). New York: Routledge.

Ahearn, L. M. (2013). Privileging and affecting agency. In C. Maxwell & P. Aggleton (Eds.), *Privilege, Agency and affect: Understanding the production and effects of action* (pp. 240–247). London: Palgrave Macmillan.

Ahmed, S. (2007). Multiculturalism and the promise of happiness. *New Formations, 63*(Winter), 121–137.

Ahmed, S. (2010). *The promise of happiness*. Durham, NC: Duke University Press.

Alexander, K., Entwisle, D., & Olson, L. (2007). Lasting consequences of the summer learning gap. *American Sociological Review, 72,* 167–180.

Althusser, L. (1971). *Lenin and philosophy, and other essays*. New York: Monthly Review Press.

American Psychiatric Association (2000). Position statement on therapies focused on attempts to change sexual orientation (reparative or conversion therapies). *American Journal of Psychiatry, 157*(10), 1791–1721.

Anyon, J. (1981). Social class and school knowledge. *Curriculum Inquiry, 11*(1), 3–42.

Anyon, J. (1997). *Ghetto schooling: A political economy of urban educational reform*. New York: Teachers College Press.

Anyon, J. (2005). What "counts" as educational policy? Notes toward a new paradigm. *Harvard Educational Review, 75,* 65–88.

Apple, M. (1992). Education, culture, and class power: Basil Bernstein and the neo-Marxist sociology of education. *Educational Theory, 42*(2), 127–145.

Apple, M. (2001). *Educating the right way: Markets, standards, God and inequality*. New York: Routledge-Falmer.

Apple, M., & Weis, L. (1983). Ideology and practice in schooling: A political and conceptual introduction. In M. Apple & L. Weis (Eds.), *Ideology and practice in schooling* (pp. 3–25). Philadelphia: Temple University Press.

Aucoin, D. (2009, March 3). For some, helicopter parenting delivers benefits. *The Boston Globe*. Retrieved from http://www.boston.com/lifestyle/family/articles/2009/03/03/for_some_helicopter_parenting_delivers_benefits/

Bailey, A. (1998). Privilege: Expanding on Marilyn Frye's "oppression." *Journal of Social Philosophy, 29*(3), 104–119.

Baltzell, E. D. (1989). *Philadelphia gentlemen: The making of a national upper class*. New Brunswick, NJ: Transaction Press.

Barr, R. D., & Parrett, W. H. (2001). *Hope fulfilled for at-risk and violent youth*. Needham Heights, MA: Allyn and Bacon.

Bassett, P. F. (2006, May 1). Affordability and "the family Ford." *Bassett Blog.* Retrieved from http://www2.nais.org/about/article.cfm?ItemNumber=148304

Baumeister, R. F. (1996). Self-regulation and ego threat: Motivated cognition, self-deception, and destructive goal setting. In P. M. Gollwitzer & J. A. Bargh (Eds.), *The psychology of action: Linking cognition and motivation to behavior* (pp. 27–47). New York: Guilford Press.

Biddle, B. J., & Berliner, D. C. (2002). Unequal school funding in the United States. *Beyond Instructional Leadership, 59*(8), 48–49.

Bishop, A. (2002). *Becoming an ally: Breaking the cycle of oppression—in people.* London: Zed Books.

Blos, P. (1962). *On adolescence: A psychoanalytic interpretation.* New York: Free Press.

Bound, J., Hershbein, B., & Long, B. T. (2009). Playing the admissions game: Reactions to increasing college competition. *Journal of Economic Perspectives, 23*(4), 119–146.

Bourdieu, P. (1977). *Outline of a theory of practice.* Cambridge, UK: Cambridge University Press.

Bourdieu, P. (1984). *Distinction: A social critique of the judgment of taste.* Cambridge, MA: Harvard University Press.

Bourdieu, P. (1986). The forms of capital. In J. G. Richardson (Ed.), *Handbook of theory and research for the sociology of education* (pp. 241–258). New York: Greenwood Press.

Brantlinger, E. (1993). *The politics of social class in secondary schools: Views of affluent and impoverished youth.* New York: Teachers College Press.

Brantlinger, E. (1999). Class moves in the movies: What *Good Will Hunting* teaches about social life. *Journal of Curriculum Theorizing, 15*(1), 105–120.

Brantlinger, E. (2003). *Dividing classes: How the middle class negotiates and rationalizes school advantage.* New York: Routledge–Falmer.

Breault, R. (2003). Dewey, Freire, and a pedagogy for the oppressor. *Multicultural Education, 10*(3), 2–7.

Bruner, J. (1990). *Acts of meaning.* Cambridge, MA: Harvard University Press.

Brydon-Miller, M., Greenwood, D., & Maguire, P. (2003). Why action research? *Action Research 1*(1): 9–28.

Butler, J. (1990). *Gender trouble: Feminism and the subversion of identity.* New York: Routledge.

Butler, J. (1991). Decking out: Performing identities. In D. Fuss (Ed.), *Inside/out: Lesbian theories, gay theories* (pp. 13–29). New York: Routledge.

Camara, W., Kimmel, E., Scheuneman, J., & Sawtell, E. (2003). Whose grades are inflated? *College Board Research Report No. 2003–4.* New York: College Board.

Campbell, W. K., Bonacci, A. M., Shelton, J., Exline, J. J., & Bushman, B. J. (2004). Psychological entitlement: Interpersonal consequences and validation of a self-report measure. *Journal of Personality Assessment, 8,* 29–45.

Case, K. (Ed.). (2013). *Deconstructing privilege: Teaching and learning as allies in the classroom.* New York: Routledge.

Chafel, J. A., & Neitzel, C. (2005). Young children's ideas about the nature, causes, justification, and alleviation of poverty. *Early Childhood Research Quarterly, 20,* 433–450.

Chase, S. (2008). *Perfectly prep: Gender extremes at a New England prep school.* New York: Oxford University Press.

College Board. (2012, February). *The 8th annual AP report to the nation.* Retrieved from http://apreport.collegeboard.org

Cookson, P. W., & Persell, C. H. (1985). *Preparing for power: America's elite boarding schools.* New York: Basic Books.

Cozzarelli, C., Wilkinson, A. V., & Tagler, M. J. (2001). Attitudes toward the poor and attributions of poverty. *Journal of Social Issues, 57*, 207–227.

Csikszentmihalyi, M., & Schneider, B. (2000). *Becoming adult: How teenagers prepare for the world of work.* New York: Basic Books.

Curry-Stevens, A. (2007). New forms of transformative education: Pedagogy for the privileged. *Journal of Transformative Education, 5*(1), 33–58.

Dale, S. B., & Krueger, A. B. (2002). Estimating the payoff of attending a more selective college: An application of selection on observables and unobservables. *Quarterly Journal of Economics, 107*(4), 1491–1527.

Damon, W., & Hart, D. (1988). *Self-understanding in childhood and adolescence.* Cambridge, UK: Cambridge University Press.

Darling-Hammond, L., & Post, L. (2000). Inequality in teaching and schooling: Supporting high-quality teaching and leadership in low-income schools. In R. D. Kahlenberg (Ed.), *A notion at risk: Preserving public education as an engine for social mobility* (pp. 127–167). New York: Century Foundation Press.

Davidson, E. (2011). *The burden of aspirations: Schools, youth, and success in the divided social worlds of Silicon Valley.* New York: New York University Press.

Domhoff, W. G. (1998). *Who rules America?* Mountain View, CA: Mayfield.

Dowling, R. (2009). Geographies of identity: Landscapes of class. *Progress in Human Geography, 1*, 1–7.

Easterbrook, G. (2004). Who needs Harvard? *Atlantic Monthly, 294*(3), 128–130; 132–133.

Education Trust. (2001). *The funding gap: Low-income and minority students receive fewer dollars.* Washington, DC: Author.

Edwards, K. E. (2006). Aspiring social justice ally identity development: A conceptual model. *NASPA Journal, 43*(4), 39–60.

Elliott, M. (1998). School finance and opportunity to learn: Does money well spent enhance students' achievement? *Sociology of Education, 71*(3), 223–245.

Erikson, E. (1968). *Identity: Youth and crisis.* New York: Norton.

Espenshade, T., & Radford, A. W. (2009). *No longer separate, still not equal.* Princeton, NJ: Princeton University Press.

Ferguson, R. F. (1991). Paying for public education: New evidence on how and why money matters. *Harvard Journal on Legislation, 28*(2), 465–498.

Fine, M., & Gordon, S. M. (1992). Feminist transformations of/despite psychology. In M. Fine (Ed.), *Disruptive voices: The possibilities of feminist research* (pp. 1–25). Ann Arbor, MI: University of Michigan Press.

Fine, M., & Macpherson, P. (1992). Over dinner: Feminism and adolescent female bodies. In M. Fine (Ed.), *Disruptive voices: The possibilities of feminist research* (pp. 175–203). Ann Arbor, MI: University of Michigan Press.

Fischer-Rosenthal, W. (2000). Address lost: How to fix lives. Biographical structuring in the European modern age. In R. Breckner, D. Kalekin-Fishman, & I. Miethe (Eds.), *Biographies and the division of Europe* (pp. 55–75). Opladen, Germany: Lieske + Budrich.

Freud, A. (1946). *The ego and mechanisms of defense* (C. Baines, trans.). New York: International Universities Press.

Frey, B. S., & Stutzer, A. (2002). *Happiness and economics: How the economy and institutions affect human well-being.* Princeton, NJ: Princeton University Press.

Garrod, A., Smulyan, L., Powers, S., & Kilkenny, R. (2012). *Adolescent portraits: Identity, relationships, and challenges* (7th ed.). Boston: Pearson Education.

Gaztambide-Fernández, R. A. (2009). *The best of the best: Becoming elite at an American boarding school.* Cambridge, MA: Harvard University Press.

Gaztambide-Fernández, R. A., & Howard, A. (2013). Social justice, deferred complicity, and the moral plight of the wealthy. *Democracy & Education, 21*(1), Article 7. Retrieved from http://democracyeducationjournal.org/home/vol21/iss1/7/

Gaztambide-Fernández, R. A., Cairns, K., & Desai, C. (2013). The sense of entitlement. In C. Maxwell & P. Aggleton (Eds.), *Privilege, Agency and affect: Understanding the production and effects of action* (pp. 32–49). London: Palgrave Macmillan.

Geertz, C. (1973). Ideology as a cultural system. In C. Geertz (Ed.), *The interpretation of culture* (pp. 197–207). New York: Basic Books.

Gibbs, N. (2009, November 20). The growing backlash against overparenting. *Time Magazine.* Retrieved from http://www.time.com/time/magazine/article/0,9171,1940697,00.html

Gibson, D., & Perot, C. (2011). It's the inequality, stupid. *Mother Jones, March/April Issue.* Retrieved from http://www.motherjones.com/politics/2011/02/income-inequality-in-america-chart-graph

Golash-Boza, T. (2013, September 20). The problems with white allies and white privilege. *Al Jazeera.* Retrieved from http://www.aljazeera.com/indepth/opinion/2013/09/2013920103353832487.html

Goodman, D. (2000). Motivating people from privileged groups to support social justice. *Teachers College Record, 102*(6), 1061–1085.

Goodman, D. (2011). *Promoting diversity and social justice: Educating people from privileged groups* (2nd ed.). Thousand Oaks, CA: Sage.

Greene, M. (1988). *The dialectic of freedom.* New York: Teachers College Press.

Hacker, J. S. (2006). *The great risk shift.* New York: Oxford University Press.

Haigler, K., & Nelson, R. (2005). *The gap-year advantage: Helping your child benefit from time off before or during college.* New York: St. Martin's Press.

Hall, G. S. (1904). *Adolescence: Its psychology and its relations to physiology, anthropology, sociology, sex, crime, religion, and education.* New York: Appleton-Century-Crofts.

Hardiman, R., & Jackson, B. W. (1997). Conceptual foundations for social justice courses. In M. Adams, L. A. Bell, & P. Griffin (Eds.), *Teaching for diversity and social justice: A sourcebook* (pp. 16–29). New York: Routledge.

Harris, J. (2007). The anxious affluent. *Renewal: A Journal of Social Democracy, 15*(4), 72–79.

Harter, E. A. (1999). How educational expenditures relate to student achievement: Insights from Texas elementary schools. *Journal of Education Finance, 24*(3), 281–302.

Hobgood, M. (2009). *Dismantling privilege: An ethics of accountability* (rev. ed.). Cleveland, OH: The Pilgrim Press.

Holland, D., Lachicotte, W. Jr., Skinner, D., & Cain, C. (1998). *Identity and agency in cultural worlds.* Cambridge, MA: Harvard University Press.

hooks, b. (2009). *Writing beyond race: Living theory and practice.* New York: Routledge.

Housing Assistance Council. (2012). Poverty in rural America. *Rural research note.* Retrieved from http://www.ruralhome.org/storage/research_notes/rrn_poverty.pdf

Howard, A. (2008). *Learning privilege: Lessons of power and identity in affluent schooling.* New York: Routledge.

Howard, A. (2009). Sorting out contradictions: Struggling to do what we say. *Independent School, 69*(1), 40–47.

Howard, A. (2010). Elite visions: Privileged perceptions of self and others. *Teachers College Record, 112*(8), 1971–1992.

Howard, A. (2011). Privileged pursuits of social justice: Exploring privileged college students' motivation for engaging in social justice. *Journal of College and Character, 12*(2), 1–14.

Howell, J., & Smith, J. (2011). *Getting into college: A cross-cohort examination of college preparations by lower-SES students.* Retrieved from http://www.advocacy.collegeboard.org

Jensen, R. (2002). White privilege shapes the U.S. In P. S. Rothenberg (Ed.), *White privilege: Essential readings on the other side of racism* (pp. 103–106). New York: Worth.

Jensen, R. (2005). *The heart of whiteness: Confronting race, racism, and white privilege.* San Francisco: City Lights.

Johnson, A. G. (2001). *Privilege, power, and difference.* Mountain View, CA: Mayfield.

Josselson, R. (2004). The hermeneutics of faith and the hermeneutics of suspicion. *Narrative Inquiry, 14*(1), 1–28.

Kalleberg, A. (2009). Precarious work, insecure workers: Employment relations in transition. *American Sociological Review, 7,* 1–22.

Kemmis, S., & McTaggart, R. (2005). Participatory action research: Communicative action and the public sphere. In N. K. Denzin, & Y. S. Lincoln (Eds.), *The Sage handbook of qualitative research* (3rd ed.; pp. 559–603). Thousand Oaks, CA: Sage.

Khan, S. R. (2010). Getting in: How elite schools play the college game. In A. Howard & R. Gaztambide-Fernández (Eds.), *Educating elites: Class privilege and educational advantage* (pp. 97–112). Lanham, MD: Rowman & Littlefield.

Khan, S. R. (2011). *Privilege: The making of an adolescent elite at St. Paul's School.* Princeton, NJ: Princeton University Press.

Kimmel, M. (2008). *Guyland: The perilous world where boys become men.* New York: HarperCollins.

Kimmel, M. (2010). Introduction: Toward a pedagogy of the oppressor. In M. Kimmel & A. Ferber (Eds.), *Privilege: A reader* (2nd ed.; pp. 1–10). Boulder, CO: Westview Press.

Kimmel, M., & Ferber, A. (Eds.). (2010). *Privilege: A reader* (2nd ed.). Boulder, CO: Westview Press.

Kleiner, B., Porch, R., & Farris, E. (2002). *Public alternative schools and programs for students at risk of education failure: 2000–01* (NCES 2002–004). Washington, DC: National Center on Education Statistics.

Kleinman, S., & Ezzell, M. (2003). The king's english: A campus fable. In M. S. Kimmel & A. L. Ferber (Eds.), *Privilege: A reader* (pp. 173–180). Boulder, CO: Westview Press.

Kozol, J. (1991). *Savage inequalities: Children in America's schools.* New York: Crown.

Lareau, A. (2011). *Unequal childhoods: Class, race, and family life* (2nd ed.). Berkeley: University of California Press.

Lawrence-Lightfoot, S. (2000). *Respect: An exploration.* Cambridge, MA: Perseus Books.

Layard, R. (2005). *Happiness: Lessons from a new science.* London: Allen Lane.

Lazarre, J. (1996). *Beyond the whiteness of whiteness: Memoir of a white mother of black sons.* Durham, NC: Duke University Press.

Leonardo, Z. (2009). *Race, whiteness, and education.* New York: Routledge.

Levine, M. (2006). *The price of privilege: How parental pressure and material advantage are creating a generation of disconnected and unhappy kids.* New York: HarperCollins.

Levine, P., Marder, C., & Wagner, M. (2004). *Services and supports for secondary school students with disabilities: A special topic report from the national longitudinal transition study-2 (NLTS2).* Menlo Park, CA: SRI International.

Lowrey, A. (2013, September 11). The rich get richer through recovery. *New York Times,* p. B4.

Luthar, S. S., & Becker, B. E. (2002). Privileged but pressured: A study of affluent youth. *Child Development, 73,* 1593–1610.

Luthar, S. S., & D'Avanzo, K. (1999). Contextual factors in substance use: A study of suburban and inner-city adolescents. *Development and Psychopathology, 11,* 845–867.

Lutz, C. (1988). *Unnatural emotions: Everyday sentiments on a Micronesia atoll and their challenge to Western theory.* Chicago: University of Chicago Press.

MacIntyre, A. (1984). *After virtue* (2nd ed.). Notre Dame, IN: University of Notre Dame Press.

Mantsios, G. (2003). Media magic: Making class invisible. In T. E. Ore (Ed.), *The social construction of difference and inequality* (2nd ed., pp. 81–89). New York: McGraw-Hill.

Maxwell, C., & Aggleton, P. (Eds.). (2013). *Privilege, agency and affect: Understanding the production and effects of action.* Hampshire, UK: Palgrave Macmillan.

McAdams, D. (1999). Personal narratives and the life story. In L. Pervin & O. John (Eds.), *Handbook of personality: Theory and research* (2nd ed., pp. 478–500). New York: Guildford Press.

McCracken, G. (1988). *The long interview.* Beverly Hills, CA: Sage.

McIntosh, P. (1988). *White privilege and male privilege: A personal account of coming to see correspondences through work in women's studies* (Working Paper 189). Wellesley, MA: Wellesley College Center for Research on Women.

McIntyre, A. (2008). *Participatory action research.* Thousand Oaks, CA: Sage.

McMahon, D. M. (2006). *Happiness: A history.* New York: Atlantic Monthly Press.

McTaggart, R. (1997). Guiding principles for participatory action research. In R. McTaggart (Ed.), *Participatory action research: International contexts and consequences* (pp. 25–43). Albany, NY: State University of New York Press.

Mead, M. (1958). Adolescence in primitive and modern society. In E. E. Maccoby, T. M. Newcomb, & E. L. Hartley (Eds.), *Readings in social psychology,* 341–350. New York: Norton.

Mickelson, R. A. (1990). The attitude achievement paradox among black adolescents. *Sociology of Education, 63*(1), 44–61.

Mullen, A. L. (2010). *Degrees of inequality: Culture, class, and gender in American higher education.* Baltimore, MD: John Hopkins University Press.

Nelson, M. (2010). *Parenting out of control: Anxious parents in uncertain times.* New York: New York University Press.

New York Times Correspondents. (2005). *Class matters.* New York: Henry Holt.

Oakes, J. (1985). *Keeping track: How schools structure inequality.* New Haven, CT: Yale University Press.

Olson, C. P. (1983). Inequality remade: The theory of correspondence and the context of French immersion in northern Ontario. *Journal of Education, 165*(1), 75–98.

Pease, B. (2010). *Undoing privilege: Unearned advantage in a divided world.* London: Zed Books.

Pekar, T. (2013, January 11). Certainty versus confidence. *Stanford Social Innovation Review Blog.* Retrieved from http://www.ssireview.org/blog/entry/certainty_versus_confidence

Penuel, W. R., & Wertsch, J. V. (1995). Vygotsky and identity formation: A sociocultural approach. *Educational Psychologist, 30,* 83–92.

Price, S. (2012). Therapy of lies. *Teaching Tolerance, 42,* 51–53.

Proweller, A. (1999). Shifting identities in private education: Reconstructing race at/in the cultural center. *Teachers College Record, 100,* 776–808.

Pollack, W. (1998). *Real boys: Rescuing our sons from the myths of boyhood.* New York: Henry Holt.

Pope, D. (2001). *"Doing school": How we are creating a generation of stressed out, materialistic, and miseducated students.* New Haven, CT: Yale University Press.

Quinn, M. M., & Poirier, J. (2007). *Study of effective alternative education programs.* Washington, DC: American Institutes for Research.

Reay, D., Crozier, G., & James, D. (2011). *White middle-class identities and urban schooling.* New York: Palgrave Macmillan.

Reichert, M. C. (2000). Disturbances of difference: Lessons from a boy's school. In L. Weis, & M. Fine (Eds.), *Construction sites: Excavating race, class, and gender among urban youth* (pp. 259–273). New York: Teachers College Press.

Rosaldo, M. Z. (1984). Toward an anthropology of self and feeling. In R. A. Shweder, & R. A. LeVine (Eds.), *Cultural theory: Essays on mind, self, and emotion* (pp. 137–157). Cambridge, UK: Cambridge University Press.

Rosenblum, K., & Travis, T.-M. (2012). *The meaning of difference: Americans constructions of race, sex and gender, social class, sexual orientation, and disability.* New York: McGraw-Hill.

Rothenberg, P. S. (Ed.). (2002). *White privilege: Essential readings on the other side of racism.* New York: Worth.

Rouse, R. (1995). Thinking through transnationalism: Notes on the cultural politics of class relations in contemporary United States. *Public Culture, 7,* 353–402.

Ryan, C. (2009). *Supportive families, healthy children: Helping families with lesbian, gay, bisexual, and transgender children.* San Francisco: Family Acceptance Project, San Francisco State University.

Schiffrin, H. H., Liss, M., Miles-McLean, H., Geary, K. A., Erchull, M. J., & Tashner, T. (2013). Helping or hovering? The effects of helicopter parenting on college students' well-being. *Journal of Child and Family Studies, 22,* 1–10.

Seider, S. (2009). Social justice in the suburbs: Challenges to engaging privileged youth in social action. *Educational Leadership, 66*(8), 54–58.

Seider, S. (2010). The role of privilege as identity in adolescents' beliefs about homelessness, opportunity, and inequality. *Youth & Society, 20*(10), 1–32.

Sidanius, J., & Pratto, F. (1999). *Social dominance: An intergroup theory of social hierarchy. and oppression.* Cambridge, UK: Cambridge University Press.

Shellenbarger, S. (2010, December 29). Delaying college to fill in the gaps. *Wall Street Journal.* Retrieved from http://online.wsj.com/news/articles/SB10001424 052970203513204576047723922275698

Smith, A. (2013). Unsettling the privilege of self-reflexivity. In F. W. Twine & B. Gardener (Eds.), *Geographies of privilege* (pp. 263–280). New York: Routledge.

Sparks, S. (2010, September 21). Research suggests a "gap year" motivates students. *Education Week.* Retrieved from http://www.edweek.org/ew/articles/2010/09/22/04gap-2.h30.html

Stoudt, B. G. (2007). The co-construction of knowledge in "safe spaces": Reflecting on politics and power in participatory action research. *Children, Youth and Environments, 17*(2), 280–297.

Stoudt, B. G. (2009). The role of language and discourse in the investigation of privilege: Using participatory action research to discuss theory, develop methodology, and interrupt power. *Urban Review, 41,* 7–28.

Stoudt, B. G., Fox, M., & Fine, M. (2012). Contesting privilege with critical participatory action research. *Journal of Social Issues, 68*(1), 178–193.

Stuber, J. M. (2010). Class dismissed? The social-class worldviews of privileged college students. In A. Howard & R. A. Gaztambide-Fernández (Eds.), *Educating elites: Class privilege and educational advantage* (pp. 131–151). Lanham, MD: Rowman & Littlefield.

Swalwell, K. (2013). *Educating activist allies: Social justice pedagogy with the suburban and urban elite.* New York: Routledge.

Tappan, M. (2000). Autobiography, mediated action, and the development of moral identity. *Narrative Inquiry, 10*, 81–109.

Tappan, M. (2005). Domination, subordination, and the dialogical self: Identity development and the politics of "ideological becoming." *Culture and Psychology, 11(1)*, 47–75.

Tappan, M. (2006). Reframing internalized oppression and internalized domination: From the psychological to the sociocultural. *Teachers College Record, 108*(10), 2115–2144.

Thompson, J. (1984). *Studies in the theory of ideology.* Berkeley: University of California Press.

Thompson, J. (1990). *Ideology and modern culture.* Stanford, CA: Stanford University Press.

Tivnan, E. (writer), & Goodman, R. (director). (2009, February 13). A hidden America: Children of the mountains [television broadcast]. In J. Diaz, K. Gray, & C. Weinraub (Producers), *20/20.* New York: ABC Television Network.

United Nations (2013). *World economic situation and prospects 2013* (E.13. II.C.2). New York: United Nations.

Useem, M., & Karabel, J. (1986). Educational pathways to top corporate management. *American Sociological Review, 51*, 184–200.

Van Galen, J. (2007). Introduction. In J. Van Galen & G. Noblit (Eds.), *Late to class: Social class and schooling in the new economy* (pp. 1–15). Albany: State University of New York Press.

van Gorder, A. C. (2007). Pedagogy for the children of the oppressors. *Journal of Transformative Education, 5*(1), 8–32.

Veenhoven, R. (1984). *Conditions of happiness.* Dordrecht, Netherlands: D. Reidel.

Wallerstein, J. S., & Kelly, J. B. (1975). The effects of parental divorce: Experiences of the preschool child. *Journal of the American Academy of Child Psychiatry, 14*(4), 600–616.

Way, N., Stauber, H. Y., Nakkula, M. J., & London, P. (1994). Depression and substance use in two divergent high school cultures: A quantitative and qualitative analysis. *Journal of Youth & Adolescence, 23,* 331–357.

Wexler, P. (1992). *Becoming somebody: Toward a social psychology of school.* London: Falmer Press.

Wildman, S. M. (1996). *Privilege revealed: How invisible preferences undermine America.* New York: New York University Press.

Wise, T. (2002). Membership has its privileges: Thoughts on acknowledging and challenging whiteness. In P. S. Rothenberg (Ed.), *White privilege: Essential readings on the other side of racism* (pp. 107–110). New York: Worth.

Wise, T. (2005). *White like me: Reflections on race from a privileged son.* Brooklyn, NY: Soft Skull Press.

Wolanin, T. R., & Steele, P. E. (2004). *Higher education opportunities for students with disabilities: A primer for policymakers.* Washington DC: The Institute for Higher Education Policy.

Wortham, S. (2001). *Narrative in action.* New York: Teachers College Press.

Index

A

A Hidden America: Children of the Mountains, 26

academic(s): influence from others and, 84, 105; lack of achievement, 123–124, 126, 163; privilege and, 58–59; rigor, 24, 45, 62, 85–86, 103, 107

achievement pressure: academics and, 45–46, 49, 72–74, 123; college credentials and, 26, 46, 64, 73, 148, 192; competition and, 41, 48, 65, 84, 194; in extracurriculars, 158, 146, 173; involvement and, 82; lack of, 126; parental goals and, 67, 70, 148, 163, 173; personal, 95

Adams, 206

Adequate Yearly Progress, 117n6

adolescence, study of, 9–11, 18n38

advantages: acknowledgement of, 31–33, 59, 62, 70, 93, 97; appreciation of, 71, 112, 168; distinction of hard work and, 58, 93, 96–97, 113

affect, 13–14, 189–194

agency, 14, 177, 196n2

Aggleton, P. 14

Ahearn, L. 177

Ahmed, S. 192, 193

Alexander, K. 103

alternative education, 124–125

Althusser, L. 178

American Dream, 67, 90, 92, 128

American Psychiatric Association, 161

anxiety, lack of, 25, 62–63, 71

anxious affluent, 194

Anyon, J. 12, 148

Apple, M. 8, 148, 178, 189

athletics, 22, 61, 76, 82, 97n3

Aucoin, D. 144

B

Baltzell, E. 87

Barr, R. 124

Bassett, P. 166

Baumeister, R. 39

Becker, B. 10

Berliner, D. 123

Biddle, B. 123

bilingual education, 147–148

Bishop, A. 5, 207

Blos, P. 9

Bonacci, A. 190

Bound, J. 64

Bourdieu, P. 87, 171, 174

Brantlinger, E. 24, 37, 56, 148, 171, 178, 192, 196n10

Breault, R. 207

Bruner, J. 8

Brydon-Miller, M. 200

bullying, 160

Bushman, B. 190

Butler, J. 8

C

Cain, C. 8

Cairns, K. 14, 190

Camara, W. 64

Campbell, W. 190

Case, K. 207

certain, 13, 177, 187–189

Chafel, J. 34

Chase, S. 11

class privilege, 7

class size, 45, 84, 103, 117n2

Colby College, 1, 203, 208

college: admissions, 26, 46–47, 74, 171; advising, 72, 171; applications, 57, 62–63; financing, 54, 62, 92, 111, 171
community: differences, 31–32, 52, 100; resources, 64, 102; service trips, 20–21, 27, 39n5, 64, 69, 108, 153–154, 167–168, 202; values, 22, 82
concerted cultivation, 105
conferred dominance, 6
confident, 13, 177, 185–187
contradictions, sorting out, 24, 36, 57, 59, 191–192, 98n5
Cookson, P. 87
Cozzarelli, C. 34
critical consciousness, 204, 207, 209n9
Crozier, G. 177, 194
Csikszentmihalyi, M. 10
Curry-Stevens, A. 207

D
D'Avanzo, K. 10
Dale, 78n5
Damon, W. 8
Darling-Hammond, L. 123
Davidson, E. 57
Desai, C. 14, 190
differentiation strategies, 183
disadvantaged students, perceptions of, 33–34, 37–38, 52, 112–113, 115, 153, 180, 196n10
discrimination, 4–5
dismantling privilege, 207
displacement, 180, 186
dissimulate, 183
dissimulation, 186
dissimulation operations, 184
divorce, impact of, 32, 65, 129–130, 137n6
domestic work, 145, 150
Domhoff, W. 87
dominant groups, 5
Dowling, R. 7

E
Easterbrook, G. 65
Education Trust, 123, 148
Edwards, K. 207
elite schools, 60n4, 78n5
Elliott, M. 123
emotion. *See* affect
entitlement, sense of, 190
Entwisle, D. 103

Erchull, M. 144
Erikson, E. 9
Espenshade, T. 64
eternalization ideological strategies, 184
euphemisms, 180, 186
executive elite, 12
Exline, J. 190
Ezzell, M. 6

F
family: activities, 88, 104; image, maintaining of, 162, 164; influence, 28–29, 32, 35, 50, 67–68, 76, 90, 106, 143–144; parental inspiration, 67, 90; parental involvement, 25, 51, 65–66, 121–122; parent relationships, 50, 65–66, 89, 105, 130–131, 151, 164; parental practices, 89, 105, 160; sibling relationships within, 150, 160, 164; structure, 23, 32, 50–51, 65, 128, 146; trips, 21, 28, 127, 150–151, 160; use of connections, 147
Farris, E. 124
Ferber, A. 5
Ferguson, R. 123
Fine, M. 8, 9, 10
Fischer-Rosenthal, W. 8
Forrest Gump, 56
Fox, M. 8, 9
fragmentation ideological operations, 179
Freud, S. 9
Freire, P. 204, 207
Frey, B. 192
future plans, 194, 198–199; career aspirations and, 22, 25–26, 30, 42, 107, 110, 172; changing of, 76–77; dreams and, 75; pressure from parents about, 143–144; uncertainty about, 74, 133–134, 153, 194, 198–199; wealth and, 87, 153, 172

G
gap year, 75–76, 79n6
Garrod, A. 9
Gaztambide-Fernandez, R. 8, 11, 14, 166, 180, 190, 191, 195
Geary, K. 144
Geertz, C. 178

gender roles: femininity, 145–146, 150; masculinity, 97n3, 150, 157–158, 163
Gibbs, N. 142
Gibson, D. 195
Golash-Boza, T. 207
Goodman, D. 5, 17n10, 26, 190, 207
Gordon, S. 10
Greene, M. 204
Greenwood, D. 200

H
Hacker, J. 194
Haigler, K. 76
Hall, G. S. 9
happiness, 14, 192–194, 197n37
hardworking, 13, 177, 182–183
Hardiman, R. 5
Harris, J. 194
Hart, D. 8
Harter, E. 123
helicopter parenting, 142, 144, 155n1
Hershbein, B. 64
high-stakes tests, 47, 84, 103, 106, 117n6, 118n14
Hobgood, M. 207
Holland, D. 8
homophobia, 161–163
hooks, b. 191
Housing Assistance Council, 123
Howard, A. 7, 11, 30, 37, 48, 57, 123, 171, 177, 180, 191, 199, 203, 204, 207
Howell, J. 113

I
identity, 7–8, 18n24, 18n38, 159, 180
ideologies, 13–15, 178–187
income disparities, 69–70, 195
independent, 13, 177, 183–185
independently wealthy, 12, 19n59
individualized education program, 99
individualism, 150, 152
inequalities, creation of, 4–5
integrity, 14, 191–192
invisible knapsack. *See* McIntosh, P.
isolated, 13, 177, 179–180

J
Jackson, B. 5
James, D. 177, 194
Jensen, R. 5, 6
Johnson, A. 7, 17n7, 56, 207
Josselson, R. 8

K
Kalleberg, A. 194
Karabel, J. 87
Kelly, J. 130
Kemmis, S. 205
Khan, S. 11, 12, 18n18, 65, 87, 177, 182, 184, 190
Kilkenny, R. 9
Kimmel, M. 5, 7, 64, 83, 207
Kleiner, B. 124
Kleinman, S. 6
knowledge versus understanding, 203, 206
Kozol, J. 123, 148
Krueger, A. 78n5

L
Lachicotte, W. 8
Lareau, A. 105, 194
Lawrence-Lightfoot, S. 17
Layard, R. 192
Lazarre, J. 35
learning differences: accommodations, 34, 99, 102; dyslexia, 102; obstacles and, 111
legitimation ideological operations, 181
Leonardo, Z. 202
Levine, M. 10
Levine, P. 110
Liss, M. 144
London, P. 10
Long, B. 64
Lowrey, A. 195
Luthar, S. 10
Lutz, C. 189

M
MacIntyre, A. 8
Macpherson, P. 10
Maguire, P. 200
Mantsios, G. 6
Marder, C. 110
Marx, K. 14
materialism, 10, 67, 70, 91, 93, 96, 168–169
Maxwell, C. 14
McAdams, D. 8
McIntosh, P. 5, 6, 207
McIntyre, A. 208
McMahon, D. 193
McTaggart, R. 205, 208
Mead, M. 9
meritocracy, 36

Mickelson, R. 171, 182
Miles-McLean, H. 144
mixed-income schools, 148
motivation: from parents, 67, 105; intrinsic, 50, 71–72; to gain success, 95, 131; to go to college, 47; to make money, 91; to work hard, 67
Mullen, A. 133

N
Nakkula, M. 10
narrativization strategies, 183–184
naturalization strategies, 182, 183–184, 186
Neitzel, C. 34
Nelson, M. 76, 142
new economy, 194
new elite, 12, 182

O
Oakes, J. 24, 148
Olson, L. 103, 171, 182

P
Parrett, W. 124
participatory action research (PAR), 3–4, 200, 203, 209n8
Pease, B. 5, 189, 207
pedagogy, 205, 207, 209n15
peer relations: activities and, 108, 114, 165; differences between, 51–54, 107–108, 147; lack of, 44–45, 62, 144, 149; others perceptions and, 38, 71, 109; romantic, 142–143; social class and, 52, 114, 179; support and, 24; the creation of, 86–87, 116, 164–165; with teammates, 83
Pekar, T. 185
Penuel, W. 8
performing arts, 157, 172
Perot, C. 195
Persell, C. 87
Poirier, J. 124
political identity, 51, 104–105, 143, 171, 181, 197n34
political correctness, 36, 39, 48, 59, 126, 180, 191
Pollack, W. 83
Pope, D. 10
Porch, R. 124
Post, L., 123
poverty, 26–27, 33–34, 112

Powers, S. 9
prejudice, 180, 196n10
Price, S. 161
price of privilege, the, 10
private school, 42, 45–46, 55, 80–81, 102, 166
privilege: activities about, 2; as identity, 7–8, 96, 114, 204; awareness of self and, 31–33, 55–57, 90, 114, 13, 135–136, 167–168, 200–203; awareness of others and, 27, 29, 31–33, 56, 102, 167–168, 200–203; commodified notions of, 6; defining, 5, 31, 33, 58, 201; distinguishing self from, 169;; imagining life without, 36, 86, 110, 171, 174; intrinsic aspects of, 39, 177, 204; lack of awareness of, 5; negative consequences of, 94; recognizing others, 52; recognizing own, 27; self-understandings and, 27–28, 32, 59, 62–63, 200–203; separating self from, 174; taking advantage of, 169; understandings of, 205–206; undoing of, 207; vocabulary about, 5
Proweller, A. 11, 37
public school, 22, 46, 64, 101, 147
public vs. private, 46, 52, 80, 102

Q
qualitative research, 12
Quinn, M. 124

R
rationalize, 180, 182
race: diversity and, 23, 60n3, 78n4, 80, 97n1, 100, 159; identity and, 5, 159; social class and, 208n4; stereotyping of 34, 37
Race to Nowhere, 10
Radford, A. 64
Reay, D. 177, 194
reference groups, 7, 56
Reichert, M. 11
religion, 151–152, 159, 168
reification ideological operations, 182, 183
reification ideological modes, 186
Rosaldo, M. 189
Rosenblum, K. 190
Rothenberg, P. 5, 203, 206

Rouse, R. 57
Ryan, C. 164

S
Sawtell, E. 64
Sawyer, D. 26
Scheuneman, J. 64
Schiffrin, H. 144
Schneider, B. 10
school: climate, 23, 45, 148; competi-
    tion, 48; culture, 20, 123,124,
    125, 165–166; diversity, 81,
    107, 165; Explore program,
    124–125; extracurricular activi-
    ties, 21, 41–42, 63, 87, 100,
    158, 162; funding, 78n3, 123,
    155–156; groupings, 23, 81–82,
    100, 115–116; magnet program,
    99, 103, 106–107, 113, 147;
    rural contexts in, 123, 136n2;
    teachers, 108, 124
scripted, 13, 177, 180–182
Seider, S. 11, 207
self-understandings: common qualities
    of, 13; identities as forms of,
    8–9; ideologies and, 178; influ-
    ences on, 199–200; sexuality,
    160, 163
Shellenbarger, S. 76
Shelton, J. 190
Skinner, D. 8
Smith, A. 207, 208
Smith, J. 113
Smulyan, L. 9
social capital, 98n4, 146
social class: defining, 55, 58, 91–92;
    differences, 93, 101–102, 105,
    126, 145, 153–154, 169–170;
    diversity 37, 52, 115, 148, 166;
    identity, 146; recognition of,
    170
Sparks, S. 76
standardization, 180
Stauber, H. 10
Steele, P. 111
storm and stress model, 9
Stoudt, B. 3, 8, 9, 11

Stuber, J. 190, 191
Stutzer, A. 192
substance abuse, 10, 53, 129–130
success: defining, 22, 68; factors that
    contribute to, 35; hard work
    and, 112; inspiration to achieve,
    111; levels of, 77; path to, 77,
    95, 101, 110, 128
Swalwell, K. 202, 203, 207
symbolization of unity, 180

T
Tagler, M. 34
Tappan, M. 5, 8, 199
Tashner, T. 144
therapy, reparative, 161, 175n2
Thompson, J. 14, 178
Tivnan, E. 26
tracking, 26, 34, 47, 78n2, 148–149
transformation, 208
Travis, T. 190

U
unearned advantages, 6, 190
unearned entitlements, 6
unification operations, 180
United Nations, 194
Useem, M. 87

V
Van Galen, J. 195
van Gorder, A. 207
Veenhoven, R. 193

W
Wagner, M. 110
Wallerstein, J. 130
Way, N. 10
Weis, L. 8, 189
Wertsch, J. 8
Wexler, P. 8, 189, 192
Wildman, S. 35
Wilkinson, A. 34
Wise, T. 6
Wolanin, T. 111
Wortham, S. 8
worthiness, 14, 189–191

For Product Safety Concerns and Information please contact our EU
representative GPSR@taylorandfrancis.com
Taylor & Francis Verlag GmbH, Kaufingerstraße 24, 80331 München, Germany

www.ingramcontent.com/pod-product-compliance
Lightning Source LLC
Chambersburg PA
CBHW070407270326
41926CB00014B/2741

* 9 7 8 1 1 3 8 2 8 6 9 3 1 *